FAITH IN TIME

FAITH IN TIME

The Life of
JIMMY SCOTT

David Ritz

DA CAPO PRESS

A Member of the Perseus Books Group

Copyright © 2002 by David Ritz

All rights reserved. No part of this publication may be reproduced, stored in a retrieval system, or transmitted, in any form or by any means, electronic, mechanical, photocopying, recording, or otherwise, without the prior written permission of the publisher. Printed in the United States of America.

Text design by *Trish Wilkinson*
Set in 11.5-point Sabon by the Perseus Books Group

Cataloging-in-Publication data for this book is available from the Library of Congress.

ISBN 0–306–81088–3

Published by Da Capo Press
A Member of the Perseus Books Group
http://www.dacapopress.com

Da Capo Press books are available at special discounts for bulk purchases in the U.S. by corporations, institutions, and other organizations. For more information, please contact the Special Markets Department at the Perseus Books Group, 11 Cambridge Center, Cambridge, MA 02142, or call (800) 255–1514 or (617) 252–5298, or e-mail j.mccrary@perseusbooks.com.

1 2 3 4 5 6 7 8 9—06 05 04 03 02

For Roberta, love of my life

CONTENTS

INTRODUCTION:
MEETING THE MAN

In the course of writing this biography, Jimmy Scott became my friend. I would have it no other way. In fact, the book could be written no other way because, at its heart, *Faith in Time* is a dialogue between friends. Over the years, my methodology of biographical storytelling has been simple: become a trusted confidante and, in doing so, elicit the candid truth. I've often but not always succeeded in winning over my subjects. Some have been remarkably forthcoming, while others have resisted. Either way, the result has been a series of ghostwritten autobiographies in which I assume the voice of the artist.

In this case, though, I'm taking a different tack. I'm following the form adopted when I wrote the life story of Marvin Gaye. *Divided Soul* started out as autobiography, but because Marvin was murdered before I could show him a manuscript, the book was completed in my voice, not his. I'm returning to that form, oddly enough, on the advice of Jimmy Scott. My practice has been to give artists control over their stories. It is, after all, their story I relate and their voice I render. I work for them. Jimmy didn't see it that way and wanted no such control. "I'm interested in your point of view," he said. "I want to read what you have to say. Stretch out. Take it wherever it leads. You make the final decisions."

In doing so, I have not abandoned my belief that Jimmy's conversational voice, like his singing voice, remains the main attraction. In the course of my research, I revisited James Boswell's *Life of Samuel Johnson*, published in 1791, the model for modern biography. I mention Boswell because when it comes to gaining access and intimacy, getting next to the artist and hanging out hour after hour, day after day, year after year, Boswell is the man. His tenacity is inspiring—as is his understanding that a genuine voice, with all its passionate imperfections, is everything. Boswell's great discovery is that Johnson's very soul is located in his real-life conversation—and that talk contains all the charms, rhythms, and mysteries of music.

Because I was privileged to live and travel with Jimmy for several years—peppering him with endless questions, engaging him in the most intimate conversations, seeing him record, watching him work the world over—I feel obligated to pass on that privilege. For all the brooding darkness that has surrounded his life, the joy of Jimmy Scott is most viscerally felt by simply being in his company. My goal is to convey that joy, which, to my way of thinking, mirrors the very spirit of jazz itself.

I've chased after a slew of people close to Jimmy—siblings, friends, ex-wives, girlfriends, musicians, producers—and have inserted their points of view. But it is Jimmy who remains star witness. I have clung to my bias that the biography of a living artist must look to that artist as its most vital source. I want to hear what others have to say about Jimmy, but my principal goal is documenting what Jimmy has to say about himself.

My passion for voice—especially the mysterious voice of jazz—has been with me since I was a kid in Newark, New Jersey. In fact, Newark is where I first heard the name Jimmy Scott. When I was eleven, in 1954, my father took me to the Mosque Theater to see Billie Holiday. I was spellbound. The wonder of black music invaded my soul. Afterward, I waited by the stage door to catch a glimpse of her. When she emerged, reporters shouted questions. One asked her which singers she liked. She named Jimmy Scott. I ran to buy his records. Two years later, I read Billie's autobiography, *Lady Sings the Blues*. When I was through, I asked my father about William Dufty, the "as told to" author. "He's the guy who actually wrote the book," said my father. "Does he get to go over to Billie Holiday's house?" I wanted to know. "I suppose so. That's his job." "Well," I said, "that's the job I want."

Two decades later, that's the job I had—I convinced Ray Charles to let me ghostwrite his book. When we first met in his Los Angeles studio, Ray was sitting alone in the dark, lights flickering across the console of his recording equipment, a ballad pouring out of the enormous speakers above our heads. The song was "Someone to Watch over Me." Ray wanted to know if I knew the singer. I did. There was no mistaking Jimmy Scott.

Five years passed. In 1982, I was working with Marvin Gaye on his memoirs when he suffered a debilitating depression and disappeared. I finally found him in Ostend, Belgium, where he was hiding from former wives and current creditors. He had brought only one tape from home. "This is all that consoles me," he said. I figured it was Sam Cooke. I was wrong: Jimmy Scott was the only singer deep enough to reach Marvin Gaye's deepest blues. As we listened to "I Wish I Didn't Love You So"—a song Marvin had earlier recorded in a Jimmy Scott mode—my mind flashed back to Newark, a year after I'd heard Billie Holiday speak Jimmy's name.

It was summertime. I'd wandered into the Third Ward, the black section of the city, and stood in front of the open door of a nightclub I was too young to enter. The sign said, TONIGHT ONLY: LITTLE JIMMY SCOTT. On the bandstand stood a man-child singing in the plaintive voice of a woman. He swung in the kicked-back cadence of ultracool jazz. His tragic/magic demeanor mesmerized me. His phrasing was otherworldly, penetrating, frighteningly sad.

Later, as I listened to him in Marvin Gaye's apartment overlooking the cold North Sea, the sadness in Jimmy's voice seemed to have only deepened.

When I finally met Jimmy, it was the nineties. We were in San Francisco. By then he was an old man who, long forgotten by the music business, had doggedly fought back. I'd heard stories of how he'd worked as a shipping clerk and an orderly at a retirement home. I'd never ceased to love his music, but I was reluctant to get involved with Jimmy. Having just completed the autobiography of a great diva—a book five arduous years in the making—I was all too aware of the distance between the unfettered glory of art and the narcissism of the artist. I thought of the film *Amadeus*. I thought of the many singers I had idolized as a kid, only to find them smaller rather than larger than life. I was feeling disillusioned with my work. I was tired of discovering feet of clay. My naive notion that inspiring music must come from inspiring people had been crushed too many times. The great diva drove the nail in the coffin.

When I heard Jimmy sing that night in San Francisco, my skepticism softened. When I spoke with him afterward, my skepticism collapsed. There seemed no separation between art and artist. The very notion I had abandoned—that a singer could be as loving as his song—was suddenly renewed. The generosity of his music and the generosity of his person were one and the same. The next night, I went to see him at a club in Mill Valley. The place was packed. I spotted Jimmy emerging from his dressing room and went to stand next to him while he waited to go on. As the band completed the opening instrumental, an older woman came up to Jimmy and, mistaking him for a waiter, asked the whereabouts of the ladies' room. I understood the mistake. In his poorly fitted and slightly shiny tux, Jimmy looked like a disheveled worker. I wondered what he would say. "I know where it is," he told her, "but it's a little tricky getting there. Let me show you." He patiently led her through the length of the club, straight to the door of the ladies' room. Then he walked on stage and drained the audience dry.

Watching him, I felt fated to learn this man's story. I had to know him. I had to give his story the poignancy he gave his songs. I had to write as beautifully as he sang. I had to be with him and learn the strange pain informing his singular style of storytelling. I had to see him after the show, when we talked half the night. I had to see him the next day. I had to fly to New York a month later and spend the weekend listening to him at Birdland, where he captivated an ecstatically appreciative audience that included Quentin Tarantino, Joe Pesci, and Ethan Hawke. "We're here to take acting lessons," said Hawke. "We're here to see how it's done."

Jimmy does it with grace. Jimmy does it with idiosyncratic timing. He does it by digging deep into the dark corners of the secret soul. His performance is musical theater of the highest order. His speech follows the same pattern of unique rhythms and riffs. You get a sense of his jazz-speak when you're in his motel room for an early morning interview. Seated upright in bed, he looks like a cocoa-and-cream-colored marionette with impossibly thin, impossibly long arms. His hair is covered with a black satin do-rag wrapped tightly around his head. He looks regal; he looks childlike. His smiling eyes are slightly askew. His teeth are small and even. He looks part Native American, part Pinocchio.

His gesticulation, like his articulation, is wholly his own. He carves the air with his hand as though he's painting words across an invisible canvas. He's wildly animated, now sliding off the bed as he laughs, now leaping up to make a point. He calls everyone—men and women, children and strangers—"baby" or "darling" or "love." His lexicon is half hipster, half preacher. He's a tactile talker, reaching out, touching your arm, taking your hand, offering you the energy coursing through his long, delicate fingers. He cuts off words like he cuts off notes, dramatically, unexpectedly. Long silences are followed by long phrases embedded in a vocabulary both endearing and elegiac.

When you express your love for a certain artist—say, Al Jolson or Al Green—he says, "Baby, I'm feeling your heart." His energy is elflike, unpredictable, staccato. His mood is exuberant. You look for the sadness you felt when he was singing his songs, but instead find joy. "Singing frees me," he says. "Releases me."

This release is not evident in many of his other activities. Food, for example, seems to give him little pleasure. He eats like a bird. His body is thin. He walks with a limp, the result of an accident suffered some thirty years ago. At times he appears alarmingly frail, at times surprisingly sturdy. His right eye is slightly crossed and seems to float freely. "It was another defect I was born with," he explains. "A weak ligament." Whether sitting or standing, whether silent or speaking, he projects intense nervous energy. He fidgets, chain-smokes, fools with his cigarettes—searching for matches, lighting up, puffing, snuffing it out, saving the stub for later, losing the stub, dashing off to buy a fresh pack. Of his many ticks, the most pronounced involves scratching; he incessantly scratches the palm of his left hand. Often he breaks the skin and must apply cream to heal the red wound. Only music stops the scratching. Only music relaxes him entirely. Seated next to him at a concert or watching him listen to records in my home, I've seen the phenomenon: The moment the music starts, his hands come to rest, one calmly resting atop the other. Music is the balm.

The great paradox of Jimmy—for that matter, the great paradox of jazz—is the tension between exhilaration and relaxation, stimulation and serenity. Jazz is on the edge of the cliff; jazz is deep in the valley. Jazz is in a hurry and jazz is patient. In telling me the story of his life, in months of walking through the scenes of his past, Jimmy is infinitely patient. The rhythms he creates are wholly original. He does more than take his time. He doesn't worry about time. Time disappears as a restraint or measure. As a singer, his signatures are idiosyncratic phrasing and radical, behind-the-beat syncopation. His career, like his singing, has lagged far behind the beat.

"If you believe in the beat," he says, "you don't need to worry about the beat. It's there. Always been there and always will. You don't have to follow it. Fact is, the beat sets you free. It's your security, your heartbeat, an expression of God, a gift. Time is a gift. Time is our life. I believe in time just like I believe in God. All that gives me faith in time. If we're in the moment, if we're truly rooted in what we're doing when we're doing it, we can work though all the bad stuff. In that sense, we can all be singers singing away our sadness."

Still, sadness is his subtext; it lives close to his surface. Sadness suffuses the sound of his unnaturally high speaking voice. The tone and timbre of that voice is the essence of Jimmy Scott. Because he never went through the changes of adolescence, his boyishness is startlingly alive. You hear it in his voice, see it in his body; his boyishness is a vital component of his quixotic charm. He lacks the tough crust that shields other grown men, projecting instead vulnerability and disarming honesty. Few seventy-seven-year-old men speak with such candor on the subject of sex.

"Kallmann's Syndrome," he says, "was little understood when I was coming up. It afflicted me and two of my brothers. My mother felt for us, but when the hospital wanted to use us in experiments, she said, 'No child of mine will be a guinea pig.' Then Mama, bless her heart, was killed in a terrible car accident. Happened when I was thirteen. The syndrome was on me, but Mama wasn't there to help me through. My testicles never descended. My penis stayed small. My voice stayed high. Facial and pubic hair never grew. Kids can be cruel. Boys especially. I might have been teased and tortured, but I grew to see my affliction as my gift. When I sang, I soared. I could soar higher than all those hurts aimed at my heart. Adults can be as cruel, maybe crueler, than kids. In my adult life, people have looked at me as an oddity. I've been called a queer, a little girl, an old woman, a freak, and a fag. As a singer, I've been criticized for sounding feminine. They say I don't belong in any category, male or female, pop or jazz. But early on, I saw my suffering as my salvation. Once I knew that, I understood God had put me in this strange little package for a reason. All I needed was the courage to be me. That courage took a lifetime to develop."

Coping with his condition, Jimmy turned to drink as a young man. The place of alcohol in his life is a subject of some controversy. Jimmy sees it as incidental. Others—especially his siblings—see it as crucial. At his advanced age, Jimmy continues to drink, though goes weeks without. His work ethic prevails. When we travel together to Europe, when he comes to Los Angeles and spends a month meeting with me every day to discuss his life, he never touches a drop. The years that I have observed him, he has never missed a gig or marred a performance because of booze. In fact, I have never witnessed a drunken episode. At the same time, the stories abound. Family members and close associates tell tales of aberrant behavior during every period of his life. The pattern is ironclad: Mild-mannered Jimmy turns aggressive, often violent, and sometimes self-destructive. When he's off the road and I visit him in Cleveland, he maintains a mellow with beer and wine and the kind of smoke that, in Ray Charles's words, "Liggett and Myers don't make."

"Do you think you're an alcoholic?" I ask him.

"Absolutely not," he answers. "Alcoholics can't control it. I can."

His siblings don't agree. "Like our dad," says Jimmy's sister Elsa, "Jimmy has the drinking habit. He's done well to work around it, but it's never gone away. It'll pop up at weird times, causing him to act in weird ways."

His manager and producer monitor him carefully. A certain apprehension about his proclivity to slip is always in the air. The vast majority of the time, though, he conducts himself as a dependable professional who behaves with decorum and grace. Beneath the grace, however, the subtext of his emotional life remains sadness. His exterior friendliness appears like a lovely curtain that, when drawn back, reveals a drama whose great theme is pain—pain over the loss of Mama, the loss of family, his inability to have children, his four failed marriages, and a career marked by deep disappointment.

During all my interviews with Jimmy's intimates—siblings, wives, and girlfriends—I hear stories of his extreme volatility, manic mood swings, and even physical violence. I trust these stories; there are too many to be ignored. But I have a hard time reconciling them with the Jimmy I have come to know. He is a natural-born performer, and even as an interviewee, he assumes a role. He has every reason in the world to be gracious with me. He wants to be loved—in his songs, in his life, and certainly in his life story. Complicating matters, though, is that part of his role as a sympathetic character requires him to candidly describe those brutal times when he was anything but sympathetic. He never appears insincere. Nor does he shy away from describing the dark pain.

Yet in describing pain, Jimmy remains a joyful speaker. Grateful to have a listener, a reader, an audience, he conveys the simple joy of being alive. Because his subject is so often sadness, his joy feels doubly triumphant, an earned state rather than an assumed attitude. To hear him speak of his heartbreak is to lessen your own and give you hope that heartbreak, like everything else in life, is fleeting.

BORN BEHIND THE BEAT

James Victor Scott, named for his paternal grandfather, was born in Cleveland, Ohio, July 17, 1925. He speaks of birth as struggle.

"My mother told stories about my birth, as did my dad. Now I'm telling stories. I know their stories and mine are mingled together. Where do their memories stop and mine begin? They said the beginning was struggle. And struggle is the first thing I felt. Gasping. Choking. As a kid, and even an adult, I've had dreams about my birth, fighting for breath, fighting for light."

He was the third of ten children born to Justine Stanard, a seamstress, and Arthur Scott, an asphalt worker, who lived in the predominantly black east side of town. On the day of Jimmy's birth, his father was called from work and told the infant was being strangled by the umbilical cord. The baby's death was all but certain. Arthur and a fellow worker named Victor rushed to their home at 2177 Forty-third Street to learn that the infant had miraculously survived. An upstairs neighbor had unwound the cord (the markings of which are visible today). For the infant's middle name, the family chose Victor, which they called him throughout childhood. ("There were so many little boys named Jimmy," he says,

"Mama started using Victor.") The principal result of the birth trauma was an ongoing mucous buildup and perpetual wheezing, which cleared up only in his teens.

"Every black family struggled," says Jimmy. "And ours was no different. Like many families, we were held together by our mother. She was the force and the power. She was everything."

Jimmy and I are standing on 101st Street in Cleveland, the location of one of the many homes in which his family lived before his mother's death in 1938. He regards the house with longing. When he describes his youth, it becomes clear that he experienced two distinct childhoods—one with his mother, and one without.

At the time of Jimmy's birth in the Roaring Twenties, Cleveland was booming. Affluent families endowed a wide array of cultural institutions: a symphony orchestra, an art museum, a playhouse, an institute of music. In an attempt to fill jobs left vacant by men gone off to war in Europe, the city recruited black workers from the South. From 1910 to 1920, the black population increased 308 percent, from 8,488 to 34,451. African Americans settled in the Central Avenue district, a black ghetto whose boundaries—Euclid and Woodland, East 14th and 104th—roughly mark the territory of Jimmy's youth.

"It was a real community back then," says Jimmy. "I'd even call it quaint. No buildings taller than three or four stories, and mostly homes with backyards. Lots of four- or five-family homes, and some single homes. You had your corner grocery stores and cafés. You had your liquor stores scattered around, and you had your churches with music spilling out onto the street. You had trolley cars with hard wires where passengers had to get out and turn the car around. You had the big entertainment boulevards—55th, 105th, Woodland—with nightclubs and barrooms and movie theaters. There were businesses—construction companies, trucking concerns, small industry—but mostly just black folk living together. Cleveland's a medical center, and hospitals like Western Reserve and Cleveland Clinic provided lots of jobs for nurses and orderlies. The women in our community worked. Outside the community, downtown was a magnet because of the record stores. Downtown had the big buildings that made us feel like we were living in an important city."

In the midtwenties the city saw the rise of Terminal Tower, a fifty-two-story skyscraper, the tallest edifice between New York and Chicago, anchored by a state-of-the-art train station set in downtown's Public Square.

"Cleveland," says Jimmy, "was about big steel, big plants, big men marching off to work. My father, who came from Missouri, was one of those men, a skilled manual laborer and also a contractor. They called him Scotty. Well, Scotty knew his game. He could lay out that asphalt with the best of them. He got the job done. He was a responsible worker but an irresponsible father. Family responsibilities—like caring, nurturing, and raising the kids—were left to Mom."

The central drama in the Scott household was the tension between mother and father. And without doubt, the central character in Jimmy's life was Justine Scott.

"She was a chubby little woman," he says, "always in motion. Always looking to help. Even with ten of her own, she was forever tending other kids in the neighborhood. If their parents were having a hard time, there'd be food at our house. She'd be feeding the hoboes, even if our food was coming from the welfare on Ninetieth and Cedar. Didn't matter—what we had, we shared. Mom shared with me all the stories about her life that I came to cherish. It was better than reading from a book. She told me, for instance, about meeting Dad. How his mother, Kissy, was a full-blooded Cherokee. How having Indian blood made us unique. How Dad came from Saint Charles, Missouri, to Cleveland, where his sister Rose was teaching a sewing class Mom attended. After class Dad would walk Mom home. They fell in love and married. Mom's future looked bright, especially when the mayor of Cleveland came home from a trip to Russia with furs for Mom to fashion into a coat. The mayor's wife wore the coat for all the city to see. With the extra skins, Mom made little mufflers for her baby sisters. Sewing and singing and playing piano, teaching us little dance steps, roller-skating with us out on the street, cooking stews and cakes and home-made ice creams, fussing after us, making sure we were fed and in bed right on time—that was the woman's life. If she didn't have to care for ten children, I'm sure she would have had a career as a clothes designer."

"My parents had conflicting sensibilities," says Nadine, Jimmy's sister born eleven months after him. "Mom's concern was family. Dad's concern was Dad. Mom was artistic—a beautiful piano player, a talented seamstress. She was interested in the home. Dad was interested in the street. With his extreme sensitivity and artistic ways, Jimmy naturally gravitated towards Mom."

Justine Stanard Scott was the oldest of twenty-six children. "They didn't all live," says Jimmy, "but Mom's family was enormous. And prestigious. The family was a matriarchy led by Hazel Mountain Walker, my mother's aunt, the sister of my grandmother Clara." In an article from the *Cleveland Plain Dealer* (February 4, 2001) celebrating Black History Month, eight prominent African Americans are cited. Among them is Justine's aunt: "Hazel M. Walker (1889–1980). First black Cleveland school principal, Ohio's first black woman lawyer, member of the Ohio Board of Education, actress." The photograph reveals a distinguished, white-haired, light-skinned woman clearly in charge. She wears glasses and an expression of utter seriousness. According to Jimmy and his siblings, Hazel ruled the roost, remaining the role model for upwardly mobile Negro life in Cleveland throughout her long and successful life.

"Hazel Mountain Walker was my principal at the R. B. Hayes elementary school," remembers Zee Mannsur, daughter of Arthur, Jimmy's oldest brother. "She resembled Golda Meir, her gray hair gathered in a tight bun at the nape of her neck. We were petrified of her. My father always spoke of her respectfully, as a great educator, but she appeared unapproachable, light-years away from where we lived."

"My grandparents cut off my mom cold," says Jimmy. "As a child, my mother couldn't attend church with the rest of the family. Mom was dark-skinned, which her mother saw as a defect. It was a sad situation."

"Mom was too smart to see skin color as a sign of status," remembers Jimmy's brother Kenny. "But unfortunately her own mother carried that attitude. She rejected her own daughter for no reason other than prejudice."

Justine's parents, Clara Mountain and Simon Stanard, lived in a large, two-story Victorian home to which the Scotts were never invited.

"The foul treatment of my mother goes back to when her grandmother died," Jimmy explains. "It happened when Mom was eighteen. My great-grandmother adored Mom, saw her talent, and encouraged her in every way, especially when it came to clothes. She had clothes made for Mom and was convinced Mom's own sewing would bring her prosperity. To help, my great-grandmother left my mother a nice inheritance. My grandmother [Clara] was infuriated, though. She didn't want my dark-skinned mother to have a thing. With the help of a relative who worked at the courthouse, Clara changed the will. Mom got nothing."

Simon Stanard worked for the Cleveland Trust Bank as a courier.

"Grandma had a ring in Grandpa's nose," says Jimmy. "They were married seventy-five years, but the poor man was pussy whipped. He was a tender lamb. Like Mom, he was dark-skinned and left behind when the rest of the family went to church. We never knew why Clara married him, except that he never gave her trouble. He was too scared of his wife to raise his voice. Clara gave the orders. And Clara, for all her bossy energy, was nothing more than her sister's flunky. Hazel Mountain Walker ran the show. She told them—she told everyone—what to read, what to say, what to

think. Everyone was intimidated because she was so highly educated. Hazel disapproved of my father and his lack of education.
She and Clara always wanted my mom to leave him."

The social stigma symbolized by Justine's marriage to Arthur—
the gaping distance between a rising middle class and stagnant
working class—haunted the Scott family throughout Jimmy's
childhood. Nothing illustrates that stigma more poignantly than
the relationship between Jimmy's siblings and their maternal
grandmother.

"Mom had a dog named Spot who died," remembers Jimmy's
sister Adoree, "and all us kids gave Spot a beautiful funeral. Mom
was too sad to see him buried, so she stayed home. When we got
back to the house, there was a woman waiting out front. 'Who's
that white woman?' we wanted to know. Turned out the white
woman wasn't white at all. It was our grandmother come to see
Mom. Her visit was a surprise. She never came before and she'd
never come again. We were never told the reason for her visit, which
made it all that stranger. She looked at us like we didn't exist."

"I wanted to know this woman," says Jimmy. "Wanted to see
where she lived and what she was like. So one time I found my way
over there. I just stood in front of their house, with that huge front
porch and those tall white columns. I peered into the picture windows to see what they were doing. After all, these were my grandparents. My family. Why couldn't I just knock on the door? I did
knock, only to have my grandmother sternly ask me what I
wanted. 'Nothing,' I said. 'Just to visit.' 'Well,' she shot back, 'the
visit is over.'"

Nadine sees a connection between Justine's devotion to her
children and her expulsion from her family of origin: "She gave us
everything she was denied. She was denied love, and so we were
loved abundantly. She was not accepted, so we were accepted un-
conditionally. She was denied understanding, so we were understood deeply. The hurt she absorbed made her a more sensitive and
tolerant woman. She took that hurt and turned it into religious

devotion. She was a devout woman interested in living the lessons of Jesus. Essentially that meant treating others, especially children, with a gentleness that we still feel to this day."

Meanwhile, Jimmy's dissatisfaction with his father ran deep: "Early on I sensed she deserved better than Dad. He wouldn't come home, or when he did, he'd be flying too high to help her out. I remember when we had a chance to buy our house on 2301 101st Street—a big house that would have provided the security that later eluded us—Dad said no. Couldn't afford the eight thousand dollars. Twenty-five dollars a month was too much for the man. Didn't want the burden. Would rather play it day by day, month by month. We'd hear Mom asking him for a real sewing machine, so she could make money doing what she did best. He refused. He refused her all the basic conveniences a mother of ten needed just to get by. So you can see why I resented him. I wanted a father who respected Mom the way we did. Wasn't enough for him to make us fritters on Sunday morning. We expected more. That's why one night we decided to attack. If we ganged together, we'd teach him a lesson. We'd make him do right. So we hid behind the door and under the furniture, and when he finally came home smelling of drink, we jumped him. 'Justine!' he yelled, 'get these fools off of me.' And just like that, Mama comes roaring out of her bedroom and goes to whipping every behind in sight. 'Don't ever do your daddy like this,' she scolded. 'You got no business judging the man. That's up to God. Your father is your father and you'll treat him as such. Am I understood?' Obediently, we answered in a single voice. 'Yes, ma'am.'"

Jimmy's mother was more than a symbol of moral authority; in her sewing and singing, in her effortless piano playing, she showed her son, who stayed close to her side, the joy of creativity.

"Jimmy was closer to our mother than anyone," claims Nadine. "He was devoted to her well-being. As soon as he became old enough, he took on the responsibility Dad had shunned, making sure Mom was cared for. As a little boy, when he was only five or six, Jimmy was running out to the train tracks and bringing home loose pieces of coal. He'd do household chores—scrub floors, wash windows—willingly, even joyfully, anything to help Mom."

"Jimmy stayed so close to Mama," says Adoree, "his arm got caught in the ringer when she was doing the wash. When she was at the piano, Jimmy was right there. When she sat and worked with needle and thread, Jimmy was watching her every move."

"Her fingers intrigued me," Jimmy remembers. "I'd marvel at how freely they moved. She could sew a hem in the blink of an eye. She could play a piano chord—one of those full-blooded church chords—like she'd studied for years. Her fingers danced like ten ballerinas. Lord, it was beautiful to watch. Her movements all natural. She had many gifts. Her greatest gift was her way of mothering, her way of giving of herself to her children."

Jimmy and his nine siblings arrived at close intervals. Arthur, born in 1921, and Shirley (1923) were followed by Jimmy (1925), Nadine (1926), Adoree (1928), Kenny (1930), Betsy (1931), Elsa (1932), Roger (1935), and Justin (1938).

"Our main memory," says Nadine, "is that Mom was always pregnant. It seemed to be her permanent condition. It made us feel like she was in a state of grace, this kind and gentle woman whose energy revolved around children, having them, loving them, protecting them."

"I remember that Jimmy's first and only bike was provided by Western Union," says Adoree. "Soon as his feet reached the pedals, he was riding around the city delivering telegrams. He couldn't have been older than eight when he was off selling *Liberty* magazines. If there was an odd job to do, Jimmy did it."

"I hawked newspapers," Jimmy recalls. "That's how I always knew what was going on in the world. I'd read those headlines about the poor little Lindbergh baby, about Hoover sweeping out and FDR sweeping in, about Dillinger and Hitler and how Edward the Seventh renounced his throne for the love of a woman. It was my first look at the wide world out there, which seemed big and confusing but wonderful. For me, the world was about work. I wanted my other brothers, Arthur and Kenny, to work as well. I wanted them to help get things for Mom that Dad wouldn't buy. But they didn't see it that way. They related to Dad. Fact is, there were times when Arthur turned on me and kicked my ass. He didn't want anyone telling him he should go out there and hustle up jobs."

"Jimmy was a little hustler," Nadine remembers. "He used his raw energy to make money any honest way he could."

"I love my brother," says Kenny, "but he could drive the rest of us kids crazy if we weren't working as hard as him. He'd get up in our business—why aren't we doing this, why aren't we doing that? He was a mama's boy, and when Mom started having church in our house, Jimmy was right there by her side."

Jimmy's father had told his mother about the Universal Hagar's Spiritual Church, whose founder, Prophet George William Hurley, often came to Cleveland and held services in private homes. The Scott household became one such home.

"It was the only good thing Scotty did for Justine," claims Jimmy. "Dad found a righteous church that fit Mom's soul. When the Depression hit hard and times got rough, Mom learned to love that church and the comfort it provided."

According to George H. Latimer-Knight, great-grandson of the founder, Prophet Hurley was born in 1884 in Georgia. In 1897, says Latimer-Night, "the spirit informed Father Hurley he was the Second Coming of Christ. At first he did not want to accept the office. So the spirit of God put him on a forty-day fast, drinking only a glass of milk and eating a cracker a day; the last three days he ate nothing. He lay on the ground so long that the grass began to grow through his skin. After this fast, he began his travels of the Eastern World to uncover the truth."

Headquartered in Detroit, Prophet Hurley came to Cleveland regularly as part of his outreach program, which extended as far as New York City. He disassociated himself from preexisting Protestant sects and preached, according to Jimmy, an enlightened form

of Christianity. His liberal biblical commentaries were peppered
with quotes from Plato and Socrates. Church literature claims that
Father Hurley argued against the "lie" that heaven is in the sky
and hell in the ground. For Hurley, heaven was supreme, a "happy
state of mind here on earth," and hell "a deplorable condition in
the bodies of human beings."

"Our house on 101st Street was Temple Number Six," says
Jimmy. "I don't know how many other temples existed, but ours
was the only one in Cleveland. Prophet Hurley showed up at least
once a month and taught the truth. I don't remember him as an
egotist. I didn't see him as a jackleg preacher. I don't recall him
claiming to be God. His main message was to lift ignorance. He
showed the spiritual side of Christ. He didn't scream about damna-
tion or scare you with stories of hell. He preached elevation of
thought. He made you think. Looking back, I can see he was influenced by Eastern religions—Buddhism for sure. We'd have twenty
or thirty people gathered together in our big living room, and he'd
inspire them in a way that made you feel warm. He wasn't over-
rambunctious and showy like so many preachers. He was a stu-
dious man who gave us all a sense of quiet spirituality.

"It wasn't so much the specific teaching, but the gentleness he
projected. When you get preached at, it's the preacher's emotions
that influence you as much as his words. Prophet Hurley's emotions were soft. He said it quietly—life is material and life is spiritual. He represented the spiritual. 'The spiritual,' he said, 'is what
gets us through.' I saw he was getting through to Mom. I saw him
helping her deal with the challenges she faced—ten children to
feed, parents who shunned her, a husband on the loose—and I
knew that the help was real. My mother had every reason in the
world to lose her temper and turn into a raging witch. But she
never did. She carried the patience of God in her heart. That was
the same patience Prophet Hurley was preaching. She learned the
lesson and passed it on to me."

Her lessons were musical as well.

"Gospel music was the first I sang," says Jimmy, "those gospel songs Mom taught us at home and had us perform for our neighbors and Prophet Hurley. Mom's singing voice was sweet and strong and right in tune. I believe my voice resembles hers. It was Mom who organized our family quartet—Nadine, Adoree, Kenny, and myself. Mom taught us how to harmonize notes, and Mom taught us how the words went with the melodies. Mom also set down the rhythm. That's when Mom would get on my case for being behind the beat. When I sang solo, though, she heard that I wasn't really behind. I just had a different feeling for rhythm than everyone else. My mother was musically gifted enough to appreciate my individuality, even as a ten-year-old boy. She'd hear me lagging behind a hymn, and instead of scolding, she'd smile. Her smile said it all. Her smile said, *I know you're different, Victor, but I know you're good.*

"Just to hear the music, sometimes Mom would take us to other churches where the sisters would be shouting, the deacons be dancing. I'd go in there and sing myself. No one had to tell me what to do. To get over in church, you had to reach people emotionally. That meant exposing your naked heart. That's a little scary, but also exciting. If you don't make the connection, you fail. If you do make it, you fly.

"At school, I had no music education except for being asked to play Ferdinand the Bull in a musical play. It was a singing part. Everyone seemed to like me, and my little girlfriends were impressed, but that was it. I never learned to read or write music, not in school—for that matter, not anywhere."

Other than church, the main musical exposure in the Scott household came from a small Philco radio.

"That little green dial was a like a magic wand," Jimmy recalls. "Turn it one way and I might hear Paul Robeson singing in some faraway concert hall. Turn it another way and there's Judy Garland. Whatever I heard fascinated me."

In discussing the music of his childhood, Jimmy fixates on these two figures. Their idiosyncrasies would later be reflected in

Jimmy's own style. When an eleven-year-old Jimmy saw Robeson singing "Ol' Man River" in the film *Showboat* in 1936, the quasi-operatic bass-baritone was thirty-eight; when Jimmy heard Judy Garland on the radio singing "Stomping at the Savoy" with the Bob Crosby band that same year, Judy was fifteen.

"Robeson was a powerful figure," he remembers. "He was tall and dignified and used his voice as an acting instrument. Up until I saw him, I thought of singing in terms of church—singing God's praise. Robeson showed me singing was a huge theatrical gesture. Singing was drama. It was a poem, a play. Robeson's singing turned singing into a spectacle. At the same time, I ran to Judy's movies because she was free with her spirit. She also had a swinging feeling to her sound, like a little girl playing on a swing in the backyard. The swing era was coming—on that little Philco I'd hear Basie and Ellington and Jimmy Lunceford and Benny Goodman playing in faraway ballrooms. Louis Armstrong was coming on, and of course, Pops was someone who freed you up the minute you heard him. But I really related to Judy because she was more or less my own age. And Paul Robeson was a god who descended from on high to instruct us on the dramatic art of singing. Together, the two of them made me forget I was trapped in this deep, dark Depression in bitter-cold Cleveland."

The same Philco radio that brought joy brought heartache. When he was eleven, Jimmy came home one day to find it missing.

"Couldn't believe it was gone," he says. "I was sick. I couldn't live without the radio. It wasn't just the romance of the music— Artie Shaw or Mildred Bailey or Bing Crosby—it was also the voice of the president. For poor folk living in the neighborhood, the sound of FDR was a song of hope. The man could speak, and when he did, when he offered up his programs of rebuilding, we felt like the government actually cared. With no radio, there was no FDR, no comforting tune from a ballroom in Times Square. Just silence. 'Where's the radio?' I asked Dad, who brushed me off with, 'Can't worry 'bout no radio, boy.' The missing radio left a hole in my heart. It was like losing a friend. Then coming back from school one day, I saw it. It was sitting in the window of a pawn shop, plain as day. Dad had pawned it. Dad needed the damn money. Dad worked during most of the Depression, but he still blew his bread on stumblebum women and whisky. To Dad, the radio was nothing more than a silly diversion. To me, it was magic. Now it was gone."

"Dad wasn't good with money," says Kenny. "But in his own way, he tried. I remember him buying linoleum for our kitchen and a bedroom set for him and Mom. Jimmy had an attitude about Dad that didn't let him see how the man was under pressure. This was the Depression, when a lot of men lost it completely. Dad never did."

The sibling dynamic was tense—big brother Arthur and little brother Kenny identified with Dad; Jimmy and his sisters were devoted to Mom.

"If Dad had had any understanding at all," says Jimmy, "he would have traded in Mom's old Singer for a modern sewing machine. Instead he brought home a washing machine. He understood dirty clothes, but he never appreciated art. Our mother was an artist."

The twelve-member Scott family somehow muddled through the Depression, moving frequently because, in Kenny's words, "we had to stay ahead of the rent collector. Our living conditions were never squalid but never too comfortable either. I remember the rats. Jimmy was the big rat killer in our family. At night, he'd boil a pot of water, turn off the lights and wait for them to scurry out of their holes. Once they did, he'd grab them by their tails and fling them into the pot. I was too scared, but big brother took on those rats without flinching."

For all his foibles, their dad worked steadily while their mom anchored the household. Justine considered her home a sanctuary to the point that church was held in the living room. She gave her brood of five boys and five girls a feeling of well-being. She literally sang the praises of God and refused to accept criticism of her husband from either her extended family or her own kids. Loyal to a fault, Justine endured harsh rejection from her mother and aunt without bitterness or recrimination. Whatever the circumstances in inner-city Cleveland, her children—and especially her second son, Jimmy—were made to feel wanted and valued. Her strength was enough to hold her family together. Her death fractured the family forever.

"As a child," says Nadine, "Jimmy was two different people. Before November of 1938, I'd say he was a happy little boy. Long as Mom was near, Jimmy was smiling. He'd come home with gifts for her, a wildflower, a piece of candy. She was his reason for living, the light of his life. Then one day the light went out, and my brother was never the same."

DARKNESS

Jimmy sends me a note from Cleveland saying he's coming to Los Angeles so that we can spend several uninterrupted weeks talking about his life. His handwriting is florid and elegant. At the end, he signs off, "Jimmy, Justine's loving son."

When I pick him up at the airport, I ask about him the phrase. "I think of her every day," he says. "I've been many things in my life. I've held many jobs and gone through many changes. First and foremost, though, I remain Justine's son. That's how I see myself. Always have. Always will."

The death of his mother is the single great fact of Jimmy's childhood. Near the same time, at age thirteen, perhaps the most vulnerable time in a boy's life, he was struck by the onslaught of Kallmann's Syndrome, which deprived him of a conventional sense of manhood. These extreme deprivations—maternal loss and what Jimmy terms "the Deficiency"—define his personality, just as they later define his art. The first, the realization of his physical abnormality, preceded the second by only months.

"When I viewed myself as being different," says Jimmy, "I wasn't thinking about my physique. If you'd ask me how I was different from the other boys, I'd probably answer, 'The way I'm drawn to

music.' Music obsessed me. Not long after my mom had us singing in
our home-grown quartet, I'd wander over to the Woolworth's five-
and-ten-cent-store every Monday, when the new songbooks came
out. People bought 'em up in a hurry, and I had to have my copy.
Those books contained all the lyrics to the new tunes. In the thirties,
great songs were pouring out every week—'The Way You Look
Tonight,' 'When Did You Leave Heaven?' 'Little Girl Blue,' 'Love Is
Just Around the Corner.' I was fascinated by the lyrics, and even better, Woolworth's had a pianist, a lovely saleslady who played the
melodies on the upright to show me how the words matched
the notes. Before I left the store, I'd buy Mom whatever she needed—
threads and needles, a pincushion or box of buttons—but I'd also
buy myself a songbook. Before long, I had me quite a collection.

"Then came a Monday when Mom said I couldn't go to Woolworth's. I was surprised because she knew how much I loved listening to the lady play the piano. 'Sorry, Victor,' she said, 'but I'm taking you and Kenny to Lakeside Hospital.' Until then, little had been
said about our physical condition. My older brother, Arthur, didn't
have it, so he grew facial hair and began shaving. But at twelve or
thirteen, I didn't think about shaving. At that age, having a small
penis wasn't a big deal. There was time for it to grow. There was
time for testicles to appear. Later I learned the condition is congeni-
tal and affects the hypothalamus, the region of the brain that trig-
gers hormones. The Deficiency is present at birth. It wasn't until the
midforties that a cat named Franz J. Kallmann, a New York geneti-
cist and psychiatrist, spelled it out, calling it a rare disorder whose
two chief characteristics are an inability to experience puberty and
the absence of the sense of smell. Nowadays it can be treated. Back
then we were still in the Dark Ages. We did know, however, that the
trick gene was carried by the women in my mother's family. Two of
her brothers were afflicted. I saw that with my own eyes.

"First there was Uncle Jack. My grandmother insisted that he
have an operation to drop his testicles, even though she was told it
was dangerous. It involved opening his scrotum. The operation

was performed when Jack was seventeen. I remember my mother telling her mother, 'You shouldn't have made him go through that.' But she did. Well, Jack returned to school and was doing gymnastics on the stationary horse when he missed a maneuver and fell on his crotch. The fall set off blood poisoning in his abdomen. The fall killed him. It was one of the few times we went to my grandmother's house. I was eight when I saw the open casket. No questions were asked; no questions were answered.

"Then there was Uncle Bern, another brother of my mom's. As my father was walking down the street, he saw Uncle Bern sitting in a doorway of a deserted building, down and out, and took him to our home. He'd been homeless for weeks. His mother had put him out. She didn't want to deal with anyone who carried the Deficiency. Not even her own sons. My mother took pity on him and had him stay with us for a while before bringing him to a hospital. He'd developed consumption. Weeks later he died. I heard my mother saying, 'This is something that can weaken a man's mind and destroy his outlook on life.'

"When Mom took us to the hospital, I understood the purpose. Even if the full implications of the Deficiency hadn't been explained, it was clear Mom was looking to save her boys from the pain ahead. At the clinic she was told there was a serum that was available only on an experimental basis. No guarantees. The doctor was eager to have us try the treatment to see if it worked. But Mom gave that man the fiercest expression I've ever seen. 'You'll not guinea pig on mine,' she told him. And with that, she took me and Kenny by the hand and marched us out. That's the last time any mention of the Deficiency was made—except when I asked my father about it and he just shrugged."

The trip to Lakeside Hospital happened in the spring. Seven months later, in early November, Justine was accompanying Shirley, her fifteen-year-old daughter, to school. Normally an A student, Shirley had been misbehaving, and as a result, her teacher had scheduled a conference.

"She and Mom were on Carnegie, a big thoroughfare," recalls Adoree, "when Shirley jumped into the street and started jaywalking across."

"At that very moment," Betsy continues, "a drunk driver was speeding around the corner. Mom saw what was happening. Her immediate instinct was to protect her child. She pushed Shirley back to the curb."

"In doing so," says Nadine, "Mom threw up her arms just as the car was on them. Back then cars had handles that prominently stuck out from the doors. Our mother's arm got caught in the door handle, and the car, still speeding, dragged her along Carnegie."

"The arm was severed," says Jimmy. "These days, maybe something could have been done. In those days it was hopeless. The doctors and nurses couldn't stop the hemorrhaging. The accident happened on a Friday. By Monday she was gone."

I ask Jimmy to describe the days surrounding Justine's death. He speaks with a sadness that makes it seem as though it happened yesterday.

"That weekend was the worst of my life. Late that afternoon, when Mom didn't come home, we all worried. Finally, Nadine showed up and said, 'Something's happened to Mom.' *But what could ever happen to Mom?* I asked myself. Mom was like the sun or the moon, a permanent fixture in God's universe. No harm could come to Mom; God wouldn't permit it. Then Shirley comes running home, crying hysterically, and races to the bathroom, where she slams the door. She won't come out, won't answer any of our questions. Now I know something is very wrong, but I don't know what. I don't know where Mom is—or Dad. My big brother, Arthur, is out, so I'm there to take care of the seven young ones. Hard as we try, Shirley won't say a thing. By now it's nighttime and there's a knock on the door. Standing there are big two policewomen. My heart is beating like crazy.

"'Where's my Mom?' I ask.

"'Get your sisters and brothers together,' says one of the women. 'They're going to have to come with us.'

"'Is my mom okay?' I want to know.

"'Take Jimmy too!' Shirley screams from upstairs. 'He's a real troublemaker. Take him!'

"Shirley was that way. She could go off on any of us kids for any reason. But this time she just wasn't contrary, she was hysterical. I wanted to go with my siblings, but first I wanted to know where we're going.

"'Juvenile Hall,' says the officer.

"'Why are we going there?'

"'Because we say so.'

"There was no kindness or understanding offered. These people were cold. We were taken from our home and brought to the detention center. That was on a Friday. We were never told why. When we asked why our father couldn't take care of us, we were given no answer. Our grandmother Clara was nowhere to be seen. So we spent the weekend huddled together, still without word. All weekend I prayed Mom was still alive. On Monday morning the policewomen brought me a government-issued suit. 'Put this on,' they said. 'Why?' 'Because you're going to see your mother.' *Oh good*, I thought to myself. *We're going to the hospital. She must be alive.* But when I looked out the window and saw two limousines, I recognized one of the drivers as the son of the local funeral director. That's when I knew. Mom was gone. We were driven to the funeral home, where Dad was waiting. My mother's mother, father, and aunt were there, seated apart from us. No hugs, no consolation. In front of us was an open casket. We were told to pay our last respects. I couldn't move. I couldn't look. I remained seated, staring at the floor. No one could know what I felt. No one could understand how much I loved her. No one could tell me that life was still worth living."

The aftermath of Justine's death was utter chaos. The siblings all tell variations of the same story. Rather than bringing the grieving survivors together, their mother's death triggered an even greater

tragedy: The family went to war. Arthur Scott fought his in-laws in
a vicious battle in which all parties, especially the Scott children,
suffered irreversible loss. The court records, sparse and frag-
mented, do not tell the story. Because all the warring adults are deceased, the siblings remain the only eye witnesses. Because they
were so young when it happened—and because they were never actually in the courtroom themselves—testing the veracity of their
versions is impossible. The result is a self-styled family mythology
developed over the years, differing in small degrees from sibling to
sibling.

"Being so young," says Nadine, "we weren't told the details.
But we did know that an ugly fight was under way—with us in the
middle."

"The fight," claims Jimmy, "was about money. And also
power. My grandmother, steered by her sister Hazel Mountain
Walker, didn't want my father to have custody. For his part, my father didn't really want custody either. The responsibility was too
much. The man could barely take care of himself, much less ten
kids. What he did want, though, was money. The driver came from
a well-off family who offered fifty thousand dollars. The accident
happened in front of a Chrysler/Packard dealership. Some of the
employees actually witnessed it, and they convinced Chrysler to
donate another five or ten thousand dollars to the family. So there
was considerable money—especially for those days and especially
for a poor family—coming our way."

"Dad always promised to keep us together," says Kenny. "It
was his intention to use that money to provide for us all."

"Money came in from people we didn't know," Nadine adds.
"An article about the tragedy appeared in the paper, and folks
started sending in their contributions."

But the generosity of the family did not match the generosity of
the public. The battle raged on.

"Dad tried to maneuver," says Jimmy, "but was outsmarted by
the other side. For a while he used Mrs. Wooding as a ploy. She

was a beautiful person, a neighbor who loved our mother and loved us as well. We called her Grandma. Dad thought if he put the money in a trust in her name, the judge would approve. But when the trial began, my grandmother and Hazel launched a full-scale attack on Dad. He couldn't survive the character assassination. His drinking and carousing were known to all. He fired back as best he could, but because Hazel was a lawyer—and an influential citizen to boot—he didn't stand a chance. The judge was disgusted by the bickering. He said, 'I've never seen such a heartless family.' He wouldn't give the money to either side, but created a little trust fund for each of the kids. Ultimately that money would disappear—where, I don't know."

"Keep in mind," says Adoree, "that these relatives—my grandparents, Hazel Mountain Walker—had huge houses, seven and eight bedrooms big. They could have taken us in. But that wasn't their interest. Their interest was in blocking my father, the man they'd detested ever since he married Mom. Other relatives were concerned. We later learned that Dad's sister, our Aunt Bess, who lived in Saint Louis, had her church donate money to bring all the kids back to live with her. But by then it was too late. We were separated and thrown into orphanages. Our family was broken."

"Adoree and I went off to one home," says Nadine. "She was ten and I was twelve. Meanwhile, Jimmy went to another orphanage with Kenny, who was eight; Betsy, seven; and Elsa, who was only six. The baby boys—Roger and Justin—were taken into different homes."

"I think of Humpty Dumpty," says Jimmy. "All the king's horses and all the king's men couldn't put us back together again."

This one stark fact—the family's inability to live in one place, in one house—haunts Jimmy to this day. Mention the subject, and you're likely to hear an hour-long disquisition. Jimmy's sweet demeanor turns sour. His anger, accumulated over a lifetime, is directed at four figures—his father, his Aunt Hazel, his brother Arthur, and his sister Shirley. "The oldest two kids should have known better," he claims. "They heard Mom say it. We all heard her say it. 'Family sticks together no matter what. Family is all that matters. Family is all we have.' But Arthur and Shirley betrayed her words and then Dad betrayed her memory when he bought them off with that trust fund money. I don't know how, but Dad got his hands on a part of the money. Once he did, he gave Arthur and Shirley their cash, and they were gone. He knew they'd split. He knew they didn't want to hang around and help, so he encouraged them to go. Meanwhile, he kept saying how he was going to buy a house big enough for all of us. But by then we—all the kids except Arthur and Shirley—were bouncing around from orphanage to orphanage. Being pulled from one place and pushed into another."

"Instability is frightening for children," says Nadine. "We experienced more instability in that period than you can imagine."

"We never knew what was coming next," Adoree remembers. "The hard part was not knowing."

"I stayed in four or five different orphanages in Ohio over the next three years," Jimmy recounts. "And in between, there was an episode with a Miss Biddie Colone."

"Biddie was Dad's lady friend," says Betsy. "She and Dad had set up a scheme where, by having us kids live with her, he could collect the money held by the court. For a short while we stayed in her house in Cleveland. Then she built a place out in Chagrin Falls, forty-five minutes outside of town in the country. They dumped us out there, but the house wasn't complete. There was no heat. We had to walk a mile to pull water out of a well. We had to walk another mile to get to the little school."

"If that was Dad's way of reuniting his kids," says Jimmy, "it was a miserable failure. We were lost out there in the country, living in a house so unsuitable that Dad had to find us another place closer to the school. By then the social workers were all over him because it was a clear case of child neglect. I still hadn't turned fourteen. Next thing I knew, Kenny, Roger, Betsy, Elsa, and I were sent to Youngstown and a woman named Eva Wade. Miss Wade was a kind soul with a loving heart who took in foster kids. She was a caterer who had cooked for the governor. Miss Wade was motherly, but I was still lonely. Loneliness was as much a part of me as my eyes or ears. I was lonely for Mom. I was lonely living in strange places and experiencing strange feelings. These were the years when the Deficiency could no longer be denied."

Jimmy stopped growing at four feet eleven inches. His hormonal deficiency remained a secret visible only in the form of stunted growth. Vivid memories of his Uncles Jack and Bern, victims of the syndrome, were enough to keep him from seeking medical help.

"The easiest thing was to pretend it wasn't there," he says. "The one person I might want to discuss it with—my dad—had nothing to say about it. I didn't even think about fixing my body because my body didn't feel broken. I could deal with my body. I felt sexual. I experienced pleasure when I masturbated. I felt drawn to girls, both physically and romantically, and I had several crushes. But I was not aggressive and, all during my teen years, remained a virgin. I couldn't help but feel small—I *was* small—and saw how that feeling could disturb my peace of mind forever. It was only the projection of Mom's thoughts into my life that saved me. Mom always said, 'Don't let your sorrows stop you. Go with what you got.' Mom made the best of her life, and I knew she wanted me to do the same."

During the tender teen years following his mother's death, Jimmy sought solace in performing arts.

"The artists who inspired me most," he says, "were young kids like Mickey Rooney, Donald O'Connor, and Judy Garland. They were my age, and they were doing it—up there on the screen, dancing and singing and expressing a kind of joy I couldn't resist. It was a joy I found nowhere else in life—not in my family, not in school, not in my little odd jobs. It was a joy that had to do with music, or show business, or going out in the world with nothing but a song in your heart. I remember going to see *The Wizard of Oz* not long after Mom died. Sitting in that dark theater and hearing Judy sing 'Somewhere over the Rainbow' was a religious experience. Judy was small in stature, but her voice was big. Suddenly I didn't feel small. When I sang, I realized my voice was big enough to hold all the feelings I felt in Judy."

Jimmy related to Judy Garland because she expressed the pain of an adult in the form of a child. She was a musical oddity whose emotional genius helped shape Jimmy's sensibility. In similar ways, Jimmy would inspire other precocious children who conveyed the frighteningly mature sounds of grown-up heartache—singers like Frankie Lymon in the fifties, Stevie Wonder in the sixties, and Michael Jackson in the seventies. In the late nineteen-thirties, for Jimmy, music and optimism were synonymous, a calming yet combustible mixture of hope and hype that defined a ballad style of high drama. Optimism fueled by restless energy was, and is, Jimmy's approach to progress.

"If you had been around him back then," says Nadine, his closest sister, "you would feel his sadness. But you also felt his sweetness. Jimmy was a boy who found pleasure in pleasing others, just as he had pleased our mother. Yet he could never do what an adult—namely, my father—should have done: Find us a home. Without a home, Jimmy was lost. So he quit school, went to work, and started searching for something we once had but lost. I'd say my brother's been searching ever since."

Jimmy's formal education was sporadic. He bounced from school to school, never staying in one for long. He lacked focus and, without parental guidance, drifted purposelessly. When he was sixteen, he left Youngstown and returned to Cleveland, where he attended Central High.

"That was uncomfortable," he says, "because Hazel Mountain Walker had become principal. When I'd pass her in the hallway, she'd look through me as though I were glass. Louis Stokes, who would later become a United States congressman, was in my class and became Hazel's protégé. For me, though, the only thing happening in school was music. Tadd Dameron had gone to Central High and played around town—the same Dameron who would become one of the most advanced writers of bebop. Tadd was a free spirit. He knew what the swing bands were doing, but he wanted to go further. Tadd was on the cutting edge."

With Judy Garland in the movie house and Tadd Dameron leading bebop bands, Jimmy found himself at the dawn of a new era. As the Depression gave way to the war years, popular music became more sentimental even as jazz became more experimental. The two genres held contrary aesthetics that, in equal measure, appealed to Jimmy's eclectic taste. In the early forties, the tender longing of Frank Sinatra's "Night and Day" and the inverted blues of Charlie Parker's "Hootie Blues" arrived within months of one another. Jimmy absorbed it all.

"It was the world outside school that called to me," he says. "I was fed up with all the different orphanages and different schools. Arthur and Shirley were long gone. Dad would show up once in a blue moon. My other siblings were still scattered in the different homes. And I was eager to break loose. I found out that the state of Ohio gives work permits for hardship cases. I convinced the state officials that, at sixteen, I qualified. I needed to work more than I needed to go to school. They believed me, and I was suddenly on the streets, learning to survive as best I could."

FUTURE OUTLOOK

*I*n 1941, a few months before the attack on Pearl Harbor drew the United States into all-out war, Jimmy went out on his own.

"He was a gutsy little guy," remembers Adoree. "Didn't matter that he was small and still looked like a child. He'd go up to anybody, anywhere, and ask for a job."

"The war woke up industry," says Jimmy. "Anyone who looked found work. They turned me down at the steel mills because I was too slight. But I convinced them to hire me at a plant that made parts for lathe machines. I found a little room in a boarding-house in the old neighborhood and started leading my life. Sometimes I'd see Dad out there on Seventy-ninth and Central, going in some bar, chasing some woman. 'Your daddy's a cunt hound,' a friend told me, and I couldn't argue. The man would never change. 'Victor,' he'd say when he saw me, 'I'm fixing to buy you kids a house. It won't be long before we're all together again.' If I asked Dad the ages of his kids or where they were living, he didn't have a clue. I'd just smile at him, remembering what Mom said—'The man's the only father you'll ever have'—and respectfully move on."

Jimmy moved from the shelter of foster homes to the unpredictability of the workplace with typical tenacity. He kept track of

his siblings and visited them at the various orphanages from time
to time. Mostly, though, his concern was with work. He also displayed a political savvy precocious for the times.

"The heavy air of racism has always hung over Cleveland like
a dark cloud," he says. "It was true in the forties just like it's true
today. But fortunately in the forties, before anyone was talking
about civil rights, we had a community leader, a black man named
John H. Holly, who began the Future Outlook League. I heard
about it and right away joined up. You paid a fifty-cent member-
ship fee and followed Mr. Holly's lead. He was organizing sit-ins at
the five-and-dime stores, bringing attention to discrimination in
employment. He had an impact that resulted in the big chains—
Woolworth's, Fisher Foods, A&P—hiring blacks, me included. The
league was a combination protest and placement center. Suddenly I
could do more than work at the lathe machine plant. Not only did
I get my best-paying gigs through Holly, but the man excited my
consciousness. He showed me that there was no reason not to apply for the job I was capable of performing. Holly was teaching a
positive way to deal with discrimination. He was beautiful."

Jimmy continued to look to Paul Robeson for inspiration:
"Robeson was an expression of our strength. Naturally we hooted
and hollered when Joe Louis beat Pino Carnera and James Brad-
dock and Max Schmeling. I was as happy as anyone. But Robeson,
who'd also been a great athlete, proved a great artist. His voice became the voice of all people looking to break free. His voice knew
no restrictions. He could sing a spiritual on a Monday, opera on a
Tuesday, and on Wednesday tear up some Shakespeare. No one ever
played Othello like Paul Robeson. I loved him because he wasn't
afraid to go wherever his artistic mind led. He showed me that art
was an adventure. Looking around the world I faced in Cleveland, I
wanted adventure. Working a hundred little jobs here and there was
fine, but I wanted more. I couldn't have used these words at the
time, but inside I was aching for some kind of creative expression.
And the only place I knew where such expressions came alive was
a theater."

The Metropolitan Theater, at Fifty-fifth and Euclid, was the magnet that drew Jimmy to the world of show business. "In our community, the creative people I knew were the singers, dancers, comics," he says. "They were the ones who expressed feelings everyday people wanted to express but couldn't. The artists lived life freely. Where did that freedom come from? How could I make it part of my life? I didn't know, but I had to find out. The place to start was the Metropolitan, and the way to start was ushering. I got the job in 1942. It was a good gig because it let me in every night to see the shows. And once I was in, I knew I was home."

Just like that, Jimmy had nightly access to two powerful currents that would shape his identity as an artist: popular singing in the form of movie musicals, and jazz in the form of live big bands.

"Before the show, you saw a movie," he says. "So here's James Cagney doing 'You're a Grand Old Flag,' followed by Ella Johnson singing 'Since I Fell for You' with her brother Buddy's big band, live on stage. Or I'd be watching Judy Garland singing her heart out in *Meet Me in St. Louis*. Soon as the lights go up, here's Cab Calloway—or Duke or Count or Erskine Hawkins. Man, they all came through. What came through most, though, was the excitement of the music and the dignity of the musicians. They wore tuxes. Looked elegant. Played precisely. Swung hard. And represented the best of our people. But not only the musicians—the tap dancers, the comedians, all the fabulous entertainers whose cultural stylings left you feeling that life was worthwhile.

"I also saw at an early age how musical stylings cut across cultural lines. The Metropolitan was in a mixed neighborhood. Besides blacks, you'd have Irish, Hungarian, Polish, all sorts of folks coming to these shows and loving every minute."

Jimmy was working two or three jobs at once.

"You couldn't make a living as an usher," he says, "so I also worked at a war plant typing up envelopes. For a while I was a busboy and dishwasher at Fred Harvey's, the restaurant in the Terminal Tower train station. That was another kind of excitement—

trains coming and going, me dreaming of riding one of those trains to faraway places. But the dreams had to wait. I had to eat, although I wasn't eating properly. That's how I got jaundice. My skin turned yellow and I had to request a leave of absence from this good gig I'd found as a shipping clerk.

"At the time my sister Shirley was back on the scene. She was married by then. She and her old man were always looking for money. Poor Shirley. Ever since Mom's death, her attitude about life got worse and worse. I know she felt guilty about what happened to our mother, and her guilt turned her devious. She devised a scheme to steal my sick-leave paychecks. She wound up telling lies about me and costing me my job.

"A little later—I must have been seventeen—I had a job at the Mayflower Donut Shop and just got paid. Shirley and her husband invited me over to their place, put booze in my Pepsi, and rolled me for my money. This it the first time I ever got drunk. That should have told me all I needed to know about alcohol. But I deceived myself into thinking liquor calmed me down. I suffered with this delusion much of my life.

"From the donut shop, I found work at a factory making khakis for the army. Of course making those khakis made me think of the war. Made me feel like I wanted to do my part. Patriotism was high, and I was ready to join up. I loved FDR and was eager to fight for freedom. Naturally, though, I flunked the physical. One look at me and they laughed. 'Too small,' they said. 'Too fragile. Too strange.'"

None of these jobs led Jimmy to permanent employment. His quixotic temperament wouldn't allow him to stay in one place for long. The key to Jimmy's future remained at the Metropolitan. His exploitation of the situation was quintessentially Jimmy: advancement through self-effacement.

"I got this idea to start up a concession for the artists who played there," he remembers. "I'd order up hand towels and soaps and organize their dressing rooms. I'd make sure everything was neat and clean. That way I could get close to the artists. It was a

nice little hustle for me. So I had my own janitorial service, sup-
ported by the theater owners, that put me in the middle of all the
backstage action. That's how I hooked up with Lem Neal and
Dickie Sims, tap dancers who needed a valet. By then a lot of the
entertainers had heard about this polite little guy who worked
hard to help them out. When Lem and Dickie asked if I'd travel
with them, I jumped at the chance. The Metropolitan had been
beautiful. It had opened up my eyes and my ears, but my feet were
wanting to travel. I couldn't wait to go down to Terminal Tower
and, instead of washing dishes at Fred Harvey's, jump on a train
and see the world. I don't even think I stopped to tell my family
good-bye. That's how excited I was about getting out of Dodge."

"Jimmy was always disappearing and reappearing in my life,"
remembers Kenny. "Once he got into show business, he'd be gone
for months at a time, and none of us would know where he was.
Then one day he'd show up and act like he was never gone."

Neal and Sims played a circuit of nightclubs, black and white,
around Ohio and Pennsylvania. Jimmy describes them as a "flash
dance team." They'd perform with other dancers as well as comics,
singers, and jazz combos. "You never knew which combination
was going to happen," says Jimmy. "It was makeshift entertainment packaged on the run."

For Jimmy, the turning point came in Meadville, Pennsylvania.
He was eighteen and in his second month of traveling with Neal
and Sims. Sharing the bill for the weekend was an all-star jazz unit
consisting of the two titans of the tenor sax, Ben Webster and
Lester Young, with trumpeter Howard McGhee, trombonist Benny
Green, bassist Slam Stewart, pianist Sir Charles Thompson, and
drummer Papa Jo Jones.

"These were the giants of jazz," says Jimmy. "Ben and Lester
drained those ballads dry. I especially loved Lester because Lester
was soft and subtle; Lester was like those painters who drew outside the lines. He was abstract. Others played solos that sounded
like stories; his solos sounded like dreams. Lester's approach hit
me hard because he took on the tradition of Coleman Hawkins—a

beautiful, big-toned, manly tradition—by turning shouts into whispers. Lester was his own man. When he got hit with heavy criticism, he laughed it off and kept to his same style. There are few real poets in the world. Lester is one of them.

"While I was ironing pants back in the dressing room, the sound of Lester's horn put me in a trance. I knew all the beautiful things he did with Basie and Billie Holiday—and yet here he was, a few feet away from me. I went to the wings and watched him. He held his sax at an unusual angle, almost horizontal. Everything about him was unusual. In my head, I sang along with his solo. I looked at the musicians, yearning to be heard by them. I looked at the audience, knowing I could hold their attention. I could reach them, entertain them, even captivate them. All I had to do was go out there and sing. But I didn't dare make a move. I'd been wanting to sing before a live audience ever since I'd been traveling with Neal and Sims, but lacked the nerve to ask. These jazz geniuses inspired me so much I finally found my nerve. I asked Sims to ask the guys—Ben and Lester—if I could sing a few numbers. Reluctantly they agreed. My moment had arrived.

"The songs I sang—'Talk of the Town' and 'It Had to Be You'—were songs already burned in my soul. I knew them as well as I knew my name. I didn't know what to do with my hands, so I just clutched the microphone. Some people danced, but most everyone crowded the bandstand to watch and listen. I heard a man say, 'That little boy sounds like a grown woman,' but I paid no attention, just like Lester paid no attention to his detractors. Besides, when I was through with the first number, the applause was loud and long. I had done it! They dug my second song even more. Man, I was flying! Until Lester approached me. We were walking off the stage when he said, 'Hey kid, you're a valet. Why don't you go back to the dressing room where valets belong?'

"I was crushed. After all, Billie Holiday, another idol of mine, had named Lester Young 'Pres,' the president of jazz. So here was this authority figure putting me down. It stung. I sulked for days. I thought I'd never get over it. It took me years but I finally understood what Pres was doing—trying to keep me from having a big head. Trying to keep my feet on the ground. Seeing a young kid about to ego-trip, he figured he'd splash some reality in my face."

The Neal/Sims gig lasted only another couple of months. Back in Cleveland, Jimmy found work in the same mode he'd pursue, with one crucial exception, for the next fifty years—as a single, that is, a freelance singer unattached to other musicians or organizations. Not until the late eighties would he have his own combo. He was a solitary minstrel wandering the landscape of American music during the second half of the twentieth century, an enchanting enigma whose way of making it in the world, like his way of making music, lagged two or three beats behind conventional time.

There's no accurate chronicle of Jimmy's early freelance years in Cleveland—no newspaper reports, no reviews—only the memories of Jimmy and his colleagues. Using borrowed rhythm sections, he gigged whenever he could in the black neighborhood of his home city, where the musical culture was becoming increasingly sophisticated. Bebop, the frenetic new jazz marked by edgy syncopation and extended harmonics, was taking hold. Charlie Parker, bebop's creator, had transported and transformed the big-band swing/blues–based music of his hometown Kansas City, taking it to New York. If the overriding goal of jazz had always been to entertain, Parker turned his back on that tradition. His interest was in pure artistic expression. By the midforties that expression was being felt in every major urban community in the United States, including Cleveland.

"Cleveland ran the gamut of jazz," says Harold Arnold, a saxophonist who led his own band in the midforties and was present in the early days of Jimmy's career. "We had the new cats who followed Tadd Dameron by playing bebop. And we had the older cats who you might call more mainstream. Jimmy got the benefit of both. I'm twelve or thirteen years older than Jimmy, and I'd been around. Been to New York. Played with Jimmy Lunceford. Knew all the swing musicians. Heard all the singers. But when I heard this little kid sing—I thought he was ten or eleven—I stopped dead in my tracks. The boy was singing like no one else. More than a high tenor, his voice is in the alto range. He sang in women's keys, which made his sound even more fascinating. His sense of syncopation was so relaxed, he was so far behind the drummer, he took you into another realm. The purity of his voice was scary. He offered up a sadness I'd never heard before. I got all this, not by hearing him with a band, but when he was working at the Loop Lounge as a singing waiter around forty-three or forty-four. I said to him, 'Look here, boy. Take off that apron and put on a suit. You need to serve up music, not meat loaf.'"

Eli Adams is another saxophonist who met Jimmy in the forties and became both a friend and colleague.

"The Cleveland jazz scene was jumping," says Adams. "Jimmy broke in a little ahead of me. I'd see him at the Cedar Gardens or the Rendezvous or the Blue Grass. He had no idea who I was, but acted like he'd known me his whole life. He encouraged my playing and made sure I felt included. His music was different than anything around us. Remember, we were caught between two mighty generations. We were taught by the old-school maestros—Louis Armstrong, Coleman Hawkins, Duke Ellington—but we also saw the birth of bebop. Jimmy was influenced by both factions. He loved both factions."

"You heard about swing cats who hated bop," says Jimmy, "or vice versa. But I noticed that the advanced players in both schools appreciated each other. When I first heard Charlie Parker, for example, it was that 'Hootie's Blues' record he made with Jay McShann's band out of Kansas City. That blew me away. Right off I heard Bird as a blues player—all the greats are blues players—but an *advanced* blues player. When I met Bird in Indianapolis in the early forties, he'd just left McShann and was advancing even further into the outer spheres of expression. I dug his every move. I dug him personally. He was an educated man, witty and brilliantly articulate. He heard me sing in the early days, when I was hustling up any little gig I could find. Sometimes I'd run into a piano player or drummer who'd bitch about me singing out of rhythm or too far back of the beat. 'Oh no,' Bird would say, 'your rhythm's right. Don't follow them. Let them follow you.' He understood what most didn't. Time is personal.

"Bird showed respect for the different forms—the swing bands, the classical cats like Stravinsky, the odd geniuses like Tadd Dameron. Tadd and Bird would meet up in New York a little later on. Tadd was writing classics like 'If You Could See Me Now,' one of Sarah Vaughan's first records, 'Hot House,' 'Lady Bird,' and 'Our Delight.' Meanwhile, Tadd would unexpectedly pop up at my gigs in Cleveland. I'd be singing when all of a sudden I'd hear some strange chord behind me. I'd look back there to see Tadd had slipped in to replace the regular piano player. His chords pushed me to new notes and different feelings. Like Bird, he encouraged me. Tadd stood for a new era where jazz would be freer. He made me feel like I was part of that era. Despite the fact that I didn't read or write music, the new music was flowing through my veins."

In spite of his musical adaptability, Jimmy had a tough time adapting to the macho world of jazz.

"Back then," remembers Adams, "the ignorant cats thought Jimmy was queer by how he looked and sounded. Some of them called him a faggot. They were off by a mile. Jimmy liked women and women liked him. His voice got to them. You couldn't call him sexy like Sinatra, but he had his own brand of sex appeal that went deep. He hit a chord in women no one else could reach."

On the matter of his own sexuality, Jimmy is blunt. "I could see getting confused," he says. "If you have small privates and no body hair, you might be doubting yourself, wondering which way to go. Especially when you hear derogatory comments from your colleagues. But the truth is that I longed to be with a woman. Always have. Still do. Being in show business at an early age, I knew

many gay men. Some showed interest in me. I declined—always respectfully, always in a manner to avoid hurting their feelings. Ever
since I was a teen, my own sexual feelings were straight ahead. I
enjoyed the company of women and dreamed, even as a young
man, of having a family of the kind that was destroyed when Mom
was killed."

If Jimmy's family of origin remained in disarray, he found solace in another family and comfort in an adopted mother. Oddly
enough, at the very moment when jazz was undergoing a revolution of tremendous creative energy, Jimmy stepped outside the revolution into a style of performance that harked back to vaudeville.
In 1945, along with his friend Eli Adams, he was hired to go on the
road with Estella Young, a contortionist-artiste who went by
the name of Caldonia but whom Jimmy called Mother.

"I met members of her troupe—dancers and musicians—who
hung out at the Majestic Hotel at Fifty-fifth and Central," says
Jimmy. "A couple of them had heard me sing in the local clubs and
mentioned me to Mother. She liked my voice. She called it unique
and said it would add to the appeal of her show. 'When can you
leave?' she wanted to know. 'Now,' I said. '*Right now!*'"

Mother would change Jimmy's life in profound and permanent
ways. When he left Cleveland, though, he was not alone. A few
months before he left Cleveland with Caldonia's troupe, Jimmy
made another startling move. At age twenty and still a virgin, he
married a sixteen-year-old girl, the first in a lifelong series of relationships marked by high hopes, dissolution, then pain.

ANGEL

As Jimmy talks about his first marriage, we're driving east
out of Los Angeles on Interstate 10. We're heading to Whittier
College to hear a concert by ninety-year-old Herb Jeffries, an important early influence on Jimmy. Jimmy's mind sweeps back to the
early forties as we listen to a CD of "Flamingo," Jeffries' seminal
hit with Duke Ellington from *Jump for Joy*.

"Herb was a stylist," says Jimmy, "an extremely light-skinned
brother who became a cowboy star. I knew his movies—*The
Bronze Buckaroo, Harlem Rides the Range, Two Gun Men from
Harlem*—but it was his singing that got me. Smooth. Relaxed.
You'd call it jazz, but you didn't have to be a jazz fan to get it.
Herb Jeffries was one of the cats who showed me that you just
don't sing a song; you sell it. That means winning over your listeners with dramatic presentation. See, Herb had much in common
with Judy Garland and Paul Robeson. Some said they were actors
first and singers second. Some said the opposite was true. But the
truth is that they were both at the same time."

When we arrive at the preshow reception, we meet a man who
Jimmy presumes is Herb's son or grandson. It's actually Herb himself, who, with a full head of hair and robust physique, looks

sixty, not ninety. He embraces Jimmy with gusto and introduces his wife, a woman several generations his junior. At the same reception, we run into Fayard Nicholas of the famed Nicholas Brothers. Still spry at eighty-seven, Fayard is with his wife, who appears to be in her forties. The concert is an easygoing romp through a suite of breezy swingtime songs, with Jeffries displaying remarkable energy. On the ride home Jimmy returns to the subject of his first marriage. The older man/younger woman connection is much on his mind.

"My first wife was Angel," says Jimmy. "That's not her real name, but she's still alive and well and I don't want to hurt her feelings in telling our story. I was twenty, and she was sixteen. At that tender age, a four-year difference is greater than a forty-year difference later in life. But the twist here is that in many ways she was older than me. I was still a virgin. And Angel was widely experienced.

"When I met her, she was a counter girl at the neighborhood drugstore. I went in there every day to have a Coke. I knew she liked me because she always put a cherry in my soda. She was a delicious-looking girl, copper skin; long, wavy, black hair; chubby body. Later in the fifties, when I saw the young Etta James, her look reminded me of Angel. Our flirtation remained innocent until we bumped into each other at a dance in a Cleveland club where the Earl Hines orchestra was playing. I was excited that night, not only to see Angel outside the drugstore, but to hear the music. Earl was not only one of the great pianists of his day—Nat Cole worshipped him—but his swing band was friendly to beboppers. He hired Billy Eckstine, Freddie Webster, a fellow Clevelander, Dizzy Gillespie, Charlie Parker, and a little girl named Sarah Vaughan. Earl was hip, and I was grooving high on the sounds when all of a sudden I see Angel. I'm used to her wearing an apron, and here she is in a tight red dress. We got to talking and dancing and feeling tight. That night I took her to my place, where she instructed me in the ways of love. I talk about Kallmann's Syndrome now, but back then I didn't discuss it with anyone. Of course I knew my penis was slight and my balls didn't hang, but I didn't know what that would mean once in bed with a woman. Angel showed me it didn't mean much. She stretched out the road map before me. By moving this way or that, by using hands and fingers and lips, by staying loose and being flexible, satisfaction came her way and mine. The girl widened my mind. Talk about putting a cherry in my Coke! It was the deepest introduction to manhood a student could hope for, a blessing and a gift. I saw her experience had been vast and was grateful for her sweet instruction. It was only afterwards that I saw her troubled soul.

"When it came time to take her home, she started crying. When I asked what was wrong, she told me the story: Her father was using her sexually. Her mother knew, but rather than protect her daughter, she became angry at Angel, as though it were Angel's fault. The situation was beyond sad. It was sick, and Angel had no way out. She'd been with many other men as a way to escape, but the escape never worked. Hearing all this broke my heart. Maybe that's why, two weeks later, we went off and got married."

Jimmy married on a whim, a wish, a prayer. His decision to marry was, like the music of his heart, an act of spontaneity, an improvised riff, a gesture of generosity and considerable hope. In the area of sex, where Jimmy was most vulnerable, Angel indoctrinated him with gentle patience. Beyond that, he felt constrained to rescue her from a home life that threatened her emotional and physical well-being.

"How else could she get out of that household?" he asks. "How else could she escape her evil father? Besides, she was the one who brought me into this new world of physical pleasure. If she could do that, the least I could do was bring her into my world of show business. Estella Young understood. That's why I called Estella 'Mother.' She arranged for Angel to go out on the road with us. I thought I'd discovered heaven on earth. But the reality was that I'd discovered hell."

Estella Young had taken her handle, Caldonia, from the enduring Louis Jordan composition of the same name. In the early forties, she had toured with Jordan, whose scaled-down jump band,
brilliant tunes, and infectious vocals became the basis of a generation of rhythm and blues. The idol of future rockers like Chuck
Berry, Jordan offered a commercial counterpoint to the noncom-
mercial bebop emerging during this same tumultuous epoch. Many
women claimed that "Caldonia" was named for them. But Estella
had actually interpreted the song in a dance as part of Jordan's
troupe. Woody Herman's version, released earlier than Jordan's,
was also a huge hit, establishing "Caldonia" as a permanent fixture in the culture of jump, jive, and jazz.

"When I met Mother," says Jimmy, "she was an older woman.
Maybe sixty. But look here: Mother had the body of a twenty-year-
old. Her face may have shown some age, but the woman had the
legs of life—long, perfectly shaped legs to make Tina Turner turn
green with envy. Mother came from Baltimore, where she grew up
around Billie Holiday and traveled in show business circles with
black movie stars. Kitty Murray, the film actress who played
Rochester's girlfriend on the *Jack Benny Show,* was her best friend
and often hung out with us. It was an exciting troupe of comics,
singers, musicians, and dancers, a complete show choreographed
by Mother, who also did the booking. In some spots—like Newport News, Virginia—we stayed for more than a year."

Jimmy's departure from Cleveland marked the beginning of a
new phase in his professional life. As a featured vocalist in an eclectic vaudeville-style show, he was, as always, something of an oddity,
but one who proved popular with highly critical black audiences.

"I first saw Jimmy Scott with the Caldonia Revue in the midforties," reports Ruth Brown, the rhythm-and-blues pioneer whose
massive hits for Atlantic Records in the fifties designated the label
as "The House That Ruth Built."

"I was a sixteen-year-old girl living in Portsmouth, right across
the bridge from Newport News, where Caldonia took over Bart

Dade's Victory nightclub. I was sneaking in—Daddy would have killed me had he known—and, believe me, I got an eyeful. The shipyard and navy base were in Newport News, so the place was popping. Caldonia was the main attraction. Some said she was a stripper, but not the crude, topless or bottomless types they have today. She was artful. Back then exotic dancing was like jazz. You had to have style and grace.

"Picture it: Caldonia comes out there in a bunch of rags, looking like a bum. One by one, she pulls off the rags until she's standing there in her long underwear. Everyone cracks up. Then she slowly peels off the long underwear, slowly revealing these skimpy panties and barely-there bra of rhinestone and lace. Now Caldonia does her thing, throwing her legs all around her head, twisting herself into a pretzel, making moves you can't believe. My mouth is hanging open. I think I've seen all there is to see, but I ain't seen nothing till I see—and hear—Jimmy Scott.

"*What's this little boy going to do out there?* I thought to myself. Newport News wasn't New York, but we raised some bad singers—Ella Fitzgerald and Pearl Bailey were hometown girls—and we knew good music. But Jimmy was something else. Wasn't five feet tall. Hardly moved his hands. Didn't dance. Didn't sway. Didn't even shake his hips. But, Lord, have mercy, this boy brought down the heavens. Phrasing for days. Sang a song, for example, called 'So Long' that took him so long to sing I thought I'd die. But I lived to record it myself—as did the R&B singer Little Miss Cornshucks—without approaching Jimmy's sensitivity. I believe sensitivity is the key. He wasn't a little boy, he wasn't a grown man, but you knew he'd lived other lives and suffered in ways we could never understand. That suffering, in a person so petite and tender, made a mighty impression. Yes indeed. Like all the clubs back then, the joint was packed with pimps and hookers, rough guys and tough gals, and every sort of criminal you could name. But when this child got to singing, tears ran down the cheeks of cold-blooded killers. The room was frozen with respect for a true artist. We'd already known we were witnessing the start of a genius generation. Bird was flying; Dizzy was coming on; Dinah was killing; soon Sarah would be scaring every singer in sight. But this little man would hold his own among the giants. His soul scorched you clean. By exposing his emotional insides, he exposed yours."

"I got good response at the Victory Club," says Jimmy, "but so did everyone else. For this particular gig, Caldonia put together a chorus line plus a helluva band, including Jack McDuff, who was stranded in Virginia before we picked him up. Later Jack got famous on the organ, but in those days he was banging out boogie-woogie piano. We also had Earl Basie, the tap dancer known as Groundhog. Groundhog was the only one that the great dancer Baby Laurence feared. A few years later, when I was hanging out with Bird, I remember Bird's drummer, Max Roach, telling me how he got many of his bebop beats watching Groundhog's feet.

"Mother also carried female impersonators, the best being Jimmy 'Chickie' Horne, who performed as Hazelle Horne. That's where Flip Wilson got his character Geraldine."

"Chickie was the best drag act out there," adds Ruth. "I saw him at the Victory Club, and later, when I went on the road, I took him with me. He called me Big Sis."

"Back then the camaraderie was deep," says Jimmy. "Most of us came from broken homes. We were looking for a new family. Caldonia provided it. We also needed discipline. Mother was strict but caring. She was a teacher. The big lesson was stage presentation. It's got to be tight and right. Rehearse, rehearse, rehearse. Professionalism meant being on time, hitting your mark, knowing your lines. Professionalism meant that if your colleagues made a mistake—if a musician played a sour note or a dancer made a wrong move—you carry on as if all is well. Never chastise a fellow artist in front of the audience. Chastisement was left up to Mother. I remember inviting a member of the audience on stage to sing with me. After the show, hands on her hips, Mother read me the riot act. 'Look, boy,' she said, 'This is *my* revue. No one gets on my stage unless *I* say so. That clear?' 'Yes, ma'am.'

"But Mother never forgot your humanity. She taught humility. I might have been getting good applause as a singer, but I also played the lowly part of a shirtless slave boy, wearing baggy pants and a turban, offering apples to the shake dancers decked out in Egyptian costumes. And just when I'd think Mother was this holy figure of divine love, I'd watch her go out there, work the crowd, collecting dollar bills with her crotch. Her thing was always, 'I *will* get paid.' And if Mother got paid, we did too."

The rapport between Jimmy and Caldonia was exceptional. Eli Adams remembers Jimmy clinging to her "like a child clinging to his mama."

"Until very recently," says Ruth, "I thought Estella *was* Jimmy's real mother. Everyone thought so. Wasn't just that he called her Mother. It was how they acted together; she took him by the hand and treated him like her sure-enough son."

"Mother would take me shopping—she bought me my first tux—not at the fancy department stores," Jimmy remembers, "but the thrift shops. 'The thrift shops are where you find the real bargains,' she'd say. The thrift shops are where I still shop today. Mother was practical, even in her attitude about music. When she heard how some beboppers were turning their backs on the audience and refusing to play to the crowd, she didn't argue; she appreciated their art. She just took their numbers, like 'Cherokee' or 'Hot House,' and choreographed them as exotic dances. Mother made it all work."

Meanwhile, Jimmy's marriage was not working at all. While he was working with Estella, Angel accompanied her husband but apparently had an agenda of her own.

"I was naive from the get-go," he says. "Thinking I could save Angel from a life of abuse, I never saw the real life she was living. While I was singing at night, she'd found a way to make money. The girl was turning tricks. Out there on the road I caught her doing just that. Walked in on her with some guy. He ran off, but I was so pissed I popped her."

This was the first time Jimmy had been violent with a woman.

"Popping a woman," he says, "was the last thing I'd thought I'd do. No one has the right to hit anyone. But seeing my wife selling herself to some guy was too much. She said she was sorry, and I wanted to accept her apology. The truth, though, is that Angel was still a girl. Sexually, she was a mature woman, but emotionally she was a child. I couldn't deal with that—couldn't deal with the cheating—so I cut her loose. I gave her a ticket back to Cleveland, and that was it. We'd only been together for six months and wouldn't get legally divorced for four years. But our relationship was finished. Fortunately, Angel straightened herself out and made a nice life for herself. She remarried and had a family and when I saw her—this was many years later—she was healthy and happy. She'd put the violent life behind her."

According to firsthand witnesses, Jimmy was most often the victim, rather than the perpetrator, of violence.

"It was well known among Jimmy's friends in the forties and fifties," claims Ruth Brown, "that he went with women who abused him. You'd always see Jimmy with some lady twice his size, twice as tall and twice as wide. He made strange choices. Don't ask me why."

I ask Jimmy why. His reply addresses the other dark theme that shadows his story: liquor.

"I started drinking as a young man," he confesses. "And I think drinking hurt my judgment when it came to women. In the forties I liked Old Kentucky bourbon. In the fifties, it was vodka. I was warned by doctors early on that I couldn't tolerate much alcohol. Wouldn't take much to get me drunk. For many years, though, I ignored the warnings."

In the wake of his breakup with Angel, Jimmy reacted in a way that both defies logic and defines his peculiar relationship to romance: He fell in love with another prostitute. This one he gives the fictitious name May, a sixteen-year-old girl who frequented the Victory Club in Newport News.

"May was beautiful," remembers saxophonist Eli Adams, who worked with Jimmy and Caldonia during their long stay in Virginia. "Like Angel, she was a big girl. Weighed at least two hundred and fifty pounds."

"A lot of these women that Jimmy picked looked like our mom," says his brother Kenny. "They had sweet faces and chubby frames. Jimmy hadn't grown to his full height. That wouldn't happen till years later. He was still under five feet, and next to those chicks he looked tiny."

"To see Jimmy and his ladies," Ruth Brown quips, "made you think of 'Jack Sprat would eat no fat and his wife would eat no lean.'"

"Jimmy and May were crazy for each other," adds Eli. "They were always kissing each other and holding hands. But they also fought like cats and dogs. He'd go upside her head—or she'd go upside his."

"May was attached to Peaches," says Jimmy, "a well-known madam who catered to the sailors. May was Peaches' star attraction. She was much admired by men, not only for her beauty but the softness of her disposition. As with Angel, I saw something good in May. She too had been abused in her young life, but her heart was pure. I thought I could help her. Sexually, she helped me feel good about myself. With all her experience, she created a satisfying physical relationship for us. We were together for over a year. Sometimes we got a little crazy—I could get jealous or she could get restless—but I took her away from a life that would have ruined her. I hope I did that by showing her some kindness. I was happy to see her turning her life around, just as my life was turning around. I was about to break into something big."

GATES

With the war won and optimism in the air, America's black music, optimistic by nature, was energized to a feverish pitch. In the midforties, big bands were still banging it out, the new bop was burning, and rhythm and blues had begun its steady ascent. Of the giants of jazz, only one artist had the savvy to successfully integrate all three genres into a single unit. Vibraphonist Lionel ("Gates") Hampton blazed through the decade—and beyond—with an impassioned approach to artful entertainment that had turned him from a Benny Goodman sideman to a superstar. It was with Hampton that Jimmy gained his first, fleeting taste of national prominence. Ironically, Jimmy's singing with Hampton ran counterpoint to all styles and genres. He stood out then as he stands out now—as an anomaly.

"Gates is a genius, no doubt," says Illinois Jacquet, the man who put Hampton's big band on the map with his ferocious tenor solo on "Flying Home" in 1942. "Part of Gates's genius was in spotting other geniuses. More cats came out of his band, more genuine geniuses—Dexter Gordon, Charlie Mingus, Wes Montgomery, Dinah Washington, Quincy Jones, Betty Carter . . . the list goes on and on. The list includes Jimmy Scott. Yet of all the geniuses Gates developed, Jimmy's the least known. Can you tell me why?"

"We called him Gates," says Jimmy. "That was our name for Hamp, and it was Hamp's name for all of us. 'Hey, Gates,' he said to me, 'you happy to be in the band?' 'Not happy, Gates,' I said, '*delirious!*' That was 1948. But the story with me and Gates started years earlier. I was playing Dayton in 1944, when a reporter from the *Cleveland Call and Post,* our black newspaper, came to the club in a panic. 'Been looking all over for you, Jimmy. Lionel Hampton's playing the Palace Theater and he wants to audition you.' Well, Gates had a strange way of auditioning. You showed up at the gig and sang live with the band, right there in front of the audience. The Palace, remember, was *the* showcase venue in Cleveland. I'd never sung there before, but I showed up, fresh as a daisy, and sang 'Why I Was Born' and 'I Wish I Didn't Love You So.' The crowd dug it, and I figured Gates did too. I was eager for the gig, of course, because the Hampton band was a breeder of stars. When he left Benny Goodman and began his own band in 1940, Hamp was already a star. From the jump, he had huge hits like 'Hamp's Boogie Woogie.' Gates was the guy who discovered Ruth Jones and gave her the stage name Dinah Washington. Gates's wife, Gladys, who ran the operation and watched the money like a hawk, schooled Dinah on high fashion and class. Like my mom, Gladys was a seamstress and designer and, before meeting Gates, custommade clothes for Joan Crawford. Between the two of them, Gates and Gladys could make your career. I thought I was ready. That night at the Palace, I thought I sang well. Afterwards, I waited for word, but word never came. Next day, Gladys, Gates, and the cats were gone. I wasn't that upset, because only a month or two later I hooked up with Caldonia."

By 1946, twenty-one-year-old Jimmy had been traveling with Estella Young for a year. The Virginia gig had run its course, though, and Caldonia was forced to change her format.

"When we left the Victory Club in Newport News," says Jimmy, "it was clear that the days of Caldonia's Revue were over.

Tastes had changed. But Mother was a survivor, and I was inspired to see how she adjusted. She started working as a single, and I was thrilled when she took me along. That's how I wound up at Gambi's in Baltimore. I went there with May and met Redd Foxx, who was emcee. Redd took a liking to me and became my big brother. Some even said we looked alike. Redd liked to party and Redd could be arrogant, but I loved his dirty drawers. In the morning he'd bang on my door shouting, 'Nigger, get up and get out of there. We need you and we love you and screw you!' Then he'd take me over to the Royal Theater, where he and Ralph Cooper, the famous black actor, were doing shows with Joe Louis. They'd do little interviews and jokes with Joe, who all the brothers and sisters were thrilled to see in the flesh. The show traveled to black theaters all over the country, and Ralph and Redd had me appear on several of them. The biggest thing Ralph and Redd did for me, though, was bring me to the Baby Grand on 125th Street in New York City. 'This boy's gotta sing in the Big Apple,' Redd kept saying. So Ralph, who was hooked up with everyone in Harlem, arranged the date. It happened in 1947."

While Fifty-second Street was famous in the forties, with clubs like the Three Deuces and the Famous Door featuring everyone from traditionalist Wingy Manone to modernist Thelonius Monk, 125th Street remained the heart of Harlem. The Baby Grand, on the corner of Eighth Avenue, just down from the Apollo Theater, attracted a decidedly nontourist crowd.

"New York was exciting," says Jimmy, "because the atmosphere was charged with music and musical stars. Lester Young was at the same hotel where I was staying, the Alvin at Fifty-second and Broadway. He remembered me from Pennsylvania, but this time he treated me like a colleague, even invited me to his concert at Town Hall, where he was headlining with Sarah Vaughan. Right down the street, I could go hear Coleman Hawkins, Art Tatum, Erroll Garner, Nat Cole, Billy Daniels, Diz, and Bird. All the styles were sizzling together in the same pot. It was beautiful. And the crowds were beautiful too—servicemen and society ladies and the out-of-town visitors curious about this jazz music. Uptown, though, wasn't about curiosity. Uptown music was the bread and butter of the community. The Baby Grand crowd was the most musically sophisticated I'd ever faced. These brothers and sisters were accustomed to hearing Ella and Billie. This was the neighborhood of Fats Waller and Willie 'The Lion' Smith. Funnyman Nipsey Russell was the emcee, and when he introduced me, when I went out there to sing in front of a borrowed rhythm section, first thing I heard from the crowd was, 'Is he a girl? He looks like a girl.' The words wounded me, but I acted like I didn't hear. I just gave the downbeat and went into 'There I've Said It Again,' a Vaughan Monroe hit I tried to refashion my own way. Afterwards, dead silence. That same voice yelled out, 'Well, *is* he a girl?' 'Whatever he is,' someone else screamed, 'the motherfucker can sing!' With that, the room exploded with applause. I stayed there a month.

"The Baby Grand opened many doors. All the cats came by after their own gigs or on their nights off. Basie, Bird, Bud Powell, Oscar Pettiford. Willie Bryant, emcee at the Apollo, was always dropping in and spreading my name around.

"The Baby Grand is where I met Billie Holiday. Of course I knew Lady Day's music from her Columbia days, when she played with Teddy Wilson and Pres. Then she signed with Decca because she wanted to sing with strings. All the singers—me included—long to sing with strings. It's like sleeping on silk sheets. Billie had just gotten back from Hollywood, where she'd costarred in *New Orleans* with Louis Armstrong. The movie was jive. Lady played a singing maid, but both she and Pops sang their butts off. Their characters might have been degrading, but their music made me proud.

"I was even prouder when Billie caught me after my set and said, 'I hear what you're doing, and you're doing it right.' She invited me to her table. It was just her and her little dog. She started talking about Hollywood. She swore she'd never play no servant again, and she never did. I knew she was high, but she was never haughty in her high. Her high showed her tender side, her need for love. Her high seemed to lift her on a cloud of sweetness that let her float over sad feelings and bad memories.

"Lady started coming to the club regularly and would often bring Sadie, her mom, who I grew to love. Then Lady disappeared. Later I learned she was in the joint, and when I returned from Cleveland to the Baby Grand a year or so later, we gave her a big party celebrating her release. She waltzed in, glowing with good health. 'Jimmy,' she said, 'I'm beating this thing before it beats me.'

"Milt Jackson, the vibist we call Bags, was also around. Bags was the salt of the earth. We became running buddies, riding over to Minton's or Clark Monroe's Uptown House, where beboppers like Bird were mixing it up with the older cats like Roy Eldridge and Coleman Hawkins. Billy Eckstine would drop in to sing. So would Billy Daniels. Back then everything was everything, and everything sounded good. Bags might sit in; I might sing a ballad; Bird might play twenty-five choruses of 'Cherokee.' Anything might happen. Off and on, I played the Baby Grand for a couple of years.

"The best thing that happened at the Baby Grand was meeting Doc Pomus, the Jewish blues singer who, because of polio, walked on crutches but raced around the city like a fire engine. Doc was Doctor Soul. Doctor Sincerity. Doctor Love. We became fast friends, and knowing I was new in the city, he showed me his hometown, from the Bronx to Battery Park. He took me home with him to Brooklyn, where I met his brother and mother, who treated me like a son. For a while, he went with Aida, my brother Arthur's step-daughter, a helluva singer herself. We all became family.

"Doc knew more about black music—loved it more passionately—than anyone in the world. His main man was Big Joe Turner, the Kansas City shouter. Like Joe, he had a huge voice and a huge heart. Like me, he had physical disabilities that never got in his way. He'd already started his songwriting, and I could hear that his talent was strong. Doc himself was a strong character, honest and real in the way New Yorkers are real. For me, the man was a pillar of support. To hear him comparing me to the important jazz singers of the day was an embarrassment. I never thought of myself that way. Still don't. But the fact someone as hip as Doc did— well, I could use all the encouragement I could get. And Doc— from the moment I met him until the day he died—provided all the encouragement I needed."

During his extended gig at the Baby Grand, Jimmy had been out of touch with his family. When he learned that Shirley was living in New York, he quickly got in touch with her. For all the difficulties marring their relationship, he still sought to reconcile.

"According to my sisters," says Jimmy, "Shirley was having a hard time. I found her living in a dump, down in a flooded basement apartment. She had her three kids with her, and the whole scene broke my heart. She scornfully took the money I offered. 'No one's ever done nothing for me,' she complained. I knew she was still guilty about what happened to Mom ten years before. No one ever blamed her; no one ever would. But she carried the guilt deep inside, and seeing her only reminded me how my family had been devastated by the death of our mother."

Between his first small success in New York at the Baby Grand and the decision by Hampton to finally hire him, Jimmy picked up gigs wherever he could. Without a manager, he relied on contacts— club owners, bartenders, musicians, friends—to set up dates.

"I played Club Delisa in Chicago," he remembers, "with Little Miss Cornshucks, who came out like a lost country girl—bandanna around her head, oversized overalls—and sat on the edge of the stage, swaying her basket back and forth, singing the blues so hard and true that by the time she was through the basket was heavy with change. In my own case, my own numbers, 'Please Be Kind,' 'You'll Never Know,' were also getting over. I made more from tips thrown on stage than the few bucks paid by the owner.

"Milwaukee was a good spot for me. I developed a little following at the Flame Club, where I almost did myself in. I was carrying a gun then, a little .22. Having a hard pistol in your pocket does something to a dude. More and more, cats were bothering me, questioning my manhood and calling me names."

"At twenty-two or twenty-three," says Eli Adams, "Jimmy still looked thirteen—and a *young* thirteen at that. Plus, he had that soft look that confused men. I always thought he was crazy to carry a gun, but I understood why he did. He was tired of being harassed."

"I figured I needed protection," Jimmy explains, "but I had no business with a firearm. Especially when I was drinking. During this engagement, I'd been hired by an arrogant, one-note piano player who, when the gig was over, paid me eight dollars after promising twenty. I got mad and called him a cheat. Next thing I know, he knocks me down and kicks me in the head so hard the scar still shows today. I limp out of there, go to my room, get my gun, and start looking for the brother. I find out where he lives and shoot out all the windows in his house. Thank God no one's home. Back at the Flame, the owner talks me out of my pistol. 'You ain't never gonna be no gangster,' he says. 'You ain't no bad guy. Only harm you'll do is to yourself.' I saw he was right and gave up the gun.

"Milwaukee was also where, for the first and only time, I tried smack. I'd been smoking reefer for some time. Reefer relaxes me. My reefer buddy had some heroin. I snorted it up and instantly got sick. Walked out of there, over to a doctor's office, to ask for help. I could hardly move. The doctor gave me some antidote. 'The bad feeling will pass,' he said, 'but never touch the stuff again.' I never did.

"I was in Milwaukee when I learned of the terrible death of our baby brother, Justin. It happened in 1948, when Justin was eleven. We had just realized that he suffered from the syndrome, too. He was living in a foster home in Ravenna, Ohio, away from his father and brothers and sisters, when he and four of his buddies went to a Saturday afternoon movie. On the way home, they drank water from a well contaminated by a nearby chemical plant. All five friends died. I got the news in a telegram from my father: 'Your

brother Justin is dead. Send money to help us pay for funeral.' By
the time I got home, the funeral was already over. I'd visited Justin
only a few weeks before he grew so violently sick. Now what was I
supposed to say? What was I supposed to feel? What was I supposed to do? I felt rage and grief all mixed together. I sent the
money, thinking how at least Mom didn't have to suffer the death
of her baby. I thought of Dad, who, no matter how many times he
promised, still couldn't care for his kids. I thought about it all, put
my pain in my pocket, and went back to Milwaukee to sing.

That same year, four years after Jimmy auditioned for Lionel
Hampton in Cleveland, he was again summoned by Hampton.

"It was in Milwaukee that Andrew Tibbs, Dinah Washington's brother-in-law, came into the club to say Gladys Hampton
was looking for me. Gates was ready. Next thing I knew, I had a
ticket to join the band in Saint Louis. From then on, life was
never the same."

The notion that Jimmy's art runs counterpoint to the world around
him seems especially true at this moment of his life. In Hampton's
stable of would-be stars, Jimmy's idiosyncratic style stood
strangely apart from the crowd-pleasing, over-the-top charts fa-
vored by the thundering band. As a remarkable vibist—his 1947
live concert working of "Stardust" remains one of the great mar-
vels of improvised music—Hamp had an affinity for other virtu-
osos. He was fluent in all styles, grunting enthusiastically as he
shaped his resounding solos. First recorded by Louis Armstrong in
1930 and then featured, along with pianist Teddy Wilson and
drummer Gene Krupa, in Benny Goodman's famous quartet from
1936 to 1940, Hamp was a dynamo of creative energy. He started
his big band at the prompting of his wife, Gladys, the power behind the throne. As big bands began losing speed in the midforties,
Hamp defied the decline and became increasingly popular. The reason had as much to do with showmanship as music—and a marriage built on sound business.

"Gladys was brilliant," says Quincy Jones, who joined the band as a teenager in 1951, three years after Jimmy. "As a woman, she was light-years ahead of her time. She'd jump in Joe Glaser's face, the tougher-than-tough guy who managed Louis Armstrong and Billie and booked Basie and Hamp. She could be cold. She had to be cold. In those days, a woman trying to do big business in the world of jazz was unheard of. She could also be warm. She was like a mother to me. The power of Hamp's shows and steel of Gladys's drive created a sensation. Amazing as it seems, Glaser was selling Duke and Basie off Hamp's popularity."

Hamp weathered the frantic permutations in jazz by offering up a smorgasbord of musical delights, all geared to satiate the audience's hunger for visceral pleasure. He got his crowds high. At movie theaters, concert halls, and dance palaces from coast to coast, he presented a full-throttled throw-down, an extravaganza of epic musical proportions.

"It was a rock-and-roll show," says Quincy. "He was the Rolling Stones of his day. He wasn't happy until he had every single fan up on his feet jumping up and down on two and four. He bopped till he dropped—and he expected . . . hell, he *demanded* the same of everyone on stage."

Gil Bernal, who played sax in the band during the same period that Jimmy joined, describes the scene and show: "Young guys like Q and myself were thrilled to be part of it because Gates's groups were already legendary. We'd seen him bring out Arnett Cobb and Johnny Griffin; we'd heard Dinah wailing and Illinois screaming, and now we were expected to do the same. Every gig was do or die. We'd be dressed in orange jackets bright as the sun. Gates would run out in a white double-breasted suit, red shirt, black tie. We'd open with 'Air Mail Special' from his Benny Goodman days. Early on there'd be a two-man tenor battle. The tenor men—in my day it was Johnny Board versus Curtis Lowe—would stomp in from the back of the hall or dance down the aisles. Sometimes they'd be up in the balcony. They'd fall on their knees; they'd fall on their backs; they'd out-honk each other until one fainted dead away while the other revived him with a towel. To calm things down, Al Gray would play a haunting ballad like 'Bewitched Bothered and Bewildered.' Then Sonny Parker, the blues singer, would fire 'em again with 'Ain't Nobody's Business.' Gates would tear it up with 'Hamp's Boogie Woogie,' chorus after chorus after chorus. Man, every night was a marathon. Benny Bailey blowing some sizzling bop, Milt Buckner on piano and organ banging out those big block chords on everything from 'Blue Moon' to 'How High the Moon.' No less than three chick singers—Irma Curry, Jeanette Franklin, and Betty 'Bebop' Carter, who was making a name for herself as a scatter supreme. In the middle of this wildness, here comes Little Jimmy Scott."

"Gates gave me the name," says Jimmy. "Gates was into novelties. He loved gimmicks. In those days, child stars like Sugar Child Robinson were all the rage. I was twenty-eight, but he told the audience I was sixteen. Some thought I looked younger than sixteen. Anyway, *Little* Jimmy Scott seemed to fit the bill. I didn't like it, but who was I to argue? This man was carrying thirty-two people up and down the road. No one was bigger than Lionel Hampton. Six trumpets, four bones, five saxes, piano, guitar, two bassists, and two drummers. Gates himself was a fabulous drummer. It was all about that intoxicating rhythm. This is where rock and roll started, right inside the Hampton big band. This is where the kids got the big beat. Gates would swing the crowd so hard that Frank Schifman, the man who owned the Apollo, swore he saw his balcony starting to sway. By the time I got on stage, the crowd was already on fire."

"Gates called him Little Jimmy Scott, but we called him Crying Jimmy Scott," Quincy reports. "Night after night, I'd be sitting back there in the trumpet section listening to this man cry his heart out. He'd just tear you up. I'd already worked with Ray Charles in Seattle, so I knew something about soul. But Jimmy's soul, shaped by the hippest jazz phrasing and delivered in that seductive rhythm delay of his, had its own luxuriant sheen. It was as though he stood in the calm eye of Hamp's hurricane. Everyone leaned in to listen. A hush fell over the crowd. You could hear a pin drop. You could sense Jimmy taking us all to an emotional level that was high and deep at the same time."

"Emotions ran high in that band," remembers trombonist Jimmy Cleveland. "Watching Jimmy work, I understood he was coming from another place. Other people compared him to Billie Holiday, but I didn't. His artistic statement was original. It was staggering to see him go out there every night and steal the show. Personally, he was unassuming and kind, but I could feel how he hurt. Once in a while I'd hear someone from the audience yell out, 'He's a faggot!'"

"People would ask me," says Hampton, "'Is that a woman dressed as a man or a man wanting to be a woman?' I'd say, 'He's just a boy.'"

"For a long time," adds Quincy, "the joke was that Jimmy wasn't a fag, he was a lesbian. He suffered from being an oddity. We roomed together on the road. Playing with Hamp down South, we once had to spend the night together in a funeral parlor, sleeping in a room with caskets containing dead bodies. Under such circumstances, you get to know a person. And I knew Jimmy was straight. He was an accommodating and good-hearted cat, but he turned weird when he drank."

"Little Jimmy Scott—he could gain a hundred pounds and he'd still be small," wrote Hampton band member Jerome Richardson in Quincy Jones's autobiography *Q*. "It seemed like every city we went to, he'd say, 'One of my ex-wives lives here.' He'd face up to cats six feet tall, and the singer Ernestine Anderson would have to talk the guy out of fighting Jimmy."

"The atmosphere of Gates's band was volatile," Cleveland claims. "We were overworked and underpaid, and we didn't like it. There was also a good-sized contingency of cats getting high. That added fuel to the flame."

"There were the potheads like me," says Quincy, "the juicers, the Nod Squad of junkies, and the God Squad of Bible readers. Jimmy fit in with the smokers and drinkers."

"When Jimmy got drunk, he'd pick on the big guys," says Clifford Solomon, another Gates saxophonist, who in the eighties became Ray Charles's musical director. "His personality completely flipped. I remember once, we were on the bus going from Chicago to New York. Jimmy got so belligerent until Leo Sheppard, our trumpet player from the West Indies, started pushing him out of the window. The only thing that saved Jimmy was that the window only opened halfway. With his head hanging out, he stayed stuck in there, but was too drunk to care. Next day he didn't remember a thing."

"Musically, we wanted to concentrate on the hip bop charts that young cats like Quincy were writing," Cleveland continues, "but Gates forced us to run those crowd-pleasers into the ground—repeating those same riffs on 'Flying Home,' blowing our brains out 'Hey! Ba-Ba-Re-Bop'—until our chops literally bled."

"If our show kicked off at nine-thirty or ten," Hamp confesses, "we might not see intermission till midnight. My policy was simple: As long as the people wanted more, they got more. They just couldn't wear me out. By the end of the show, I was so worked up—throwing my mallets in the air, jumping on my tom-tom, sweating like I'd been hit with a bucket of water—that they'd have to drag me off."

"We complained to the union about no overtime," says Cleveland. "We complained that blowing so hard and long was compromising our health. Hamp passed the complaints on to Gladys, and Gladys didn't care. Hamp's head was in the wrong place. He didn't think the public would accept true art. So he gave them all that raucous rock and roll."

"I appreciated Gates's sense of entertainment," Quincy says. "In his own way, he saw the future of our music in its visceral appeal to fans. He had a vision of how music could reach out and grab you by the throat. His enthusiasm was infectious. I loved being there. It was the learning experience of a lifetime. It didn't matter that we starved."

"The pay was ridiculous," remembers Solomon. "Twenty dollars a night, twenty-two if you soloed. We were lucky if we worked four or five nights a week. Gladys was notoriously cheap. She traveled first-class with her own separate entourage. She had her poodle and her parrot and her Jaguar driven by Curly Hamner, the good-looking dude who did a little tap dancing and told a few jokes on the show. She also traveled with Leo Moore, her gay valet who, before she entered a room, always announced with proper English accent, 'Lady Hampton is on her way.'"

"Give Gladys credit," says Quincy. "She made Gates a rich man. Her business acumen set him up for life."

"It was Gladys," adds Solomon, "who turned Gates into a Republican. He's worked for the Republican party for over fifty years."

"Gates would go in a club where all the cats were hanging out and set up the bar," Illinois Jacquet recalls. "We ordered whatever we wanted. The check would come, Gates would reach in his pocket and pull out a dime. 'Damn,' he'd say, 'Gladys forgot to give me my allowance.'"

"I was proud to be in the show," says Jimmy. "When we passed through Cleveland and played the Palace, my brothers and sisters got to see me on stage with the great Lionel Hampton. It was an honor. But it was also difficult. I had to pay for my own clothes. On a hundred twenty-five dollars a week, I could afford only one suit. But I needed two suits for those times when one was being cleaned. I asked Gladys, and she refused. That's when I quit—for the first time. That was in 1950, only a few months after I had cut some sides with the band."

In January 1950, at the Decca recording studios in New York City, Jimmy Scott recorded four songs with "Lionel Hampton and His Orchestra." One of those sides struck a chord with the public. The result was greater interest, and even greater confusion, surrounding Jimmy's incipient career.

FOOL

At the start of the fifties, the jazz world was in the midst of a drug epidemic. Many of the innovators of the new music were hooked on heroin. The great guru, of course, was Charlie Parker, whose every move was emulated by a small army of disciples. Bird's sound, both as reaction to and reflection of midcentury America, was the most exciting since Louis Armstrong's. But where Armstrong's moods were informed at least to some degree by the flavor of marijuana—Louis smoked daily—Parker's brilliance was jolted and ultimately undermined by heroin.

Since they met in Indianapolis in the early forties, Jimmy had been tight with Bird. As he moved in and out of Hampton's band in the early fifties, the singer found himself in the center of the hyperkinetic world of bebop. He also developed intimate relationships with seminal rhythm-and-blues artists he met on the road— Little Willie John, the fabulous soul singer from Detroit, and Jesse Belvin, the great crooner–composer from Los Angeles. Big Maybelle, perhaps the most underrated singer of this entire epoch, was Jimmy's best friend. Like Bird, Maybelle died of her addiction. The same was true for Billie Holiday, with whom, over the next several years, Jimmy became especially close. Jimmy worked in a world of extreme highs and lows. His audience sought, as audiences always seek, extravagant emotional stimulation. He sought such stimulation himself, viewing his own habits—smoking cigarettes and reefer, drinking booze—as mild next to the hard habits of his junkie friends. Consequently, he saw no reason to stop what he was doing.

"Bird was playing the Regal Theater in Chicago," Jimmy remembers, "when I went backstage to visit. This was the early fifties. I'd been seeing him off and on since Indianapolis in the forties. I loved him. He always made me welcome. He had an advanced mind and new musical vocabulary all the cats were scrambling to learn. He took to me, I believe, because he saw that, like him, I was different. Now on this particular night when I opened his dressing room door, I caught him by surprise. The needle was in his arm. He kept shooting up, but as he did he glanced over his shoulder and looked me in the eye. 'Jimmy,' he said, 'if I ever catch you with this shit, I'll kill you.' He said this out of concern and self-knowledge. He knew it was killing him. I also knew enough about life not to judge him. He had pressures on him I couldn't begin to understand. He reacted the way he reacted. That was his business, not mine. I took him the way he was, the kind of towering genius who comes along once every hundred years. As a man, like all men, he had limitations. As a musician, he had none."

An extraordinary glimpse into the Scott–Parker relationship is provided by a recording that was taped off the radio by a fan from a live broadcast. The recording also exemplifies Jimmy's luckless history with musical documentation. In the summer of 1950, Bird was playing Birdland, the basement club on Broadway only a few months old and named for him. Jimmy, who'd quit Hamp's band a few weeks earlier, happened to drop by.

"Bird saw me coming down the stairs," recalls Jimmy. "He and Fats Navarro, the trumpet player, were into 'Wahoo,' one of Tadd Dameron's lines. Bird nodded to me. He knew Tadd and I were tight and was happy to make the connection. Bud Powell was on piano, and Art Blakey on drums. Watching Bird work was always a great pleasure. I dug the whole set. Towards the end, he motioned me towards the bandstand. This wasn't unusual. Whenever Bird was playing, he'd want me to sit in. '"Embraceable You" all right?' he asked. '"Embraceable You" is fine.'"

"Embraceable You" survives as a glowing record of the rapport between saxophonist and singer. Bird states the melody with customary gusto followed by a flight of embellishments that, even for the great bopper, astonishes. Jimmy follows. At twenty-five, he sings with the security of a veteran.

I once spoke with the late Betty Carter, Jimmy's colleague from the Hampton band, about the experience of singing with Bird. It happened in Detroit when Betty, like Jimmy, was just getting started. "It was the most intimidating moment of my life," she told me. "Like singing before the Lord Himself. I thought I had my bop chops together, but just being on the bandstand with Bird unraveled me. I tried to change my phrasing to suit his, but it didn't work. Afterwards he encouraged me. He said he appreciated me, but I felt like I blew it."

On "Embraceable," Jimmy doesn't blow it. For all Bird's brilliance, the singer sounds unaffected by the saxophonist's style. Jimmy goes his way at his own pace, his rugged individuality manifest in a delivery as ethereal as it is direct. He is neither intimidated nor nervous. He doesn't try to make his mark or prove a thing. He merely is. Even at this nascent age, his style is firmly in place. In basic ways, the Jimmy you hear in 1950 is the Jimmy you hear today. Fats Navarro, who died from drug addiction shortly after the live date, takes the final horn solo, another expression of sensitive reflection. Then Jimmy closes it out as Bird opened it up: transforming a Gershwin tune into a meditation, a mixture of hope and despair.

The history of the recording is a study in negligence. Bootlegs abounded for years, none of them crediting Jimmy as the singer. In 1977, Columbia Records commissioned Gary Giddins, a fine critic, to produce and annotate a two-LP reissue, *One Night in Birdland*. Dan Morgenstern, director of the prestigious Institute of Jazz Studies at Rutgers University, researched the project and wrote the liner notes. Those notes list Chubby Newsome, a *female* rhythm-and-blues singer who had a small hit with "Hip Shaking Mama," as the vocalist on "Embraceable You." Morgenstern writes extensively about Newsome's background and derides her performance. When I called Morgenstern twenty-five years after the record was reissued, he graciously acknowledged his mistake. I also contacted Giddins, who still didn't know Jimmy was the vocalist. When he listened to the record again, he concurred that it was Jimmy and was amazed that the error had gone undetected for so long. The documentation of an important jazz singer joining Bird on the bandstand is no small matter. For two eminent scholars to mistake the singer—and gender—reflects the neglect Jimmy has suffered. To add insult to injury, in the late nineties Swan Records issued a CD, *New Bird*, that included the same track, with no vocalist listed.

Mistaking Jimmy for a female was a pattern perpetuated by his first recordings made with the Hampton big band a few months before the Birdland date. Like the session with Bird, these are precious artifacts. Unlike the live Parker date, they are formal affairs, carefully rehearsed and arranged. The saddest similarity between Jimmy's dialogues with Bird and Hamp, though, is that the singer remained uncredited on both.

The Hampton sessions yielded four songs, the most famous of which, "Everybody's Somebody's Fool," proved the only hit of Jimmy's six-decade career. (Correspondence from Universal Recording Corporation indicates that, a year before "Fool," Jimmy had cut four songs in Chicago without Hampton. Jimmy has no memory of doing so, though, and no masters can be found.) "Fool" stayed on the rhythm-and-blues charts of *Billboard* magazine for six weeks, reaching number six. The label read simply, "Lionel Hampton, Vocal with Orchestra." And as recently as 1988, with the publication of Joel Whitburn's *Top R&B*

Singles, 1942–1988, the attempt to rectify the exclusion only made matters worse. Whitburn mistakenly credits Irma Curry, Jimmy's colleague from Hamp's band, as the singer.

In spite of that, the song is sublime. Jimmy soars. Hamp plays a solo that breaks your heart, his sensitivity attuned to Jimmy's. The reeds are rich, and the story—a lesson in humility—underlines the recurrent theme of quiet heartbreak so prevalent in Jimmy's life. "Everybody's Somebody's Fool," along with the other three numbers—"I Wish I Knew," "Please Give Me a Chance," and "I've Been a Fool"—constitute a makeshift suite boldly announcing Jimmy's arrival on the American music scene.

It sometimes seems that great vocalists each sing but a single song. Billie Holiday's is "Lover Man." Marvin Gaye's is "What's Going On." Sarah Vaughan's is "If You Could See Me Now." Everything else becomes variations on a theme. Like a miniature landscape painted on a brooch, the signature song carries an imprint of the singer's life. For the rest of his life, Jimmy will incorporate the sound and meaning of "Everybody's Somebody's Fool" wherever he goes. Everything he sings will be an extension of the song. With its heady mix of self-effacement and sorrow, spiritual hope and romantic disappointment, the song stands, even as played by Dexter Gordon in 1965 or sung by Michael Jackson in 1972, as an emblem to Jimmy Scott.

"Regina Adams wrote the lyrics and was trying to get someone to record it," says Jimmy. "Everyone was ducking her because the song needed work. It lacked a melody. But I was polite and said I'd sing it as long as Gates approved. We were leaving Detroit, heading for New York, when I mentioned it to Doug Duke, a white boy who played a mean organ in the band. When we got to the city, Doug helped me write a melody and smooth out the form. Bobby Plater, the saxist, wrote a lovely chart, and with Gates smiling through his solo, we cut it in two or three takes. A month or so later, when the seventy-eight came out, I was a little surprised that my name wasn't on the label as either singer or writer. Instead, the name Gladys Hampton appeared as one of the composers. Doug wasn't listed either. I'm not the complaining type, but I did say something to Gladys. I was respectful. I understood the conventions of the time. Band leaders like to grab credit for themselves, their wives, and their managers. I have to say, though, losing that credit hurt. And Gladys did nothing to correct the inaccuracies."

As "Everybody's Somebody's Fool" circulated, confusion about the singer intensified. B. B. King was a deejay at WDIA in Memphis at the time. His first hit, "Three O'Clock Blues," wouldn't be released for another year.

"Hamp was huge," says B. B., "and naturally we played him along with Lloyd Glenn, Amos Milburn, and Roy Brown. Back then, we didn't think of rhythm and blues as one thing and jazz another. It was all good. All their voices touched us, and when I heard this voice on 'Everybody's Somebody's Fool' I loved it but couldn't place it. First off, I thought it was a woman. But then, no, it's a man. Young man who sounds like an alto sax. Young man with a sound all his own. It was a hit, but it was a hit that went against the tide. Back then those deep-throated male voices—Billy Eckstine and Nat Cole—were dominating. Jimmy slipped in under the radar. Certain voices will be heard, no matter how different they are. Certain singers—Lonnie Johnson, Ella Fitzgerald, Bobby Bland—are so distinctive you'll never forget them. Well, I never forgot Jimmy's."

Ray Charles was twenty when he first heard the song. "I was out on the road with Lowell Fulson, playing the blues circuit with T-Bone Walker and Joe Turner. I mean, these were *serious* blues cats. But when that song came on, we all stopped to listen. We all loved big bands and big sounds. Hamp's sound was lush. And on top of all that lushness, here's a man singing in a woman's key. A man phrasing like a jazz horn and kicked back in the beat like Lester Young. I asked around until I found out from my friend Quincy, who'd joined the band, that his name was Little Jimmy Scott. I've always been into stylists. I'd gotten by imitating stylists like Charles Brown and Nat Cole. Scott's style was too light, too different, to imitate. But the way he told the story, with so much sadness pouring out of him, impressed me deeply. Years later, when I started singing ballads, I thought about Little Jimmy Scott."

"My name was already out there," says Jimmy, "because of the shows I'd done with Caldonia, the gigs I'd played on my own, and the touring with Gates. But because no singer was listed, people who didn't know me were curious. Bill Cook was a big-time deejay in Newark who loved the record. He also discovered and managed Roy Hamilton, the singer who hit big with 'Unchained Melody.' Bill knew it was me singing 'Fool,' but in order to promote it he ran a contest—Name the Singer. Folks called in from all over. Many swore it was a woman. Some said it was Ella, some said Billie or Maxine Sullivan or Nellie Lutcher or even Rose Murphy. 'That ain't no woman,' a female fan who'd been a regular at Gates's shows finally said. 'That ain't no one but Little Jimmy Scott.'"

The pop world of the early fifties was still overwhelmingly white. On the black side, Jimmy's friends were enjoying successes of their own—the Dominoes with "Sixty Minute Man," Percy Mayfield with "Please Send Me Someone to Love," Charles Brown with "Black Night," Ruth Brown with "Teardrops from My Eyes." But it would be years before black music sold to white audiences in large numbers. In the field of jazz, despite the revolutionary fervor of bop, the best-selling album was a throwback to the swing era, Benny Goodman's 1938 Carnegie Hall concert.

At the dawn of the LP era, Broadway shows like *South Pacific* would lead the way while the pop single market was dominated by schmaltzy ballads: Perry Como's "If," Mario Lanza's "Be My Love," Patti Page's "Tennessee Waltz," Nat Cole's "Mona Lisa." In a different world, one in which music—not demographics, marketing, or race—was the only consideration, Jimmy might well have crossed over. His straight-from-the-heart style was only a few degrees off the mainstream mark. A year after "Fool," for example, Johnnie Ray hit the top of the charts with "Cry." Deeply influenced by Jimmy (as well as Kay Starr and Dinah Washington), Ray would soon be the biggest singer in the country.

"At times I felt like the smallest singer in the country," says Jimmy. "Here I was with a hit record. Cats like Johnnie Ray were telling me to my face that they flat-out copied me. Fans were showing up at all my shows. Yet I was still scuffling hard to make a way. I knew show business was about timing. Caldonia had taught me that. The window of opportunity is small. When it's opened, you've got to slip on out. But once you're out, where do you go? Who do you trust? How do you get over?"

THE JAZZ LIFE

*J*azz is rooted in improvisation and a fanciful view of time. So is the jazz life. It's a romantic view: the jazz artist as a syncopator, an inventor making it up on the spot, abandoning convention, moving ahead with the certainty that excitement lies in the unexplored and unknown. The jazz life is about discovering who you are—where to go, how to live, what to play—along the way.

From the time he was sixteen and left school, Jimmy led the jazz life. He made decisions about switching cities the same way he decided how to sing a song. He didn't think about it. He riffed over the chord changes. Because the jazz life was also the high life, those decisions were made under the influence of powerful musical and chemical stimulation. In the fifties, the two could hardly be separated. The whimsy with which he moved is striking. He lived here and there, searching for domestic harmony, fighting for professional recognition, struggling to make ends meet. He fashioned a strategy for survival based on a model of creative spontaneity.

In his midtwenties, Jimmy experienced an alienation common to jazz musicians. Having quit the Hampton band, he was cut off from popular taste and, as a result, from financial security. There was also the matter of being black in racist pre-civil-rights America.

But Jimmy's alienation goes deeper still: Even within the world of black jazz, he stood apart. The ambiguity of his singing style, combined with the ambiguity of his physicality, pushed him further into the margins of musical culture.

"People were harsh with Jimmy," remembers Ruth Brown. "You'd go to his show and hear someone yell out, 'He sounds like a freak, he looks a freak, he *is* a freak.' But Jimmy was a gentleman. He just stood there and took it. Maybe that's why he befriended other artists who might be seen as freaks—Big Maybelle, Little Willie John, even Billie, whose sex life was surely freaky."

"Funny," says Jimmy, "but I saw myself as a normal guy looking for normal happiness. A home. A wife. A nice income. Of course I learned about discrimination firsthand. Discrimination hit us because of our music and our color. I'd felt it when I went out on the road and saw where we couldn't stay, where we couldn't eat, how the police brutalized us on a whim. I saw white cops beat up black men just for the fun of it. It happened in the South and it happened in the North. At times I'd get angry, frustrated, and discouraged. But I tried to see it as a spiritual challenge. My mother said, 'Look at folks individually, not as a group.' That single statement saved me from turning racist myself. So I watched it go by. I knew racists were on the losing side. I knew love finally carries the day. It was just a matter of being patient for that day to arrive. I witnessed injustice and suffered with the rest of the cats. Didn't feel like a victim, though, because the joy of making music—night after night—was stronger than any oppression. The bad guys could only offer up ignorance. We were offering up light. Our music was about love."

Jimmy's jazz life was about the next gig, the next recording date. Centered in Manhattan, the music attracted a host of hustlers, managers, agents, artists and repertory (A&R) men, and label owners—many lovers of the art form, many coldly indifferent, some honest, some devious, all hungry to score.

"There were the sinners and saints," says Jimmy. "And maybe because I was too trusting, I often got the two groups confused."

Trust is a challenge resonating throughout Jimmy's turbulent life. He struggles with the idea. What woman to trust? Which manager is honest? Who's real? Who's jive? In his romantic and professional liaisons alike, Jimmy swung back and forth from feelings of openhearted trust to angry suspicion.

Trust was the big issue he faced after quitting Hamp in 1950. In looking for work, he encountered two characters who would influence his career, both positively and negatively, for the decade to come. The first was Teddy Reig, the man record producer Jerry Wexler calls "the hipster's hipster." Jimmy calls him "the hustler's hustler." A three-hundred-pound-plus, six-foot Jewish promoter born in Harlem in 1918 and raised among the thieves and geniuses of the jazz world, Reig was an impassioned fan who mastered the art of networking at an early age. "Teddy had wonderful taste," says Wexler, "and cosmic chutzpah. Teddy was the embodiment of Norman Mailer's 'White Negro.' He had a green card into the black nation. He married a black woman and, like Mezz Mezzrow, Symphony Sid, and Johnny Otis, lived black. Before any of us, he also understood how to make a buck off music—and brilliant music at that. Teddy was the guy who produced Bird's landmark recordings for Savoy. Teddy produced the first-ever sessions for Miles and Getz. Basie adored Teddy, and Teddy was responsible for Basie's best stuff, his Roulette records. Then there's Teddy's Latin connection. He put out superb records on Machito and Candido. Teddy was a freelancer and wheeler-dealer who suffered no fools and took no prisoners. He could be rude and crude. He smoked enough reefer to launch a rocket. Some considered him a liar and schemer and self-serving schmuck. I liked him. I liked the music he made. I liked the fact that he delivered. Were it not for guys like him, the world of recorded jazz would be considerably poorer."

"Teddy was so loud and obnoxious I was embarrassed being around him," says his colleague Lee Magid, who succeeded Reig as A&R director at Savoy. "He thrived on combative relationships. Label owners hated him, but he served their needs. They needed a conduit to jazz musicians, who spoke a language of their own. Teddy spoke that language, but when he translated to the owners, something got lost in the translation. That loss was usually a pile of cash that wound up in Teddy's pocket."

"Here was this big, brash guy who said he could take me places," Jimmy reflects. "When I asked Bird about him, Bird just shrugged. 'If he can make you money,' said Bird, 'go with him.' Of course Bird didn't have much business sense himself, but he made it plain that Reig understood the music. That was important to me."

Reig introduced Jimmy to Jimmy Evans, a booking agent who, according to Wexler, was "a short, fierce, one-eyed Italian with connections to the darkest corners of show biz."

"Reig and Evans worked hand in hand," says Jimmy, "with kickbacks between them. It wasn't about nothing but money. Reig made big money producing Paul Williams's 'Hucklebuck,' an R&B instrumental stolen from Bird's 'Now's the Time.' Reig made even more money when he got Evans to book Paul all over the country. Evans booked other R&B acts—Jimmy Reed, Little Esther, and Big Maybelle."

"Evans was an asshole," claims Magid. "No one else would deal with the junkies. He'd put together shows with Bird and Sticks McGhee, the guy who hit with 'Drinking Wine, Spo-Dee-O-Dee, Drinking Wine' on Atlantic. Evans had no sense of music, no integrity, no feeling for anything but copping a commission."

"Evans sent me on the road with pianist Paul Gayten," Jimmy remembers. "Paul was beautiful. When Louis Jordan broke down the big bands, Paul was one of the first to follow with a band of his own. He carried Annie Laurie on the show as well as Larry Darnel, both great singers. Paul loved driving a big Cadillac, but I noticed that as soon as we dipped below the Mason-Dixon line, he put on a chauffeur's cap. We toured for a few months and got recorded down in New Orleans."

That date, rescued from the archives and reissued by scholar-singer Billy Vera as *Little Jimmy Scott Live in New Orleans* on

Specialty in 1991, reveals the strength of Jimmy's live shows from the early fifties. He sings five numbers, including "Everybody's Somebody's Fool," with his usual brand of disarming sincerity.

Back in New York after the tour, Jimmy signed with Regal, a short-lived label run by Freddy Mendelsohn, who would be around longer than the label as Jimmy's producer.

"If Teddy Reig was the sinner," says Jimmy, "Freddy was the saint. Freddy was the one producer who understood me. He treated me with respect and looked for the right songs. Freddy was a gentle soul. He couldn't always stand up to the rough guys who ran the business, but he found a way to serve the artists he believed in. He always believed in me. For twenty-five long years, the man never gave up on me."

The early sides Mendelsohn made with Jimmy are exquisite. Unfortunately, they were never released in album form and remain hard to find. "My Mother's Eyes," with its painfully personal connotation, is especially fine. "I remember seeing George Jessel singing it in a movie," says Jimmy, "and I couldn't help but cry." The rare gem, though, is "The Masquerade Is Over." Although originally recorded by Betty McLaurin, it's Jimmy's version that has prompted everyone from Nancy Wilson to Stevie Wonder to Aretha Franklin to sing the song. Jimmy created the standard. Like "Fool," "Masquerade" carries heavy poignancy. The lyric, a lament to lost love with its operatic reference to Pagliacci, hints at a tragedy far deeper than standard pop fare. The tragedy seems especially suited to Jimmy's persona.

The small-label scene in the early fifties was catch-as-catch-can. Unlike today, the majors—Decca, RCA, Columbia—had an indifferent attitude toward intensely ethnic music. If an artist—say, Armstrong or Hampton—proved tremendously popular, the majors were interested. For the most part, though, edgy bebop and rhythm and blues were left to independents. Those little labels were makeshift operations, run by a variety of characters—some knowledgeable fans like Herb Abramson, Jerry Wexler, and the

Ertegun brothers at Atlantic; some cold-blooded businessmen like
Herman Lubinsky at Savoy or Syd Nathan at King. Jimmy stepped
into this entrepreneurial minefield without benefit of counsel.

"In those days you never heard of an artist hiring an entertainment lawyer for protection," says Jimmy. "Maybe those guys existed, but I didn't know a single one, and neither did my buddies
like Percy Mayfield or Big Maybelle. When we all had our first
little hits, there was no one to advise us. We went along with the
booking agents and the record companies not because we were
foolish, but because we had no choice. If you wanted to work, you
signed on the dotted line."

Jimmy wanted to work—and he did. He often worked in a way
that mirrored the practices of the labels themselves. He sometimes
slipped around, singing for whichever label would record him. He
struggled to survive just as the labels themselves were struggling.
Business practices were substandard. Advances were minuscule,
royalties a pipe dream.

"We understood we were being cheated," says Ruth Brown,
"but we had to eat. It was a simple choice—abandon the business
altogether or take the terms offered. We took what we could get."

Yet within this universe of exploitation, loyalty could occasionally be found. Fred Mendelsohn went broke with Regal but took
Jimmy with him when he went to work for Teddy Reig's Royal
Roost Records (sometimes shortened to Roost). Over the next few
years, Jimmy recorded some twenty songs for the label. A number
of those interpretations—"After I'm Gone," "Talk of the Town,"
"Be My Sunshine," "Rain in My Eyes"—still stand as Scott mas-
terpieces from his early epoch and are available on the Billy
Vera–produced box set, *Little Jimmy Scott: The Savoy Years and
More,* released in 1999. Typically, the instrumentation is sparse.

"Freddy liked using Terry Gibbs," says Jimmy, "because Terry
had Hamp's flair. Freddy was hoping to catch the same smooth
vibe I'd caught with 'Fool.' I loved the idea because vibes—
whether Terry or Gates—relaxed me."

Despite the relaxed precocity of many of Jimmy's early sessions, there were no hits on Regal or Roost.

"We came close with 'I Won't Cry Anymore,'" Jimmy recalls. "I cut it first, and they were playing it on the radio when Tony Bennett covered it for Columbia. They snatched my version and replaced it with Tony's, whose label, Columbia, had all the juice. It was a hit for Tony and, along with 'Because of You' and 'Cold, Cold Heart,' kicked off his career as a million-seller artist. Over the years, every time I see Tony, he apologizes. 'No need to apologize, baby,' I tell him. 'It wasn't your fault that you were with the right label.'"

Improbably enough, there *was* a Roost hit in 1952, though not by Jimmy. Guitarist Johnny Smith and saxophonist Stan Getz's version of "Moonlight in Vermont" raced up the charts, where it remained for months.

"Getz and I were the first two artists on Roost," Jimmy remembers. "I liked Stan. He was a nice Jewish boy from the Bronx whose god was Lester Young. Stan had beautiful technique. When Pres was in town, Stan would bug me to take him over to the Alvin Hotel so he could sit at the master's feet. Pres was flattered by Stan's appreciation, but Pres, like Bird, didn't get off on disciples. Because Pres was such an individual, he expected everyone else to be. For all his fine musicianship, Stan was insecure. He felt like he had to run with the big boys. He got into the dope thing and ran up against the law. He went through crazy personal stuff, but his music never faltered. I believe his music expanded; his music got lovelier as Stan got older. Whatever he learned from Lester—and he learned a lot—he expanded on the lessons until he became a master himself."

You can hear the young Getz solo behind Jimmy on "Do You Mind If I Hang Around?" one of a series of singles cut for Coral, a subsidiary of Decca, in 1952.

"In those early ears I flipped labels pretty much the way the labels flipped artists," says Jimmy. "I thought I'd have a better shot with Coral because Coral was big time. Coral thought they could have a hit on me the way 'Fool' hit with Decca. They rushed me in and had me sing 'Wheel of Fortune,' which had already been cut by Johnny Hartman. Everyone smelled a hit and everyone started recording it—Dinah, Arthur Prysock, Helen Humes. The smash was cut by Kay Starr."

Billy Taylor was the pianist and arranger for one of the Coral sessions where Jimmy was backed by, among others, trombonists Tyree Glenn and Kai Winding and saxophonist Stan Getz. "I was astounded by Jimmy's musicianship," says Taylor. "It didn't matter that he couldn't read or write music. His instincts for back phrasing were phenomenal. He interpreted the lyrics like Olivier interpreting Shakespeare. There was something aristocratic about him. They called him Little Jimmy, but I saw him as Prince Jimmy. He had a great dignity about him. A subtlety of expression. A finesse that, even in the golden era of great jazz singers, stood apart."

Gil Askey, a trumpeter who later became a musical director for Motown, played in saxophonist Lucky Thompson's band, backing Jimmy on his second Coral sessions. "Jimmy sang 'Why I Was Born,'" remembers Askey, "with such sadness my heart just ached. When we were through, I put down my horn and wiped away tears. I was embarrassed until I saw all the other cats were teary-eyed too."

When the Coral releases didn't hit, Jimmy went back to Regal.

"They'd have us sign contracts," he says, "but the contracts were loose. Contracts meant nothing. Fifty bucks here. Hundred bucks there. The labels knew what we were doing, and we knew what they were doing. They needed records and we needed cash. Over at Roost, the cat who understood that better than anyone was Sonny Stitt. Before it was over, I bet Stitt made two hundred albums with forty different labels. 'Long as I get it up front,' he'd say, 'I'll sign anything.' He learned that—like he learned so much—from Bird.

"Some say Bird resented Stitt for sounding so much like him. Not true. Bird loved Sonny and encouraged him, like Bird encouraged everyone. The jazz press painted them as rivals, but Bird was

above rivalry. One night in the early fifties Bird and I went to Bop
City, a club down the street from Birdland, to hear Stitt. Sonny
was burning, and Bird was the first to jump up and applaud. He
wouldn't sit in because he didn't want to steal Sonny's shine. It was
Sonny's time. Bird just sat back and smiled like a proud pappy.
Few weeks later, I remember walking down Broadway with Milt
Jackson when we spotted Sonny passed out in front of the Brill
Building. I mean, he was wasted. We scooped him up and took him
over to the Alvin Hotel, where the night manager, a guardian angel
of lost jazz souls, gave him a room out of harm's way."

In the approximately two-year period that Jimmy was out of
the Hampton band, he had a small apartment on Edgecombe Avenue in Harlem that he describes as bare-boned: "I was recording
and working a few clubs but just scraping by. I was up in my place
on Edgecombe when I heard a knock on the door. It was Bird. Now
it was Bird who was wasted. 'Hey, Jim,' he said, 'can I crash here? I
just need some peace and quiet.' 'Sure, Bird,' I said and helped him
over to the bed. Getz came by a few hours later and couldn't believe
Charlie Parker was asleep in my pad. 'I'm on way to Wilmington,
Delaware, to catch this new trumpet player,' he said. 'Thought you
might want to come along. You think Bird wants to come too?' 'I
think Bird wants to sleep,' I said. So Stan and I ran down to
Delaware and saw a musician the likes of which I'd never heard before. His name was Clifford Brown and, as fate would have it, a
few months later he and I would be playing in the same band. Next
day, when I got back to Harlem, there's Monk and the Baroness, an
aristocratic friend to all the beboppers, carrying Bird out of my
apartment, taking him to the hospital."

By 1952, Jimmy was back with the Hampton big band.

"The band had a more youthful spirit," Jimmy recalls. "Quincy
was writing charts and Monk Montgomery, Wes's brother, was also
aboard. Monk was one of the first guys to play the bass guitar anywhere. That bumped up the groove and led to heavier rhythm and
blues. Without Monk Montgomery there's no James Brown. Hamp
liked that heavy beat. Fact is, Hamp had a good appreciation of all

the styles. Without Betty Carter, for instance, who was singing alongside me in Hamp's band, there's a hole in the history of jazz. Betty was bad because Betty took chances the way Bird took chances. Betty's inspiration was Ella, but Betty was Betty. She'd sculpt any song in any shape that felt right. She had the courage of her convictions and didn't care if the critics didn't get it. We got it. We got all the bad young cats in Gates's group. That included the trumpeter I'd just seen in Delaware. Even before Getz took me to hear Clifford Brown, Tadd Dameron had hipped me to him. 'Diz, Miles, Fats—they're all going to be scared of Brownie,' warned Tadd, who'd used Clifford in his band. Tadd was right. Brownie was Gabriel. He came into Hamp's band in fifty-three with the sweet sound the world was waiting for. He was the next Louis. And at a time when we were all doing too much drinking, Brownie was doing nothing. Clean as a whistle. A bebop Boy Scout. Beautiful brother.

"With new musical stimulation, the second time around with Hamp was generally cool. Irma Curry had been forced to sing 'Fool' in my absence and, man, was she glad to see me back. 'I'd try to imitate you, Jimmy,' she'd say, 'but the people don't believe me. They want you.' That let me know I had a little fan base— nothing huge, but there were people who dug my sound.

"Gates dug me enough to ask me out to Hollywood, where he was shooting a Jax beer commercial. Playing a young sailor, I cavorted with two chicks on a yacht while singing about the delights of drinking Jax. Never saw a dime, but it was nice seeing those palm trees along Wilshire Boulevard.

"When Ike won the White House in fifty-three, I'd voted for Adlai Stevenson. But Gladys and Gates had worked for Ike, and the band was asked to play at the inaugural ball. We shared the bandstand with Jeannette MacDonald and Nelson Eddy. I escorted Lily Pons to the microphone, where she sang an Italian aria that gave me goose bumps. Gates had me sing 'Why Was I Born.' It was quite a thrill, but not enough of a thrill to ever leave the Democrats.

"Gladys's thriftiness made me leave the band for the second and final time. Never could get that lady to give me a raise. Tried to bring it up with Gates, but Gates would only smile and say, 'Ask the boss.' I never heard a man refer to his wife that way before. At the time, I saw it as stupid. Later I saw it as smart. After all, the boss made Gates a millionaire many times over."

Jimmy's second time around with Hampton lasted less than two years. By mid-1953, he was back out on his own, dividing his time between Harlem, Newark, and Cleveland, following the gigs wherever they led. His jazz life was as scattered as ever. He was recording but making little noise on the sales charts. His relationships with women—his search for righteous romance—remained much on his mind. In considering the male/female dynamic, he was moved by the partnership of Lionel and Gladys Hampton, a marriage he had studied with growing appreciation.

"I thought about their relationship in a new light," he says. "I was raised to think a man and woman come together for love. Sure, there was a degree of love between Gladys and Gates, but the main thing was business. It was a partnership. He made the music, she watched the money. He let her go out and play in her way, and she let him do the same. Who was I to judge the arrangement? It worked for them. In my own life, I'd yet to find a relationship that worked for me. I was determined to settle down. I wanted peace and quiet with the right lady. I wanted love. But love is like a beautiful dream of heaven. The dream has you floating on clouds. The dream calms and comforts your soul. But a minute after you wake up, you can't remember a thing. In the same way, love keeps appearing and disappearing, a soft glow way off in the distance, a light of hope rising and setting like the sun."

JERSEY

*J*immy and I are driving the New Jersey Turnpike from Manhattan to Newark, the locale that became his second home. I point to the Pulaski Skyway, a dark icon from some gothic fairy tale. I think of my own childhood in Newark and the music that first fired my imagination, the hot amalgamation of bebop and blues heard in the downtown clubs and bars of the Third Ward.

"Newark was always good to me," says Jimmy as we pull into the city. "It was a refuge from New York—a little kinder, a little lighter on the pocketbook, an easier alternative. But in the fifties, Newark was also jumping. Bird came to Newark. Savoy Records, the label with Bird's best stuff, operated out of Newark. James Moody came from Newark. Sarah. Ike Quebec. Babs Gonzales, the scat singer and hipster supreme. You could work in Newark. And because you weren't more than a half-hour from New York, it was convenient. Newark let you live, let you breathe. Unlike New York, Newark might even give you a break. When I first arrived in the early fifties, I felt welcome. I stayed at a black-owned hotel, the Coleman, on Court Street. The Coleman Brothers, a famous gospel group, ran the place and fixed it up with a recording studio and radio station."

"I was working as a waitress at the Coleman Hotel in 1951," says Earlene Rodgers, a highly significant individual in Jimmy's private and professional life over the next fifty years. "The jukebox had 'Everybody's Somebody's Fool,' and I used all my tips to play it again and again. The song and the singer went straight to my heart. Then one day the bandleader Paul Gayten shows up with his singer Annie Laurie. Accompanying them is a little boy I presume is their son. He's so thin I give him an extra glass of milk and a heaping portion of potato salad. He's a sweet thing, friendly and polite. Next day he comes in alone and I'm sure to serve him extra greens and a big slice of apple pie. 'You need to fatten up,' I say. When he shows up a third time, I pile his plate high with meat loaf. Back in the kitchen, one of the cooks peeks into the dining room and says, 'Hey, that's Little Jimmy Scott. That's the singer you keep playing on the box.' I'm shocked. I'm so embarrassed I can't even go back out there to collect his dirty dishes. I'm treating him like a boy, but he's really a man.

"Turns out Jimmy and I had a friend in common who'd shown him my picture. Later I learned he liked the way I looked because, being short and round, I resembled his mom. But seeing me in my waitress uniform, he didn't realize I was the girl in the picture just as I didn't know he was the singer of the song. When we finally figured out who we were, he came over to the house—I was living on Williams Street in the Third Ward—and I felt quite attracted to his sweetness."

Earlene Rodgers was born November 30, 1928, in Newark's Central Ward. She describes herself as a natural caretaker. "When I met Jimmy," she says, "I was living with my mother. Now fifty years have passed, and I'm still living with her."

"I was attracted to Earlene's innocence," says Jimmy. "In that neighborhood of Newark, so many of the girls were turning tricks and hustling for pimps. Earlene went the other way. She was good as gold. She liked to mother me. She cooked and cleaned and cared for her own mother with such devotion I couldn't help but respect her. The only thing that bothered me was this man hanging around the house who was high on dope. He acted so rowdy I kicked him out. Just shoved him out the door."

"The man was my husband, John," says Earlene. "See, Jimmy didn't know I was married."

"'Girl,' I told her, 'you could have gotten my ass murdered. Why didn't you say you're this fool's wife?'"

"I didn't tell Jimmy because I didn't want to run him off," Earlene confesses. "Once Jimmy knew, he went away for a while. But he came back. There were strong feelings between us. Soon John was gone, and whenever Jimmy came to Newark he'd stay over. That went on for four, five years."

"Earlene was the most supportive woman I'd ever known," says Jimmy. "Always in my corner. Always cheering me on. Wasn't interested in herself as much as she wanted to help others."

"The funny thing about those early years with Jimmy in Newark," Earlene recalls, "is that our relationship was not physical. He wouldn't even get undressed in front of me. We'd sleep together all cuddled up, but never have sex. I didn't push it because our relationship was good in all other ways. I loved hearing him sing. His voice gave me goose bumps. His music was satisfaction enough. I was deeply in love with him, but I realized early on that he liked me fine, but for him, it wasn't love. It was comfort and convenience. Besides, I knew he was still seeing May."

"My thing with May went on for a while," Jimmy admits. "She had turned her life around and was on the straight and narrow. I was working in Milwaukee when May and I parted ways. The breakup was amicable and happened only because May wanted to go home and help her mother, who'd just adopted a baby. I couldn't stand in her way. I wanted good things in May's life and was happy to learn she later married and had a fine family of her own. Around the same time, I'd met a white woman who was a brilliant legal secretary. I'll call her Fredrika. She frequented the Flame Club in Milwaukee, where I was playing about every night. Handsome woman with a well-spoken manner. She came on strong and invited me back to her place, where she lived with her two kids in an apartment with no furniture. I could see she was kind of crazy, but she was quiet with it. If I was twenty-seven or twenty-eight, she had to be ten years older. In those days, it took a spirited white gal to pursue a black man. I thought we had a cool thing together.

"The gig at the Flame lasted seven months or so. When it came time to go back to Cleveland, Fredrika said, 'I'll find someone to stay with the kids here. I'll come to Cleveland with you.' It wasn't what I had planned, but I didn't argue. We found a little place in Cleveland, and we weren't there a week before the cops were banging at the door with a warrant for her arrest. Fortunately for her, she wasn't home. Unbeknownst to me, Fredrika was a world-class check forger. Someone back in Milwaukee had dropped a dime and told the law where to look. I was questioned myself but could honestly say I didn't know anything. Naturally that ended our relationship and made me wonder how I could have lived with this woman without knowing who she was. Maybe I was fooled by her exciting mind. Maybe her brightness blinded me. Either way, I never figured her as a criminal genius."

In hearing Jimmy describe his relationships with women, I wonder about the emotional intimacy, whether he was really close to any of them.

"As close as they would allow me to be," he says. "With women, you think you're close to them but then learn you aren't. It's a subtle thing."

Meanwhile, Jimmy's subtle genius as a singer was finding appreciation among the black clubs of Newark.

"I took Jimmy around when he first came to town," says Carl Brinson, known as Tiny Prince, a lifelong Newarker and promoter who, in the fifties, owned and edited *After Hours*, an entertainment listing serving the black community. "Jimmy walked into a jazz scene second only to New York. We had it covered. Hot spots like the Caravan, the Key Club, Fredericks' Lounge, Lloyd's Manor, and Teddy Powell's Holiday Inn—he played 'em all. I helped him book gigs in every club in town. Even took him to Paterson and Passaic. Jersey loved Jimmy. We started claiming him as our own.

"He might not have been a national star, because after 'Fool' he really had no national hits. But Little Jimmy Scott set Newark ablaze. Here, he was a big fish in a little pond. He was a local hero. They all came here to gig—Billie Holiday, Al Hibbler, George Shearing, Buddy Johnson, Illinois Jacquet, Arthur Prysock—you name 'em. But no one had the cachet of Little Jimmy. Little Jimmy was Newark's secret weapon. On any given weekend, we could go down and hear the best jazz singer in the country, bar none. The fact that he was little known outside the city made him that much more special to us."

"The Newark scene," says Jimmy, "was an escape hatch for me, a place where I could go, gig, and feel like family. I'd look at Newark as a swingin' small town. Bill Cook the deejay put me on his TV show *Stairway to the Stars,* a pioneering program by and for blacks. Tiny and a cat we called Geronimo found me gigs. Earlene let me lay up at her place. I could relax in Newark. Stay months at a time. Between Harlem, Newark, and Cleveland, I got by, even without a hit."

Working in the fifties, Jimmy was arguably among the best jazz singers in the United States. But unlike his peers, his musical environment was almost entirely makeshift. Consider his colleagues: Ella, Billie, Sarah, and Dinah wouldn't dream of traveling without their own musicians. They trained and maintained trios and quartets of peerless accompanists. Jimmy went it alone. In terms of musicians, he picked up whoever, whenever, however. He couldn't even entertain the notion of a permanent band. A more aggressive businessman, or an artist who understood the need for an aggressive businessman, might have organized his life differently. But Jimmy's view of himself was strictly that of the itinerant singer, a modern big-city balladeer equivalent to the itinerant country blues man.

"It was me and my voice," he says. "It was the cheapest and only way. If Dinah got sick, for instance, and couldn't make a gig, she'd have me take her place. She had a nickname for me. 'Fat Daddy,' she said, 'if you show up for me, no one will be disappointed.' That wasn't true, but I thanked her anyway and ran off to Chicago or Detroit or Pittsburgh. I'd sing with whoever she was using. I'd sing with whoever anyone was using."

The closest Jimmy had to a steady accompanist was a keyboardist named Chickadee. For years, they'd share gigs together at Paddock's in Cleveland. No matter where else he might be living, Jimmy came back to Cleveland on a regular basis. His hookup with Chickadee strengthened his Cleveland fan base.

"We were a popular attraction in the neighborhood," says Jimmy. "Truth be told, Chickadee was more than an accompanist. He was a star in his own right. A local star who never showed up on the national scene, but he sure lit the sky over Cleveland. He came by way of Saint Louis, and his thing was the Hammond B3. Baby, I've known some organists—Milt Buckner in Gates's band was a monster—but Chickadee burned down the barn. He made the thing smoke. His harmony was reeking so strong, cats from everywhere came to cop his licks. To hear Chickadee mix up that 'One Mint Julep' was something else. He could sing Nat Cole but mostly sang blues. When I sang my ballads, he laid down the chords so steady and pretty, it was like having a quartet behind me. We'd turn it out, night after night, month after month, year after year. Paddock's was the place.

"Everyone fell by Paddock's. Even Dad. When I was in town, that might be the only place I'd see him. I'd hear someone say, 'Scotty's here,' and look up and see him at the bar. Chickadee and I might be doing 'Imagination' or 'The Masquerade Is Over.' The crowd might be hanging on our every note. We might get a standing ovation. But Dad never looked my way. He was too busy checking out chicks. At the break, I'd go over and pay my respects.

"'How's everything, Dad?'

"'Fine, Son.'

"I'd wait for a word about my singing. An acknowledgment, a compliment, a signal that he was proud. None came. I'd wait for a question about my career. How are the gigs going? When's your new record coming out? None came.

"'Seen the kids lately?' I'd ask.

"'Saw Kenny the other day. Bumped into Nadine at the store.'

"'That's good.'

"He'd take long sips from his drink, I'd take a taste from mine, and we'd let the silence build and build until I'd finally get fed up and say, 'Okay, Dad, I better go back to work. See ya around.'

"'See ya, Son.'

"That was it. Later, while I was singing some song, I'd see him slip out with some lonely lady looking for a little attention."

"I've been at Paddock's," says Jimmy's brother Kenny, "when Dad showed up angry and drunk. Once I remember him coming up to Jimmy, after not having seen him for a long time, and saying, 'Boy, you still ain't shit. I can still smack your ass whenever I want.' Jimmy just nodded his head and walked away, tears in his eyes. Maybe Dad was jealous because Jimmy was a little star at Paddock's, or maybe it was just Dad's temperament when it got to drinking. Either way, it cut Jimmy deep."

"At Paddock's," says Channie Booker, the woman soon to be Jimmy's second wife, "everyone was paying attention to Jimmy and Chickadee. They were the shit. The flashy hookers and hard hustlers made that scene, not looking to score but just loving the sounds. Some called him Little Jimmy Scott; others called him Crying Jimmy Scott. But everyone saw him as some kind of strange angel, a jazz angel, who broke you down and reduced you to tears, no matter how many tricks you turned or cats you iced. He fascinated me. At the time we met, in 1953, I was twenty-five and Jimmy twenty-eight. I was known around town because I worked at Prince's barber shop at Ninety-sixth and Q. I was the first black female barber Cleveland had ever seen."

"Channie was out there," says Jimmy. "The girl was something else. Glowing copper skin. Dyed blond hair. Dressed like a showgirl. Dressed to show off all the curves of her fine, brown frame. She was a loud-spoken lady, but she impressed me because she had an art. She cut men's hair in a most creative fashion. There was a demand for Channie, especially in our community, where she was a novelty. She'd been married once and had a three-year-old daughter. I'd never met a woman like Channie. She had spunk and drive. She was assertive. She talked like she knew what she wanted. She was willing, even eager, to go back to my room that very first night. It was a sweet connection, at least in the beginning."

"In the beginning and in the end," Channie adds, "our connection had a lot to do with drinking. We were both deep into the bottle."

"I admit it," says Jimmy. "Our relationship sailed along on a sea of booze. I was dipping into that sea as much as Channie."

"I don't think any of the moves we made—the courtship, the decisions, the fighting, the making up—none of it was done in the light of day," Channie continues. "Our years together were all about the dark nights of drinking. I loved the little man, and I believe he loved me. But that didn't stop us from nearly killing each other. When we got married five or six months after we met, neither of us knew we were about to go on the wildest ride of our lives."

THE SLAVE BARRACKS

As Jimmy approached thirty, he entered into two key relationships, one personal, the other professional. Both proved ruinous. His marriage to Channie and his contract with Herman Lubinsky of Savoy Records were futile attempts at domestic and commercial success. He tried valiantly, but whether it was his naïveté, his drinking, or his inability to confront the complex problems plaguing his psyche, he failed to find what he was looking for in the fields of romance and music.

His new romance began promisingly. Channie Booker, born November 11, 1928, had known the Scott family in the forties.

"When Jimmy told us he was going with Channie," says sister Betsy, "I was happy because I knew her from my childhood. When I was a ten-year-old girl staying in a foster home in Cleveland on 144th Street, Channie lived across the street. I saw her as a big sister. She was an energetic woman who went out of her way to befriend me. I liked the idea of having her as a sister-in-law. Maybe that would help put Jimmy in closer touch with the family."

"Jimmy complained about our lack of family unity," remembers sister Nadine, "but his relationship to us has always been inconsistent. He'd be gone for months, show up, and then disappear again. By marrying Channie, we were all hoping we'd see more of him."

"Channie was someone you could get close to," observes sister Elsa. "The family liked the idea that Jimmy was marrying a girl from the neighborhood."

"My sisters might have known her from the old days," says Jimmy, "but if I did, I didn't remember her. When I met her at Paddock's, I was seeing her for the first time. What I saw was an extremely cool chick. Beautiful, glamorous, and ambitious. She could be loud and outspoken, but she was also funny. Being around Channie was never boring. In many ways she was smart; in other ways she wasn't. She was unique. She had a flair for hair, and I felt that this could benefit us both. I saw myself putting her to work as a barber."

"I'd never lived anywhere but Cleveland," says Channie. "Given Jimmy's talent, I thought he was wasting his time in Cleveland. New York was the place. My cousin Louis McKay, who'd married Billie Holiday, was living in New York and always asking me to visit. 'Come on, Jimmy,' I urged, 'why don't we move to New York?'"

"I had given up my Harlem apartment on Edgecombe Avenue, but I was ready to move back," Jimmy recalls. "All I needed was an excuse. Channie became that excuse. I thought she could make good money in New York. Red Saunders had a popular barber shop on Seventh Avenue in Harlem that attracted all the celebrities. I mentioned to Red the idea of giving Channie a chair, and he dug it. 'A pretty lady barber could bring in business,' he said. Eventually I planned on buying Channie her own boutique where she could carry women's clothing. She had strong fashion sense and an aggressive way of selling."

At the same time, through the combined efforts of Teddy Reig, Freddy Mendelsohn, and Jimmy Evans, all of whom had close ties to Savoy Records, Herman Lubinsky became interested in contracting Jimmy, giving him another reason to move from Cleveland.

"No one else was offering me any deals," says Jimmy, "so it wasn't much of a decision on my part. Besides, in the world of jazz, Savoy was a big-time label. They were headquartered in Newark but cut the records in New York. At that moment in my life, New York seemed the right place for me."

According to Jimmy, New York was the wrong place for Channie.

"Once we got there," he claims, "she went wild. The city overstimulated her. Cleveland had her rooted in some reality, but New York was a fantasyland. Channie needed family. Suddenly I was part of Billie Holiday's family. 'You were my brother before,' she said, 'and now you're also my cousin.' But Louis and Billie were having problems of their own and didn't make for great company. When Louis wasn't around, when I'd see Billie at my gigs or when I went to hers, she was hurting. She'd tell me how much she wanted kids and a house in the country. 'I just wanna cook and change diapers,' she said. I could feel how she hungered for the simple life. But there was nothing simple about dealing with Louis McKay, an overpowering man. And nothing simple about surviving New York City, where a cabaret card law kept her from working nightclubs. Her drug history came back to haunt her. 'Be sweet to this cat,' she'd tell Channie. 'A good man is hard to find.' Channie never heard a word she said."

"When we first moved, we got a place on Hancock Street in Brooklyn," Channie recalls. "My little girl stayed in Cleveland with her father and grandfather. From there we went to the city and the Flanders Hotel in midtown. Finally we found a permanent place on Thirty-third Street on the West Side, right across from the central post office."

"Three-thirteen and three-fifteen West Thirty-third Street were notorious buildings," says Jimmy, "filled with hustlers and whores. The super was a hustler himself who'd just gotten busted and was sent off to jail. He hired me to take his place. I liked the job because I

could work during the day—collect rents and do janitorial chores—
and gig at night."

"I mopped and cleaned those buildings from one end to the
other," Channie claims. "There were forty-eight apartments, all
occupied by street people. Our salaries were tiny, but we got by.
Jimmy's thrifty. He insisted we stay there, but I wanted out."

"I wanted Channie to pursue her art," claims Jimmy. "Her art
was hairstyling, but she wouldn't focus on the work. Instead she
was running all over New York. I never knew where she was. All I
knew is that the burden of making money had fallen a hundred
percent on me. That's why I put all my efforts into my recording
career. It seemed reasonable that, if I worked hard and gave my
heart and soul to my singing, I should be able to make a decent living making records at Savoy."

Savoy Records is famous in the annals of American music for producing a large number of important classic recordings in the field
of jazz, rhythm and blues, and gospel. And the label's owner, Herman Lubinksy, is infamous for his underpayment, or even nonpay-
ment, of everyone with whom he worked.

Seymour Stein, the record executive who, decades later, helped
reshape Jimmy's career, describes Lubinsky this way: "When I was
working at *Billboard* magazine, my boss, Paul Ackerman, used to
take trips to Newark. Instead of saying, 'I'm going over to Savoy
Records,' he'd say, 'I'm going to the slave barracks.' We knew that
meant he was going to see Lubinksy."

Music producer Joel Dorn calls Lubinsky "a human hemor-
rhoid and close personal friend of the Devil." Lee Magid, who
worked for Lubinsky, calls him "a horror story, a wanna-be big
shot, a cigar-chomping cartoon character—five feet four, bald, myopic, with a Napoleonic complex and heart of stone. At a time
when the business was run by cheap sons of bitches, this son of a
bitch made the others seem generous."

Barbara Kukla, author of *Swing City*, an exhaustive study on
the history of jazz in Newark, confirms this characterization of Lubinsky: "In my forty years as a reporter, I've never heard a person
described in such derogatory terms. Lubinsky's maltreatment of
musicians is legendary."

"Lubinksy would cheat you," adds Jimmy, "but Lubinksy still
got the good cats. You looked at his roster and saw everyone—
Erroll Garner, Don Byas, Billy Eckstine, Dexter Gordon, Fats
Navarro, Leo Parker, Miles, Getz, Diz, Bags, and of course Bird.
You had to be impressed."

"My father was born in 1896 in Connecticut," says Lubinsky's
son, Herman Lubinsky, Jr., who at age sixteen went to work at
Savoy around the same time Jimmy joined the label. "He learned
electronics and owned and operated the first radio station in New
Jersey under the name Alex Smith. That was in the twenties. In the
thirties he started a business selling radio tubes. Later he opened
the Radio Record Shop at Fifty-eight Market Street in downtown
Newark specializing in electronic parts and black music for collec-
tors. He got into recording music in the early forties during a musicians' union ban. He made all kinds of records—hillbilly, Latin,
Jewish—but concentrated on black gospel and jazz. In the midforties the guy who got him into big-time jazz was Teddy Reig."

"Reig told me he met Herman at the Three Deuces on Fifty-
second Street," says Jimmy. "Herman was over there scouting talent while secretly recording with his portable tape machine. He
was always secretly recording someone. Anyway, they'd kicked
him out of the Deuces because he never spent a dime on liquor—
wouldn't even buy a beer—when Reig saw him on the street.
Teddy said he could get him all the musicians he wanted. In those
days label owners like Lubinsky knew nothing about the music so
they depended on guys like Teddy. Teddy could gather up the cats
and run the sessions. Reig and Lubinsky played a cat-and-mouse
game for years. They didn't like each other, but they needed each
other. Teddy had his side hustles, his own little labels or sublabels.

Sometimes they'd make him money; sometimes they'd leave him broke. Teddy couldn't stop double-dealing. But no matter how many deals he had going, he saw Herman as a source of money. You see, Herman was always in the black. Because Teddy had influence over musicians Herman wanted, Teddy had Herman's number. He could always scam him out of a few bucks.

"So Herman would turn certain sessions over to Teddy. Meanwhile, Herman had also hired Freddy Mendelsohn as a producer. When Teddy and Freddy were at the Savoy at the same time, they'd play good cop/bad cop. Teddy was the scoundrel and Freddy the sweetheart. When Freddy came over to Savoy to make records, I felt better about singing there because I knew Freddy was sincere. Also add Jimmy Evans, the booking agent, to the mix. Evans was tight with Teddy and Herman. Evans fed musicians to Reig, who fed musicians to Lubinsky. The merry-go-round was spinning too fast for anyone to jump off. The money was small but consistent. Herman never wanted to give me a one-record contract. His contracts were based on time—a year or two or even more. I didn't pay much attention because I realized I had no bargaining power. I'd get fifty or a hundred bucks for a gig, a session, it didn't matter. If I wanted another advance, Herman added time to my contract. He was a sharp lawyer."

"My father wasn't a lawyer," explains Herman, Jr., long retired from the music business. "But some of the musicians thought he was, because of his cutthroat deals. I'm sorry to say he dealt with his family in much the same way. He couldn't give, financially or emotionally. I ran away when I was seventeen, thinking I'd escape him and make it on my own. I didn't. I came back and worked the counter at the store selling radio tubes. On Friday, Dad would fire me for undercharging someone a nickel. Mom would intervene, and Monday I was back at work. Dad was afraid of being exploited so he kept everyone at arm's length. His defense mechanism was ironclad. He was also volatile—pleasant one minute, belligerent the next. When Little Jimmy Scott came to the label I thought, *Now*

here's a true gentleman. He has perfect manners and a kind disposi-
tion. Dad will take it easy on him. But Dad didn't take it easy on
anyone. He and Jimmy did a strange dance together that went on
for a long, long time."

Jimmy, the least confrontational of men, was no doubt intimidated by Lubinsky, the most confrontational of men. In their dealings over the next twenty years, Jimmy simply took what he could
get. He doesn't recall a single episode in which he expressed to Lubinsky the anger and resentment he harbored inside. There were
times when Jimmy temporarily left the label and recorded for others; there were times when Lubinsky threatened Jimmy with lawsuits. But the men never had a single face-to-face encounter.

"I never wanted to give him the satisfaction of seeing me all
riled up," says Jimmy. "So I simply stayed away from him."

In total, Jimmy cut some sixty sides at Savoy, a modest number
considering the time span. The quality ran from superb to mediocre. The range of material was narrow. The main vehicle remained the ballad. When producer Freddy Mendelsohn gave him
material he saw as commercial, the results were banal and sometimes painful.

"For the most part, the Savoy sides that Jimmy made with
Freddy Mendelsohn in the fifties are not great records," says Billy
Vera. "The productions lack verve and the instrumentation isn't
very exciting. The excitement comes with Jimmy's vocals. His interpretations, his phrasing, his feeling for the lyric—these are the ingredients that make them treasures. Jimmy elevated the material; he
soared above the musical environment and turned dozens of classic
performances. If you're a singer interested in jazz, you need to study
the Jimmy Scott Savoy catalogue. It's a basic text."

The text began on February 5, 1955, his first Savoy session, re-
sulting in four sides. The jewel is "When Did You Leave Heaven."

"I was eighteen years old when I first heard it," says jazz singer
Nancy Wilson. "I was playing clubs around Ohio and, because of
Jimmy's version, fell in love with the song. I had fallen in love with

Jimmy's sensitivity the moment I'd heard 'Everybody's Somebody's Fool.' From then on, I followed his career and based my style on his. It was more than his phrasing, which, of course, was compelling and unique. It was what he did with words. Jimmy is a singer of the word, not the note. The note must serve the word, not vice versa. That lesson has served me for a lifetime. Later I'd record many of his songs: 'Fool,' 'The Masquerade Is Over,' 'When Did You Leave Heaven.' When people in the know heard my versions, they often said they heard Little Jimmy Scott. I complimented them on their good ear and gave Jimmy the glory. Without his example, I—along with so many other serious singers—would be lost."

The initial Savoy session that produced "Heaven" was far from easy. Mendelsohn was the producer and, motivated to put Jimmy in the best musical light, hired a group of top-flight musicians, including veteran saxophonist Budd Johnson, pianist Howard Biggs (known for creating the Ravens), guitarist Mundell Lowe, and bassist Charles Mingus, the hard-core bebopper who'd played with Hamp and Bird and would become a major force in modern music. Because Mingus was himself an experimenter, it came as a surprise that he stormed out of the session because of Jimmy's unconventional rhythms.

"It happened at Rudy Van Gelder's studio in Hackensack, where so many of the Savoy sides were cut," says Jimmy. "Van Gelder was considered the greatest engineer of the day. Things were going smoothly when all of a sudden Mingus starts yelling, 'This guy can't keep time! He's fucking up the time!' Next thing I know, he's out of the studio on his way home. Kenny 'Klook' Clarke stopped him. Mingus respected Klook as one of the hippest drummers. He had to listen to Klook. 'Be cool,' Klook told Mingus. 'Give Jimmy some slack. He's right on time.' Mingus came back and behaved. The whole episode shocked me because I saw Charlie as one of the deepest cats around. His musical expression was beautiful, and I was sure he'd be the first to appreciate someone who also did it differently. Maybe he was just having a bad day."

Bad day or not, Jimmy and Mingus never worked together again.

"I cut those first four songs at Savoy with hope in my heart," says Jimmy. "I really believed the records might hit. I thought these were vocal interpretations that the jazz public would appreciate. But whatever concerns I had for myself were overshadowed by the news that arrived a week later. It happened in March. One of the cats phoned—Bird was gone."

On March 12, 1955, at age thirty-four, Charlie Parker had collapsed and died at the apartment of Baroness Pannoica de Koenigswarter at the Stanhope Hotel on Fifth Avenue.

"His last months were hard," says Jimmy. "I got glimpses of him running through the clubs. He looked like a different man. I knew he couldn't keep up the pace. I don't claim to understand Bird in all his complexities. I do know that he was an educated man. He told me he'd wanted to be a doctor. He had ambitions and intelligence beyond music. He had so much energy burning through him, so many ideas, he couldn't contain them all. His artistic expression and his addiction conspired and exploded and took him out early. God bless Bird. His genius inspired everyone he touched. He was a genuine friend who never looked at me as an oddity but as an artist. To have his approval was all any of us wanted. It was better than a hit record."

Jimmy had no hit records at Savoy or, for that matter, for the rest of his long and winding career. His early sides for Savoy— "Time on My Hands," "Imagination," "Very Truly Yours," "Street of Dreams," "Recess in Heaven," "If You Only Knew"—were aimed at a jazz audience. With all due respect to Billy Vera's reservations, the productions are intoxicating. Spare and elegant, they offer just the simplicity that Jimmy requires.

Later in 1955, *Very Truly Yours,* Jimmy's first Savoy LP, was released. The cover shows a slender young Jimmy at the microphone. He appears delicate, forlorn, lost in the music. The songs— "Time on My Hands," "Imagination," "When Did You Leave

Heaven," "Someone to Watch over Me," "Street of Dreams"—are
dreamy, elegiac. *Very Truly Yours* proceeds at a snail's pace, with
Jimmy pleading his case with polite urgency. There are also strange
and unfortunate moments, especially when Cissy Houston (Whit-
ney's mom) shadows Jimmy on "Someone to Watch over Me" with
operatic inflection.

"Savoy cut a huge amount of gospel records," says Jimmy,
"and Cissy was signed to the label. They liked the effect of a high
voice behind me. I didn't, but I kept quiet. This was my first album
and I didn't want to rock the boat."

Despite the absence of promotion, Savoy hoped that songs like
"Don't Cry Baby," "Guilty," and "The Show Goes On," releases
geared for jukebox play, would catch on.

"I got some play," claims Jimmy. "When I worked the clubs
around Newark and Philly, my two best towns, they had me on
the box. They knew my material. But nothing took off. Some said
that was because I was too jazz for the pop fans. Others said I was
too pop for the jazz fans. My fans said, 'Just keep doing what
you're doing.'"

On many of Jimmy's first sides for Savoy, his subtle interpretations of ballads remind the listener of Miles—or vice versa. This
was the same period when Miles formed his great quintet with
John Coltrane, Red Garland, Paul Chambers, and Philly Joe Jones.
Miles's sensitivity in handling standards—"There Is No Greater
Love," "It Never Entered My Mind," "When I Fall in Love"—
brings to mind a lonely singer. That sense of romantic alienation,
where love is but a distant dream, combines with a painstakingly
patient approach to time. The results, for both Jimmy and Miles,
are love songs that approach prayer.

"Seeing Jimmy Scott live and in person in the midfifties was a
shock," says Chuck Stewart, famed jazz photographer. "It happened
at one of those big teen shows in Philly. It was the kind of musical

program being promoted in big cities across the country. Rock was about to be born, and even though there were some doo-wop acts like the Cardinals, the showstoppers were Screaming Jay Hawkins climbing out of a coffin to sing 'You Put a Spell on Me' and Bill Haley and the Comets doing 'Rock Around the Clock.' In the middle of all this, they introduced Little Jimmy Scott. I wasn't waiting for a little man who sang like a fallen angel. It was incongruous to see him there—he was a million miles away from rock and roll—but he was strangely effective. He held the crowd in the palm of his hand."

"Jimmy Evans put together these packages," Jimmy explains, "and couldn't care less about the mix of music. At thirty, I didn't exactly see myself singing to teenagers, but I was happy for the exposure. The best thing about those shows, though, was meeting Little Willie and Big Maybelle. I'd first met Maybelle in Indianapolis back in forty-four, when we were teens. This was a child who could sing Sarah Vaughan under the table. Maybelle was fierce. She was also enormous. She had the most beautiful face you'd ever want to see—smiling eyes, gorgeous cheekbones, a smile that lit up the room. But, oh Lord, the child had a terrible complex about her size. Dope was her leaning post. But high or not, she tore up those ballads. Freddy Mendelsohn loved her. He championed her early on, just like he'd championed me. He produced her first records, and when he jumped to Savoy he got Lubinksy to sign her up. We became label-mates, and I was happy when her first single, 'Candy,' hit big. I related to her style and I believe she related to mine."

"Listen to Big Maybelle, and you'll hear the female corollary of Little Jimmy," observes Jerry Wexler, who during this same period was producing Ray Charles's first major hits. "The irony, of course, is that Jimmy is a small man with a woman's sound while Maybelle is a large woman with a man's sound. They're flip sides of the same coin. Maybelle may be earthier, Jimmy may be more ethereal, but their common currency is heavy soul. They meet at the crossroads of rhythm and blues and jazz. Later, when Jimmy left Savoy, Lubinsky had Maybelle singing Jimmy's songs.

For all the difference between them, it's easy to mistake one for the other."

"Maybelle was my sister," says Jimmy. "Just like my career, hers just sort of limped along. Quincy Jones had produced her doing 'Whole Lot of Shaking Goin' On,' but it was the cover by Jerry Lee Lewis that made the money. Maybelle survived on the road and road alone. She and I worked together in every little joint up and down the East Coast. We'd often switch songs. She'd sing 'Masquerade' and I'd sing 'Candy.' When she was straight, she was sweet as candy. When she was high, she withdrew. She didn't react like Billie, who became happier. Maybelle got morose. She'd start to crying, and next thing you know, she'd disappear into the night with the wrong guy.

"Meanwhile, Jimmy Evans was the wrong agent for us, though we were both afraid to drop him for fear of not working at all. Maybe we should have looked around for a different agent, but we didn't think that way. We were dependent on the Lubinksy network for money, and Jimmy Evans was a big part of that network. Jimmy liked the fact that Maybelle was dependent on dope. He helped keep her hooked. That way he could control her. He also liked spreading the word that I was a junkie, even though I wasn't. That meant other agents wouldn't touch me. I'd show up in Detroit, say, and a cat would come to the club talkin' 'bout, 'Little Jimmy, I got what you're looking for.' I wasn't looking for nothing except a little money to live on.

"The money was always funny. Lubinsky did Maybelle like he did me. He'd parcel out little loans to her and use them to extend her contract. Jimmy Evans did her even worse. He'd double or triple his commissions, thinking she was too loaded to notice. Evans owed her so much money that one time she went out to his house on Long Island, stood on his front lawn, and shouted so loud all the neighbors could hear. 'I work for this man all day long cleaning his house,' she yelled, 'and he won't give me a dime. I mop his floors, I scrub his toilet, I wash his dirty drawers, and the motherfucker won't give me my hard-earned pay. He's cheating me! I want everyone to know that Jimmy Evans is cheating me!' To see a three-hundred-pound black woman in the middle of the white suburbs screaming bloody murder was enough to scare even cold-blooded Evans. He called me and said I had to come out there and calm her down. 'The only way to calm her down,' I said, 'is to give her some money.'

"He did, but eventually he got even. In the early fifties, when they were auditioning actresses to play Beulah on the TV show of the same name—Ethel Waters, Hattie McDaniel, and Louise Beavers all had the role at one time or another—Maybelle was asked to read. She would have been perfect. She was dramatic and had great comic timing. But Evans was afraid a big-time Hollywood role would lead her to a big-time Hollywood agent. He wanted her to keep working the clubs, so he manipulated the situation and got her high before the audition. She messed up and never had another chance like that again."

Jimmy's chance at the big time didn't come, at least not yet. His dealings were with small-time labels cut off from the mass market. No major label approached him, because most major record executives hadn't heard of him. In the midfifties, the pop ballads were the Four Aces' "Love Is a Many-Splendored Thing," Al Hibbler's "He," Dean Martin's "Memories Are Made of This." Given the right song on the right label, Jimmy might have had a hit. His voice had the power and emotional punch, but his style remained idiosyncratic. At a time when a big seller was Frank Sinatra's *In the Wee Small Hours,* an album whose caressing ballads were close to Jimmy's sensibility, Savoy didn't really know what to do with its singer. He wasn't Sammy Davis singing "Birth of the Blues." He wasn't Nat Cole singing "A Blossom Fell." He wasn't Johnny

Mathis singing "Chances Are." Who was he? At the dawn of a revolution in pop music, when teenagers would drive the market in radical new directions, Jimmy continued doing what he had always done. He scuffled. He made the best of a bad situation. That situation included not only his tenuous relationships to the music business, but his marriage to Channie, which, with every passing year, grew more insane.

WYANDANCH, LONG ISLAND

*I*n 1956, searching for calm domesticity, Jimmy bought a small house outside New York City. The purchase represented an effort to control the uncontrollable elements of his unstable marriage. Home ownership had been a lifelong dream, a way to put together what had come undone in his traumatic childhood.

"Jimmy always talked about having a house," says Channie. "A house reminded him of the family he had before his mother died."

"My father never owned a house in his life," Jimmy explains. "He never bought a place where my sisters and brothers could feel like family. I was determined to have a home. That's one of the reasons I took the day job as a custodian on Thirty-third Street while working whatever music gig I could find. I saved some money and started looking for a place. Out on Long Island, in a town called Wyandanch, they were constructing little bungalows that cost ten thousand dollars. It was less than an hour from the city. The area was nice. In the fifties, everyone was moving to the suburbs. So why not? Manhattan was hard. I was tired of chasing after thieving tenants for their rent money. I dug the Island. Dug the quiet.

Channie and I were having our problems, but maybe we could work them out in a place of tranquillity."

"Jimmy wanted to put some distance between himself and the jazz world of New York," says Channie. "People in that world spread rumors that Jimmy was a junkie. But Jimmy never touched dope. He and I were too busy drinking to worry about heroin. Besides, unlike the junkies, Jimmy was a worker. He worked hard to buy that house on the Island. It had two bedrooms, a mirrored bathroom, a kitchen, and a dinette. It also had a carport, where Jimmy parked his Coupe de Ville Cadillac and I parked my Dodge Coronet. Looking in from the outside, you'd think we were a happily married couple. But the happiness never stayed. I loved Jimmy's sweet soul, but when he got juiced he'd get mean as a rattlesnake. He has the quirkiest moods of any man in the world—angel by day, devil by night. After every gig, he'd be nasty drunk. Even worse, he wouldn't have a dime."

"Channie was obsessed with money," claims Jimmy. "*My* money. I still had jobs, even on the Island. I was a stock clerk at a plant store and worked in a factory making plastic molds. Lubinsky wasn't about to give up any good advances. I might have gotten a couple of hundred dollars for my second album on Savoy, if that much."

The album *If You Only Knew*, released in 1956, includes three songs by Charlie Singleton and Rosemarie McCoy, the writers of "Very Truly Yours"(the title tune), "Oh What I Wouldn't Give," and "I'll Never Deceive."

"As one of the few black female songwriters," says McCoy, "I was a rarity. As a singer, I had performed with Jimmy at Leon's Cocktail Lounge in Hackensack, so I knew what he could do to an audience. But to see him in the studio was a revelation. We had some nice charts in a straight-ahead, jazzy style. Jimmy was at the top of his form. I was blessed in that I'd written for Dinah Washington, Ruth Brown, Big Maybelle, Pearl Bailey—I knew them all. And every last one of those ladies loved Jimmy. Every last one of them, from Dakota Staton to Della Reese to Shirley Horn, was deeply influenced by his approach. No man has ever taught women more about singing than Little Jimmy Scott. His timing, his patience, the way he prolonged the story—I just sat there and took mental notes."

If You Only Knew has lovely moments. Jimmy skips along on the title track with breezy nonchalance. (More than forty-five years later he's still breezing along singing the same song.) The highlight, though, is another heavenly metaphor—"Recess in Heaven." Jimmy loves singing about lost angels and, augmented by Budd Johnson's lush tenor, paints a divine picture of idealized love. Still in his early thirties, his voice remains a powerful instrument, his vibrato a wonder of firm control. Some of the songs, such as "I'll Never Deceive You," are attempts at radio-friendly fare, with lackluster results. But at its best—the opening notes of "Oh What I Wouldn't Give," for example—the record is thrilling.

"The record didn't sell," says Jimmy. "You never know why, but one thing's for sure—Lubinsky didn't spend a cent on promotion."

"My father avoided payola more out of frugality than morality," says Herman, Jr., speaking of the 1950s scandal in which some music industry figures bribed disc jockeys to give their records air time. "He didn't want to pay off anyone. The reason he recorded so much gospel was because gospel didn't require promotion."

"After Freddy Mendelsohn produced *Very Truly Yours*," Jimmy remembers, "he got fed up and quit because Lubinsky wouldn't buy any ads or slip the deejay a little something for airplay. I had another issue with Lubinksy. Around this time Don Redman, maybe the greatest arranger in the history of jazz, wanted to write an entire album for me. Don was coming over from England just to do it. Redman had led his own big band; he'd written for Fletcher Henderson, Basie, Dorsey, Harry James. Don was the cat. He was also willing to do it for modest bread. But even modest was too much for Lubinsky. He offered Don a below-scale wage. Don was insulted and refused. I didn't blame him. Nor did I blame Freddy when he up and quit, going to work for Syd Nathan at King, the Cincinnati label where James Brown got big. 'I want to take you with me,' said Freddy, who never gave up on artists he liked. 'Are you willing, Jimmy?' I was. Teddy Reig and Jimmy Evans were also in the mix. They were looking to hurt Herman. Herman Lubinksy was always fighting the world. So they arranged for Henry Glover, King's man in New York, to set up the session. Freddy supervised."

Between 1957 and 1958, Jimmy cut a dozen singles for King Records. Under pressure to produce hits, Mendelsohn seems to have lowered his standards. The material he fed Jimmy was crass—simplistic chord changes, stale background singers, dopey lyrics. The two exceptions are "Somewhere Down the Line," a semisatisfying blues number, and "Home," a lament of lost familial happiness that rings especially true coming from Jimmy.

"I wasn't comfortable with most of the material," he says, "but was willing to go along for the ride. Syd Nathan, who looked like Herman's brother, gave me three hundred fifty dollars. I never saw a cent more. Never heard a word from Lubinsky about breaking his contract. I think that's because he and Syd were tight. It's also because I had no hits on King. It wasn't a happy time."

"Out on Long Island, we were fighting like cats and dogs," Channie recalls. "We'd go at it. Jimmy was never crazy violent. But he'd push me, and I'd push him. There was no punching but lots of smacking. I wasn't satisfied."

"Channie was running around on me," claims Jimmy. "I knew that early on, but wanted to give her the benefit of the doubt. I wanted to hold on to the idea of a faithful wife and a real family. But my original family and my new family were in tatters. Channie and I tried to look on Louis McKay and Billie Holiday as family. Sometimes we'd see them in the city. But that family was no different than ours—Louis and Billie were on the brink of collapse. When Billie got high, she'd hold your hand and call you brother. Now Billie's highs were all lows. Looking at her, I didn't know how long she could last. The trust between her and Louis was gone. You could see it in her eyes, feel it in her music.

"Betrayal is hard to take. I took it for a long while, but when Channie had her man drive her back to our house in full daylight, I lost it. She'd been out all night. It was two in the afternoon when they pulled up in his car. I was in the front yard mowing the lawn when I saw them both get out of the car. They kissed good-bye. They were rubbing it in my face. Before I knew it, I took the lawn mower and heaved it through his windshield."

"We came to blows that day," Channie remembers. "I think I might have been a little stronger than Jimmy, but he wouldn't back off. I wouldn't back off because I knew he had his woman in Newark—Earlene. I knew he was leading a secret life in Jersey, so I saw no reason not to do as I pleased."

"Newark was a refuge," Jimmy admits, "but never as a place to cheat. With a single exception, I never cheated on any of my wives. It's not my nature."

"I never had sex with Jimmy while he was married to Channie," says Earlene. "I think that's why Jimmy respected me. I'd go see him at clubs and ask after his welfare. I knew he was unhappy, but Jimmy is loyal and likes to try and stick it out. He doesn't end relationships easily. I saw him put the pain in his music. That made me love him—and his music—even more."

"If it wasn't Earlene," says Channie, "it was someone else. A girlfriend warned me. She said, 'Channie, your man's got a woman and he's singing to her every night at the club.' The club was out on the Island, and on a Friday I sneaked in there without warning Jimmy. Sure enough, Jimmy's on the bandstand eyeing this broad. Soon as he finishes his set, he makes a beeline to her table. I get there before he does and start going after the bitch. Next thing I know, the bouncer is going after me. Fists are flying when suddenly here comes Little Jimmy going off on the big bouncer! 'That's my wife,' he tells the bruiser. 'Get your hands off her!' I had to laugh—

Jimmy protecting *me!* By the end of the evening, we were all so loaded we could laugh about it."

"The problems with Channie and her crazy jealousy got so serious," says Jimmy, "that I found myself running over to Newark every chance I had. Newark was the one place I felt safe."

By 1957, Jimmy started living two separate lives—first with Channie on Long Island, the second in Newark, where he'd rent rooms in boardinghouses.

"When I first met Jimmy he was living alone in Newark," relates Joe Pesci, the actor who began as a singer. "I was a teenager, raised in the Italian North Ward and in love with jazz. I thought I knew jazz until one night I slipped into the Front Room, a club where Jimmy was singing. The sound of his voice turned my world upside down. All the magic, all the mystery of grown-up life, was in his voice. He gave jazz a twist—an individual turn—I'd never heard before. I related in every way. Just as he was called Little Jimmy, they were calling me Little Joe. My first album, in fact, was titled *Little Joe Sure Can Sing.* All I wanted to do was sing like Little Jimmy Scott. I became his disciple. I'd follow him around after gigs, see if I could help him in any way. He was living hand-to-mouth. I didn't ask a lot of questions, but I knew a hard relationship was ending. I also saw how he needed romantic torture to sing like he did. He brought that experience into his art. His life was strange and a little secretive. But as a mentor, he couldn't have been more open. People might have been fucking him over—wives, girlfriends, agents, and managers—but he never whined. He'd listen to me sing and encourage me on. Sometimes he'd disappear for days at a time, but when I caught up with him—in his little room on Gillette Place or in some coffee shop on Broad Street—he'd smile and welcome me into his world. The world of Jimmy Scott was a world of singing. We'd sing together nonstop for hours, sometimes all night. He'd teach me phrasing and harmony. He'd teach me songs I still remember. As an instructor, he was a steady guide with a gentle touch. He became my guru. I became his shadow."

"Jimmy was a towering influence on a whole generation of young singers," says Frankie Valli of the famed Four Seasons. "Like Pesci, who I knew since we were kids, I grew up in Newark. I heard Jimmy early on. I remember seeing him at a club somewhere in the Third Ward. Many of the joints where Jimmy played weren't much more than a bar and a few tables. There wasn't even a bandstand. Sometimes it'd be just Jimmy and a pianist. But that's all he needed. When I heard that voice, that cry, that phrasing, those emotions coming out of that little man, I'd found what I didn't even know I'd been looking for. I found Truth. I became a Jimmy Scott follower. I still am. He never got the name of an Ella, Billie, or Sarah, but his talent is just as great. His talent inspired me at a time in my life when I needed a musical mentor. He'd let all us kids hang out with him—didn't matter that we were white—and patiently showed us the way. 'Baby,' he'd say to me, '*you* set the beat. *You* make the rhythm section wait on you.'

"It wasn't only aspiring jazz singers who were influenced by Jimmy. There's a whole school of doo-woppers—Sonny Till of the Orioles, Frankie Lymon of the Teenagers—who heard Jimmy's high tenor and copped his licks, blending his style with their own multi-harmonies. Jimmy's control in the top register, combined with his feeling for romance, shaped many a soul singer. Listen to Marvin Gaye."

"I heard Jimmy Scott back in the fifties," Marvin Gaye told me in the seventies, "when I sang doo-wop with Harvey Fuqua and the Moonglows. We looked to Jimmy as a master. My entire career I longed to sing ballads—like Frank Sinatra or Nat Cole or Perry Como—but with the depth of Jimmy Scott. He had that tear in his voice. That aching soul. When I finally got to record those ballads, I had a tape of Jimmy Scott songs by my side."

"I believe we caught him in his prime in Newark," Valli continues. "He'd always be an astounding artist, but to see him in those days, when he was still scuffling, wearing his heart on his sleeve and singing for his supper, was unforgettable."

"Little Jimmy was always singing around in Newark somewhere and gambling in the hallways of Hillside Place," writes poet-playwright Amiri Baraka in *Autobiography of LeRoi Jones*. "We all dug his 'The Masquerade Is Over' and imitated him every day, including his caved-in chest stance and sway as he whispered his tragic blues."

A hero among hipsters, Jimmy achieved cult status in Newark. In Newark he didn't need a booking agent like Jimmy Evans, whom he never really trusted. Others found him work.

"I found him gigs here and there," says Tiny Prince, the Jersey entrepreneur and Scott booster. "He took whatever the owner paid, sometimes a small cut of the door. 'You count the money,' he'd tell me. 'I trust you.' Jimmy never cared about money and never really took care of business. No matter what condition he might have been in, though, the women came out to see him, to touch him, to get him to sing their song."

Bill Cook, a Newark deejay, ran Cookie's Caravan on South Bedford in the heart of black Newark, where Doc Pomus saw both Big Maybelle, whom he called the "most passionate female singer ever," and Jimmy. Doc's eyewitness account from his journals:

"Jimmy was frail and Indian looking. He had a long, narrow face that he kept framed with oversized, thick glasses. His clothes were always so long and loose he looked like some kind of myopic scarecrow. And he walked with a slow, strange stagger-shuffle. But I swear that weird-looking dude could holler. He sang the slow notes slower than anyone and had an uncanny way of bending notes. It was like he was trying to find out how much he could control and try a note without messing up his perfect pitch. He snagged behind the beat further than anyone. Every time I was certain that he finally got too far back, he somehow returned. His meter was always impeccable. He had a wide vibrato, and the combination of his timing, pitch, and soft, sweet sound gave every song a dreamlike, love-fantasy quality. Jimmy and I were real tight and used to go visit his sister Shirley and her husband, who lived in an army barracks in the Canarsie section of Brooklyn. They were a proper couple so we made sure that we were never stoned around them. Jimmy was gentlemanly and quiet by nature, so it was easy for him to maintain his cool. I was rowdier, so it was a little more difficult for me."

"Shirley was on welfare from the Catholic Church and living in deep poverty," says Jimmy. "It was depressing going over there. I tried my best to keep up my spirits, but her vibe got me down. She was becoming bitter about life's cruel turns. I knew that was an attitude to avoid, which is why hanging out with Doc was so beautiful. Doc was a positive person, always interested in creative expression. He was deep into his writing. Ray Charles was singing one of his songs—'Lonely Avenue'—and the Drifters were getting ready to sing 'This Magic Moment' and 'Save the Last Dance for Me.' Doc had a rare gift. He appreciated jazz, but his appreciation embraced all black music as one. That's why he could switch tracks and write top-ten radio hits. He could take a pure blues singer like Big Joe Turner, Doc's idol and dearest friend, and give him a song like 'Boogie Woogie Country Girl' that appealed to everyone. He appealed to the kids with Dion and the Belmonts' 'Teenager in Love.' I could talk music with Doc because, unlike the critics and snobs who had to stuff everyone in a little box, Doc didn't need boxes. He saw the big picture. Some jazz writers, for example, might wonder why I considered Little Willie John and Jesse Belvin among the greats. Doc didn't wonder; he knew. He understood Willie and Jesse just like he understood Big Maybelle. He knew they were stone geniuses.

"Little Willie had a bunch of big hits on King before I got to the label—'All Around the World (If Grits Ain't Groceries, Eggs Ain't Poultry and Mona Lisa Was a Man),' 'Talk to Me, Talk to Me,' and 'Fever,' which Peggy Lee made even bigger. Willie was a pistol. In fact, he liked carrying pistols. Since the incident in Milwaukee, I'd given up guns, but Willie never would. He was a singing fool, but he looked on life as being cruel. He saw his smallness as being unfair, so he'd test the waters with tough guys. That got him in trouble and finally landed him in prison.

"I understood the challenge of being small. I ignored snide remarks, but some things you can't ignore. There was the time I was playing Philly with pianist Red Garland, the best accompanist I'd ever had. Red had left Miles and was on a creative high. He'd find your key, blend the melody with beautiful block chords, and follow wherever you led. Red followed me into the Philly clubs—Martin's on Market Street or Gus Lacy's Mister Silk's Third Base, where the neon sign read, 'Always Touch Third Base Before You Go Home.' The Philly fans were cool, but the Philly cops were cruel. It was a mellow gig, when suddenly the cops burst in and accused me of transferring dope. They banged my head on their car as they shoved me in the backseat. I started to bleed, but they ignored it. At the station they made me strip and stand naked in front of the guys in the precinct. They pointed to my privates and howled. Didn't matter that I had no dope. Didn't matter that the charges were manufactured. The cops frequently manufactured charges to hassle musicians, especially black musicians. But this was something else. This was about humiliating me. They wanted a good laugh and got one at my expense.

"Same thing happened in Newark. I was standing outside the Caravan on a cold December night, when a cop hauled me off to the station. I recognized him because a week before he'd asked me to play the policeman's ball. I couldn't because I had another gig. But he didn't accept my excuse. He got mad and decided to punish me. Down at the station, it was the same strip-search routine as Philly. They wanted to see me buck naked. They wanted to hoot and holler. I simply took it. I let them laugh. To resist was to prolong the ordeal.

"There was no solace at home. Channie and I held on, hoping for a change in our feelings, but things only worsened. There was a bad scene after a gig in Connecticut. I was doing a show with Big Maybelle. Must have been in fifty-eight. We were all drinking. When Channie showed up in my Coupe de Ville, her man was sitting next to her. Without my knowledge, she collected my money from the club owner. Not only that, they threw me in the backseat. I went off. I wanted my money. I started attacking them both. Punches were thrown. I got a black eye."

"Jimmy owed me that money," claims Channie, "so I felt in the right. He was so mad, though, he climbed over the seat and, while I was pressing the accelerator, he put his foot over mine and pushed the pedal to the floor. 'If you don't give me my money,' he threatened, 'I'll kill us all.' We must have been going a hundred, swerving all over the road, until I managed to slam on the brake. Screaming, I jumped out of the car when the cops showed up. They knew who Jimmy was, so they let us go on the promise it wouldn't happen again. With all of us back in the car, it *did* happen again, Jimmy going crazy by jumping on the accelerator. We took off like a rocket ship, burning so much rubber that the cops heard the noise and came running. This time they threw Jimmy in the slammer. I let him stay there. Next morning I went back to see about him. They took me to his cell, where he was sitting between a foul-smelling drunk and a nasty toilet. He looked so sad and helpless. I'd taken all his money, so he didn't have a dime to pay the fine. I paid it and took him home."

"I'm sure I stayed with Channie longer than I should have," says Jimmy, "but I've always been that way with women. I kept hoping it'd get better. Finally, though, I ran out of hope. The fighting only got worse, especially when she told me she was pregnant by her man. That happened in July of 1959. The reason I remember is because Billie died that same month. When we went to the funeral, I had to wear dark glasses to cover up another black eye Channie had given me. The pain I was feeling was no greater than the pain Billie felt her entire life. She died in the hospital with cops outside the door. She died under arrest. She lived under arrest.

Now she was spiritually free in a way the material world never let her be. I listened to her last great record, *Lady in Satin,* where she finally had the full orchestra and strings she'd been longing for. Her voice had a different quality. For me, it's a deeper quality. Truer. Wiser. She knew she was dying, and these were her last gifts to us. I treasure them to this day. On the day of her funeral, we sat in the Apostle Roman Catholic Church on Columbus Avenue in the first pew reserved for family. We were the only family she had—Louis, Channie, myself, and her half-sister, Kay Kelly. I walked to the casket and saw her in her pink gown and pink gloves. She was a picture of peace. The cemetery was in the Bronx, and as they lowered her in the ground, I heard her music inside my head. I heard her singing, 'God bless the child that's got her own.' *God bless Billie,* I said to myself, *and the music that sprung from her soul.* The week Billie died, my marriage died as well."

MOTHERLESS CHILD

*J*immy and I are sitting in the Newark train station. He loves the ambiance. "When I was a kid," he says, "train stations gave me a thrill of coming and going. I saw all the movement as a sign of hope. If you hang in, you *will* get where you're going." Today is Sunday and no one seems to be going anywhere. The station is nearly deserted. A few homeless men sleep on benches. A family of Latinos shares a box lunch. I inch closer to Jimmy and ask about the end of the fifties.

"When Channie and I split up for good after five years of marriage, I gave her the house. I didn't have the heart for a fight or the money for lawyers. She'd go on to have boy twins with her man. I let bygones be bygones. I wanted to forget the whole affair and move on with my life. It'd be twenty years before I saw her again.

"I stayed here in Newark. Newark took care of me. At thirty-four, I had my blessings. I had my health. I had my people. I had my old friends like Tiny Prince and Geronimo. I had young cats—Pesci and Valli—who'd do anything for me. I was still working the clubs. Winter was harsh that year. I was playing the Caravan in December to only half-filled houses when one Thursday night I noticed a young woman I'll call Eunice sitting in the back. She was no older than nineteen. Her facial features were a striking combination of Asian and African. When she got up to leave, I noticed she didn't have a coat. A snowstorm was howling outside, and worried about her health, I offered her my coat. She sweetly refused, but promised she'd be back the next night. I believed her and decided to buy her a coat. Well, Eunice did return, and when I presented her with the coat, tears welled up in her eyes. At evening's end, she came back to my little rented room. After the nightmare with Channie, it was satisfying to be with a gentle woman. For a while I moved in with her and her mom, who was raising a little baby girl. Eunice was a sweetheart, but I soon learned she'd been dibbling and dabbling with prostitution. 'No more,' she said after we'd been together a few weeks. I was convinced she was sincere, and I moved out of my rented room and got us our own apartment. We were cool until my brother Kenny moved in. He'd come from Cleveland to run a private parking lot on the East Side of Manhattan. Kenny was my blood and welcome to live with me anytime. But seeing Eunice's stockings and undies hanging in the bathroom made him uneasy. Eunice got the idea he didn't approve of her. Tension mounted. Finally I had to ask Kenny to leave. In one way or another, I was still having problems with my family.

"I was having worse problems with Savoy. I followed Freddy Mendelsohn back to the label. Lubinksy was happy my King singles had flopped. He said he harbored no ill will and was willing to make another record. So I signed another contract and got another two hundred dollars. This time, though, he wanted a hit. 'Jazz doesn't sell,' he said. 'Sam Cooke is selling, Brook Benton is selling. Connie Francis just covered "Everybody's Somebody's Fool,"and it's selling. There's no reason why we can't sell Little Jimmy Scott.' With that, Lubinksy sent me and Freddy back into the studio with strict orders to come up with a smash. I liked the idea of making money, and I went along."

The Savoy archives reveal problems Lubinsky was having with getting Jimmy to the rehearsals. "I might have missed one," Jimmy

claims, "but that was rare." Yet a telegram Lubinsky sent to Jimmy
at 79 Sherman Avenue in Newark suggests otherwise: "Please call
us on the phone. You have missed three appointments and the situation is serious as this is costing us money. Phone in the morning as
rehearsal is for two P.M. Friday March 25, 1960. Biggs is waiting."
"Biggs" refers to arranger Howard Biggs.

The Fabulous Songs of Jimmy Scott, released later that year,
flopped. (For the first time, by the way, the "Little" was dropped
from his name.) It would be fifteen years before he'd make another
record for the label. *Fabulous Songs* was the sour note that ended
Jimmy's relationship with the team of Mendelsohn, Reig, Evans,
and Lubinsky. The album garnered virtually no attention from the
marketplace or critics.

"After we cut the original tracks, Freddy and Howard added
strings," says Jimmy. "I didn't mind because I was hoping strings
would help sell the thing. But the strings were stilted. I re-recorded
'Fool' and 'Masquerade,' only this time they didn't sound fresh.
The arrangements cramped my style. Some of the songs were
pretty—'The Way You Look Tonight,' 'Please Forgive Me'—but
with the corny tempos and over-tinkly piano, it all felt cheesy. I
couldn't blame Freddy for putting it together the way he did. He
knew the only way I'd have any money was by having hits."

"Jimmy always sang his heart out," says Herman Lubinksy, Jr.
"On that last album it's almost as though he tried too hard. With
all of us straining for a hit, you can hear the pressure in his voice.
The only thing that really came off was 'Sometimes I Feel Like a
Motherless Child.' It's one of the most beautiful things Jimmy ever
did. I heard him sing it in the studio and I heard him sing it live.
I'm glad to see he's still singing it today because it says so much
about his true feelings. 'Sometimes I feel like a motherless child . . .
a long way from home.' Along with 'Fool,' 'Masquerade,' and
'Heaven,' it's become one of his signatures."

Another selection from *The Fabulous Songs*, "An Evening in
Paradise," certainly fits Jimmy's description as cheesy, with its

cascading harps and syrupy strings, but the song gets to the listener, just as it got to Bill Cosby, who featured it on one of his
Cosby Show episodes in the eighties. It sounds like something
from *South Pacific,* a cousin of Bloody Mary's "Bali H'ai," but the
melody is seductive and Jimmy's full-blooded reading irresistible.

"My dad never promoted *The Fabulous Songs,*" says Herman,
Jr., "just as he never promoted any jazz. But he did try to promote
a single recorded by Jimmy that wasn't on the album. 'I May
Never' was close to rock and roll. We thought it had a shot at
some chart action and booked Jimmy on *Teen Bandstand,* a New
York TV show on Channel Five. I took Dad's Cadillac and drove
Jimmy to the studio in the city. Five minutes before he was due to
sing, he told me he'd forgotten the lyrics. He wanted to leave, but I
wouldn't let him. 'This is your chance, Jimmy,' I said before pushing him out in front of the camera. He made up the words he'd forgotten. He did the best he could, but the song died."

"In those days I wasn't especially comfortable on television,"
says Jimmy, "especially on a teen show singing a song that really
didn't fit my style. No wonder it didn't sell."

The Fabulous Songs, along with his singles for King and Savoy
in the late fifties, represent a sad ending to a once promising phase
of Jimmy's recording career. As a big-band vocalist at the end of the
big-band era, Jimmy had one hit in the early fifties and, with more
focus and less flitting about, might have had more. But by the end
of the fifties, in the new world of pop, rock, and rhythm and blues,
he didn't stand a chance. He was—and remains—a jazz singer specializing in deep, romantic ballads. Yet in spite of his high standings
among his colleagues, in spite of more than a dozen small masterpieces recorded for Decca, Coral, Roost, and Savoy, the critics were
indifferent. The historians ignored him. He wasn't given as much as
a mere mention in any of the major jazz books of the period.
Leonard Feather, Nat Hentoff, Ira Gitler, Barry Ulanov—no one
paid him the least attention. Given the cold critical and commercial
climate, it's no wonder Jimmy was eager to leave Savoy.

"Lubinsky wanted me to make more rock-sounding records," he says, "but I just wasn't willing. I tried a few, and a few were enough. The lyrics were trite, the rhythms were rough, and I couldn't apply anything I'd learned about singing. I couldn't be sincere. I'd rather just sing in the clubs than try to record something I couldn't feel.

"I could always go home and gig with Chickadee, who was still playing Paddock's. Chickadee was still the baddest organist around. His reputation had grown over the years to where even Lubinsky wanted to sign him. Fact is, Chickadee is the only cat I know who screwed Herman rather than the other way around. Savoy gave him a couple of hundred dollars to cut a record. Chickadee took the money and disappeared. Lubinksy called me in Cleveland, hysterically demanding I find Chickadee. 'Sorry, Herman,' I said, 'but it looks like this is one chickadee who flew the coop.'

"Eunice was showing less interest in me as well. She wandered off with another cat. It wasn't devastating, because, although I dug her, the hold wasn't that great. She was a good kid, but it turned out we didn't have much in common. Besides, I felt like I needed some time alone. Inside me, something was changing. I thought it was an emotional change, but it turned out to be physical."

"On one of his trips home to Cleveland," remembers sister Nadine, "Jimmy came over to visit. Something was very different about the way he looked. It took me a couple of seconds to realize it, but he was taller! Inches taller!"

"For several months I'd been worried," says Jimmy. "I'd be stretched out in bed when I'd suddenly hear noises inside my body. My bones were creaking and my muscles were moving. Didn't know what it was. Finally I went to the doctor, who told me, plain and simple, I was growing. He called it a delayed hormone development. Said it sometimes happens to people with the Deficiency. Within months I went from four feet eleven to five feet six. I was more confused than jubilant. I was worried whether there'd be health consequences. But there weren't. While my height shot up, the other traits of the Deficiency remained—no body hair, lack of smelling, small privates."

"At the time this happened," reports Nadine, "Jimmy was about thirty-five. The doctors told him that because of the growth, an operation to stimulate more hormonal development was possible. But Jimmy refused. He was afraid of the needle."

"I was afraid of entering uncharted territory," adds Jimmy. "Besides, fooling with my hormones might mean changing my voice. Whatever the problems that came with the Deficiency, my voice was the one thing I could count on."

In the early sixties, the space race was on. The Kennedy White House was seen as Camelot, Castro was making noise, and jazz was especially fertile: John Coltrane was reinventing "My Favorite Things"; Stan Getz was discovering bossa nova; Miles Davis was hiring Herbie Hancock and Tony Williams; Dexter Gordon was making his great Blue Note recordings; Charlie Mingus was reaching back to his roots with *Oh Yeah*. That meant Jimmy's highly romanticized style was hardly in the vanguard, despite his appreciation of the new forms.

"For a while, rootsy jazz was all the rage," says Jimmy. "I saw it coming with Jimmy Smith's *The Sermon*, a monstrous expression of magnificent ideas. Horace Silver had that same gospel/blues vibe with 'Sister Sadie,' and Cannonball picked up it with *Them Dirty Blues*. Jesse Belvin was another cat who sang rootsy. But Jesse could also sing ballads as beautifully as Nat Cole. Many of us thought Jesse was going to be bigger than Nat. In 1960, though, along with his wife and driver, Jesse was killed in a terrible car crash in Arkansas. I still haven't gotten over it.

"The real return to roots happened with Ray Charles. See, Ray had a jazz group that played R&B and bop with the same feeling. Ray combined everything. He made church songs secular and gave modern jazz soul. Everyone followed Ray. He had his tight little

band with Fathead Newman and Hank Crawford, and he was flying high with 'Hit the Road, Jack,' written by Percy Mayfield, the
Prophet of the Blues. Percy and I were always tight. His 'Please
Send Me Someone to Love' and my 'Everybody's Somebody's Fool'
came out together. Ten years had passed since then, but Percy and I
hadn't lost touch. The man was a natural-born poet who mixed the
language of the Louisiana swamps with the big-city blues. He was
living out in L.A., where Ray had hired him as a staff writer. It
was Percy who wrote Ray's most perfect blues, 'But on the Other
Hand, Baby.' 'Ray's always asking after you,' Percy would tell me.
'Ray has all your records.' I thought Percy was just trying to make
me feel good—he knew I didn't have a record deal—but I had to believe him when Ray called and asked me to appear on a show he
was headlining at the Apollo. This was 1961."

"I was there," says producer Joel Dorn. "I was a teenager and
had come to see the Coasters and Ray Charles. The Coasters were
on fire. They had 'Searchin'' and 'Young Blood' and 'Yakety Yak,'
not to mention 'Charlie Brown' and 'Poison Ivy.' They were funny
and funky and had the place rocking. Now here comes Little
Jimmy Scott. I'd never heard of him and was impatient because
Ray was next. With one note, Jimmy turned my impatience to
speechless fascination. He stopped my train. He turned the mood
so misty blue no one knew what to do. He slew that crowd, the
world's toughest. He sang 'Fool' and 'Masquerade' and 'Motherless Child' with such depth of feeling I felt myself transformed. I'd
been baptized in some religion whose name I didn't know. I'd been
knocked on my ass. The music of this marionette man, whoever he
was, would haunt me the rest of my life."

"I felt funny on some of those big-name shows," says Jimmy.
"I didn't have an act. Didn't even have a band. I'd been knowing
Ray since the early fifties. Ray and I were always cool. So at the
Apollo, Ray let me use his cats. I never felt I had the punch those
shows require. But I did have Caldonia's lessons embedded in my
mind. She used to say, 'Ain't much difference from stage to stage.

Just go out there and give it up. If you're not faking it, folks feel you.' It's that feeling that gets you over.

"The sixties were a new time, and I was still feeling determined. I saw singers like Jackie Wilson, who had a dramatic voice, making it big. Nancy Wilson was singing 'Save Your Love for Me' with Cannonball and selling records. In one way or another, I could relate to these singers just as they said they could relate to me. I wanted to stay on the path that led back to making good music."

With his relationship to Savoy souring and his Newark gigs drying up, Jimmy looked for more work on the road.

"Can't remember who booked it," he says, "but I found a gig at the Royal Peacock in Atlanta, Georgia, where I was on the same bill as Mary Ann Fisher."

Mary Ann Fisher's fame resides in her role as the first female vocalist hired by Ray Charles. Like Jimmy, Mary Ann had survived a traumatic childhood. Her father had been lynched by white racists. When Ray discovered her in 1955, she'd been singing in local dives in her hometown of Louisville, Kentucky, for ten years. Ray's sidemen invited her to sit in with the band during a gig at the army base in Fort Knox. He and she soon connected, according to Michael Lydon's meticulously researched book, *Ray Charles, Man and Music*: "Within days Mary Ann and Ray became lovers. . . . That Ray had been married a month before didn't matter; he told her he was single. Ray rehearsed with Mary Ann daytimes, and soon she had a segment of the show, singing blues and late-night ballads like 'Black Coffee.'"

"Ray and I hooked up before he had any Raelettes," says Mary Ann. "His 'I Got a Woman' had just come out, and his little band was smoking. 'Fish,' he said to me, 'you're the soul sista I been looking for.'"

"Fish had a bubbly personality and spunky spirit," remembers Fathead Newman, Ray's sidekick and favorite tenor saxophonist. "Some of the cats called her the black Mae West. She could be bawdy, but she could also sing. Her voice blended with Ray's. In fact, Ray wrote the song 'Mary Ann' for her. For a while, they were very close."

"Fish was the prelude to the Raelettes," says Ray. "At the time, I could only afford one girl singer. A few years later, I was able to have three. That's when I took a vocal group called the Cookies and turned them into the Raelettes."

"Ray's the man," Mary Ann exclaims. "Everyone wanted to get close to the genius. The genius was getting so high he'd jump sky high when he laughed. The genius was singing so hard that, after the show, it looked like he'd been caught in a rainstorm, soaked through and through. In those days the genius was wild with his partying ways. I held on long as I could—four long years. When the dope scene got too wild, I decided to leave. That was early 1959. I loved Ray and I knew he loved me, but Ray isn't exactly a one-woman man. After we broke up, I went with Rick Harper, Ray's trumpet player, but that relationship also went south. I was on my own, billed as 'Mary Ann, Featured Vocalist with Ray Charles,' when I bumped into Jimmy in Atlanta. Of course I knew who he was. Back then there wasn't a black singer—especially a black *female* singer—who hadn't stolen a lick or two from Little Jimmy Scott. Even Ray praised his style. Ray's a highly competitive artist, so whenever he praised another singer, we took note. Meanwhile, with my new career as a solo singer, I was a little insecure. Jimmy was a sweetheart. He saw my fears and did his best to encourage me. I appreciated that. Unlike most men, Jimmy had a generous heart. He loved giving."

"I saw Fish had a complex," says Jimmy. "She had doubts about her looks and talent. I didn't have doubts about either. She was a pretty girl with short hair covered up by a cute wig. She could sing you a blues and she could sing you a ballad. But she worried all the time and needed someone to say, 'It's okay, baby, you can do it.' I quickly became that someone. We started cooing that first week in Atlanta. I loved being around her. Fish was funny and had lots of fire. At the time, she was living in New York, but soon was living with me in Newark. Eunice was long gone, and I had cut what I thought was my last side for Savoy. I didn't have a record deal and neither did Fish. We were both scuffling for gigs. Sometimes she found one for me; sometimes I found one for her. Then sometime in 1961 she was called to California to work at Memory Lane, a nice club in South Central L.A. She flew out alone. A few weeks later she called and asked, 'What do you think about coming to L.A.?'

"'Is there work?' I wanted to know.

"'Memory Lane wants to book you. Folks out here are asking after you. Plus, I saw Ray the other day and he wanted to know where you were.'

"Didn't take long to decide. Southern California was the center of the entertainment world, where Paul Robeson and Judy Garland had made their movies, where Nat Cole had recorded his hits, where the weather was warm and hope was high. California was just what my slow-moving career needed—a shot in the arm. I was tired of nasty East Coast winters and cold-blooded East Coast labels. So it was good-bye, Newark; good-bye, New York City; stop off in Cleveland and say good-bye to the family. But keep on moving. Keep on dreaming. My dream of being a successful artist leading a comfortable life was alive and well. Hollywood, after all, was where dreams came true."

BROTHER RAY

Ray Charles and Jimmy Scott are a study in contrast. Both appeared on the national scene in the late forties. After a dozen years, Ray had become an international star in the wide world of popular music, while Jimmy remained an obscure figure in the narrow world of jazz. Ray is aggressive, assertive, always in charge. Jimmy can be tentative, passive, reluctant to lead. Ray's music varies greatly as he jumps from genre to genre. Jimmy's greatness is rooted in a single form, the ballad. By 1962, when their lives converged, Ray was a wealthy man at the top of his field and about to go higher. Jimmy was broke, in need of a break. When Ray gave him that break, it looked as if Jimmy's life would be altered. It was, but not in the way either man expected.

Ray was living in Los Angeles, where he was doing most of his recording.

"Fish [Mary Ann Fisher] would come by from time to time to say hello," remembers Ray, "and mention Little Jimmy Scott. That caught my curiosity. I'd set up my own label with ABC distributing, and was looking for artists to record. Turned out the artists I loved most weren't being recorded—cats like Percy Mayfield and

Jimmy Scott. My country-and-western material was starting to hit, so I wasn't worried about money. I just wanted to make sure these singers made the right record. I called my label Tangerine, after my favorite fruit, and signed up Percy Mayfield and Jimmy Scott."

"By the time Ray said he was ready," says Mary Ann, "Jimmy was already out here."

"California had just the mellow I needed," Jimmy remembers. "I loved the look of the place and the attitude of the people. I was ready to settle down and live in L.A. forever. Fish had found a nice little place in mid-city off LaBrea. We were a happy couple. I worked a few clubs and now was getting ready to go into the studio with Ray. You gotta remember that Ray was the hottest thing going. He already had his 'What I Say' and moved on to 'Georgia on My Mind' and 'Ruby.' He and Quincy did 'One Mint Julep,' and now you were hearing his 'I Can't Stop Loving You' wherever you went. Everything he touched turned to gold."

For all Ray's forward thinking, he's essentially a musical conservative, an attitude that brought him to Jimmy. In 1961, just a year before working with Jimmy, he recorded *Ray Charles and Betty Carter*, a magnificent sandpaper-and-silk album of twelve duets arranged by Marty Paich. "Two singers with Hampton's band from the early fifties really knocked me out," Ray remembers. "The first was Jimmy, and the second was Betty." Ray often chose material and musicians from earlier eras. His breakthrough album on Atlantic, *The Genius of Ray Charles*, is loaded with orchestrated ballads and blues by his heroes from the forties—Louis Jordan, Buddy Johnson, Charles Brown. He saw Jimmy in the same light, an inspiration to cling to.

Ray can be mercenary. Known for his thrifty ways, his reputation for paying his musicians minimally is legendary. His motivation to make money by making music is a self-proclaimed mantra of his career. His single greatest innovation—the secularization of gospel—was a brilliant stroke of artistic invention fashioned as an

Justine Stanard Scott, Jimmy's mother.

Arthur Scott, Jimmy's father.

Sister Shirley,
Aunt Rose,
sister Nadine,
and Jimmy.

As infant. From left,
Nadine and Jimmy.

At age 12, Nadine and Jimmy.

At 14, with
a fistful of
candy.

In Cleveland,
at 15, about
to break out.

Age 19, wearing his first tux,
bought by Caldonia.

The early
fifties,
recording
for Savoy.

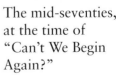

The mid-seventies,
at the time of
"Can't We Begin
Again?"

At a teen rock and roll show in Philly, 1955. PHOTO CREDIT: CHUCK STEWART

Doc Pomus, the eighties, at the time he was championing Jimmy's cause.
PHOTO CREDIT: SHIRLEE HAUSER.

The comeback years, performing in 1986. PHOTO CREDIT: CHUCK STEWART.

Jimmy's triumphant appearance in Milan, with designer Saverio Palatella, 2001.
PHOTO CREDIT: NICOLA GOODE

Jimmy taking a break at the piano, 2001.
PHOTO CREDIT: NICOLA GOODE

Jeanie McCarthy and Jimmy in Cleveland, 2001.

In his Cleveland backyard, 2001. Jimmy and his sisters; from left,
Nadine, Adoree, Elsa, and Betsy. PHOTO CREDIT: DAVID RITZ

Scott and Ritz in Los Angeles, 2001. PHOTO CREDIT: ALAN MERCER

attempt to sell songs to a larger market. Starting out penniless, he understandably saw music as his single strategy for survival and financial security. Along the way, though, he never played anything he didn't feel. Ray was both corruptible and incorruptible, willing to "corrupt" purer forms of gospels and blues, unwilling to tackle material from which he felt emotionally estranged.

"I'd heard from the cats that Ray could be tight with a dollar," says Jimmy, "but when he called me over to his house on Hepburn, where he was living with his wife, Della, he was generous. 'Jimmy,' he said, 'I want to make a great record with you and I'll advance you twenty-five hundred dollars to do it.' Well, that's about a ten-times bigger advance than I'd ever gotten out of Herman Lubinsky. Man, I was thrilled—and grateful."

"Jimmy's the nicest guy you'll ever meet," Ray testifies, "and I knew he'd be easy to work with. The two arrangers I'd been working with—Marty Paich and Gerald Wilson—were the best. They'd been working with me on my country-and-western songs, and I knew they had the sensitivity Jimmy required. I also knew I wanted an album of nothing but beautiful ballads. If you're going to produce B. B. King, get him to sing blues. If you're going to produce Jimmy Scott, get him to sing ballads."

Ray had a vision that Teddy Reig, Freddy Mendelsohn, and Herman Lubinsky all lacked. He didn't think in terms of singles, but a suite of songs. In fact, Ray was an early originator of concept albums. His initial albums on ABC included *Genius Hits the Road*, songs named for cities and states, and *Dedicated to You*, songs named for women. The album he produced for Jimmy—*Falling in Love Is Wonderful*—was recorded just after Ray's *Modern Sounds in Country and Western Music* and just before *Modern Sounds in Country and Western Music, Volume 2*, both bold concepts.

Ray calls his concepts "little jive ideas," but they're deeper than that. They go beyond the usual formula of short, disconnected scenes and project rich, musical landscapes. Many of Ray's sixties albums, including Jimmy's, survive as high benchmarks of American popular music.

"The concept with Jimmy," says Ray, "was romance. Make a romantic record you could listen to late at night with your lady. I wanted the kind of record you could play over and over again, where you wouldn't be bored and the mood stayed steady. There's nothing worse than when you finally get your lady ready and the record changes up on you. You're into let's-go-nice-and-slow and the record is into jumpy-and-loud. A good lovemaking record is like lovemaking itself. Getting there's half the fun. You sure as hell don't want to get there too soon. The thing about Jimmy is his timing. He never gets there too soon. His timing and the sadness in his voice make for a romantic record made in heaven."

"We started off by going over to Ray's house every morning," Jimmy remembers. "These were the hallelujah days for Ray, when he was still getting his daily high. Sometimes we'd have to wait for the man to arrive with the goods before Ray would be ready. Once he got fixed up and came downstairs, though, he was roaring. Not roaring to party but roaring to work. Ray wasn't like Billie or Maybelle, where dope had them floating in space. Ray's down to earth. Ray's a worker, and the dope made him work even harder. If anything, he gained concentration. He never dropped a stitch or missed a beat. Ray's dope was like coffee; it woke him up and wired him to work. He couldn't wait to get to the studio. But first we went over the songs together. Most of the suggestions came from him; a few came from me. Being a singer himself, Ray was considerate of my feelings. 'If you don't like the story,' he said, 'don't sing it.' Like me, Ray's main thing is the lyric. 'You're the actor,' he said, 'so you need to dig the script.' Also like me, Ray digs the classic songs, the old songs that hold memories. He also wanted songs I hadn't recorded before, so I'd sound fresh. We made only one exception, 'Someone to Watch over Me,' because we both loved it and because my first version, back in fifty-five with Cissy Houston shadowing me, wasn't to my taste."

"Ray's concept was clear," says Gerald Wilson, who arranged and conducted seven of the ten arrangements. "He wanted the music relaxed. He pointed to Sinatra. He always loved the strings Alex Stordahl wrote in the forties and the ballads Nelson Riddle and Gordon Jenkins arranged in the fifties. At least four of the songs on the album were closely identified with Sinatra: 'Why Try to Change Me Now,' 'Someone to Watch over Me,' 'How Deep Is the Ocean,' and 'Sunday, Monday or Always.' Ray knew just what he wanted—a calm, consistently sweet sound. He didn't want heavy horns, but rather violins and cellos with a touch of an oboe or a flute. We recorded at United Sound on Sunset Boulevard in Hollywood. I've never seen smoother sessions."

While working with Ray in the seventies, I saw many sessions he produced. He supervises with strong purpose and steely control. He intimidates neophytes and veterans alike. If he doesn't get what he wants, he can be brutal. Even the venerable B. B. King, who sang a duet with Ray in the eighties, told me, "I was scared to death I couldn't please him." I've seen him dictate note-for-note solos for saxophonists to follow. I've seen him reduce background singers to tears. When it came to Jimmy Scott, though, Ray was apparently a different man.

"I've never seen him so mellow," says Mary Ann, who witnessed the sessions. "I believe Jimmy's gentleness rubbed off on Ray, who's usually a little gruff. It was more a lovefest than recording session. It's something Ray had been wanting for years. For Jimmy, it was the dream of a lifetime."

"Ray supervised," adds Gerald Wilson, "but he did so from the piano. He played on every track. And he made sure we wrote charts that gave his piano space. If you listen to the record carefully, it's really a long and intimate conversation between Ray's sensitive piano and Jimmy's sensitive voice. The strings are there to complement and elevate the conversation. Ray could have hired any pianist in the country—Oscar Peterson, Hank Jones, you name 'em—but Ray wanted in on the action. Ray wanted to play behind the great Jimmy Scott. As beautiful as Jimmy's vocals are, Ray's background piano is the essence of taste, elegance, and restraint. Not to mention bluesy. Ray can't help but be bluesy. He surprises you with every solo."

The biggest nonmusical surprise during the making of *Falling in Love* was the sudden reemergence of Arthur Scott, Jimmy's dad.

"Dad had been talking about going to California for a long while," says brother Kenny. "He'd semiretired from work and had some social security. With Jimmy in L.A., he thought it'd be a good time to move out there. Dad didn't own a car, so he took the bus and stopped over in St. Louis to visit family. He had some distant cousins in L.A., but he told me he'd rather live with Jimmy. I didn't say anything, but I wondered, *What's Jimmy going to say about that?*"

"I said okay," Jimmy recalls. "What could I say? I kept hearing Mom's words: 'You only have one father. Respect him.' I had to take him in. I wasn't entirely reluctant either, because finally Dad would get a chance to see me record. He'd never expressed interest in my career. He might not be impressed by me, but he'd have to be impressed by Ray. Ray was the biggest star in the country.

"The day I took Dad over to the studio to meet Ray and watch me record was a big moment. There were all these classically trained musicians, there was the famous conductor Gerald Wilson, who, aside from his arranging, had an orchestra of his own. There was a battery of engineers and there was the genius himself, running the whole operation, who made it a point to shake Dad's hand. With me in the center of all this action, standing at the microphone and singing in this big-time Hollywood studio, Dad had to be impressed. He wasn't. Or if he was, he didn't tell me about it. 'What time's the session over?' he asked me during a break. 'I got a woman waiting for me at the bar and I need a ride.' Dad would never change."

"I don't think Jimmy's dad was impressed by anyone but himself," says Mary Ann. "When he moved in with us, the vibe between me and Jimmy changed altogether. This man everyone called Scotty was the opposite of his son. He was demanding and selfish. Jimmy was a gentleman while Scotty was a player. He thought I was taking too much of his son's time and, from the beginning, angled to break us up. He looked at Jimmy as his chauffeur. 'Take me to the bar, take me to the restaurant, take me to this chick's crib . . . ' The *take me*'s never stopped.

"Scotty changed Jimmy's outlook on life. When Scotty wasn't around, Jimmy was peaceful and calm. But with Scotty on the set, Jimmy got riled up. His father reminded him of all the family love he'd been missing. He still wanted that love, but Scotty wasn't giving. Scotty was taking. It was good that Jimmy was busy making the album. The record gave him a way to get his mind off his father."

"The record was completed in just a few sessions," Jimmy recalls. "I don't think we did more than two takes on any one tune. There wasn't any overdubbing either. It was all-the-way live. The fiddlers were fiddling, Ray was playing, and I was singing, all at the same time. In my mind, that's the way to make records. When it was over, we were thrilled. 'This is the material the public wants, Jimmy' said Ray. 'This is exactly what I was looking for.' Now it was just a matter of putting it out. With ABC backing Tangerine, we weren't worried about distribution. My plan was to stay in L.A. and, based on good response from the record, start working more clubs. With Ray's enthusiasm and support, I was even hoping I could make a few appearances on TV."

Before the record was released, though, a major development changed the nature of Jimmy's domestic life. Mary Ann adopted a little boy.

"His name was Tracy," says Mary Ann, "and his mother, a friend of mine, couldn't care for him. So I decided to raise him. He came to us when he was just a month or two old. Jimmy loved the infant, and for a while it looked like our little family was going to live happily ever after."

"I adore little babies," says Jimmy, "and saw this as a chance to be the daddy I always wanted to be."

"When Tracy was a few months old," Mary Ann continues, "I got a gig in Atlanta. The bread was too good to pass up, so I asked Jimmy if he could take care of the child. I knew I'd be gone for several months. Jimmy said sure."

"Things got complicated when Dad decided he wanted to go home to Cleveland," Jimmy states. "'Fine,' I said, 'I'll buy you a plane ticket.' 'I ain't flying,' he said. 'Fine,' I said, 'I'll buy you a bus ticket.' 'I ain't taking no bus,' he said. 'Then how are you going?' I wanted to know. 'I want you to drive me. It's the only way I'll feel safe.' I thought, *Well, he is my father,* and I agreed."

When Jimmy tells me how he left L.A. to drive his father to Cleveland, the same father he describes as neglectful and abusive, we're driving past Ray Charles's studio on Washington Boulevard in mid-city Los Angeles. I'm incredulous. Didn't Jimmy have more of a responsibility to his own future than to his father's whims? After all, he had planned on pursuing his career in California. Los Angeles was where he would promote the Tangerine album.

"Maybe I saw it as a chance for him and me to finally bond," he muses. "With Mary Ann off in Atlanta, I had the baby with me. I was a father, Dad was a grandfather, and in our own way, we had a family. Besides, with the Tangerine record coming out, I knew I'd be back in L.A. in no time. All in all, I felt it was the right thing to do."

When the record came out, Joe Adams, Ray's longtime manager, was listed as producer. "I never saw him anywhere near the studio," says Jimmy. "He had no musical input whatsoever." It was Adams, however, who conceived the cover photograph featuring a Cesar Romero–looking model pondering his female counterpart seductively situated before a roaring fireplace. Wine glasses are by their side, along with recent albums by Ray Charles. Jimmy's picture appears nowhere on the front, but only on the back, still looking like a teenager as he listens to playbacks with Ray and Marty Paich and reviews a score with Gerald Wilson. The insulting idea was that a model, and not Jimmy, was cast into the romantic role.

"Of course it hurt," Jimmy admits. "It's your record and you want to see your picture. But I understood that Joe wanted to sell product. He figured a big, handsome guy was more of a romantic figure than me. I was in no position to argue. Besides, all that counted was the music. And the music was so powerful that all of us—Joe, Ray, the big shots at ABC—were convinced we had a bestseller."

Falling in Love Is Wonderful is pure inspiration, a work that favorably compares to the greatest albums of the genre—Sinatra's *In the Wee Small Hours*, Billie's *Lady in Satin*, and *The Genius of Ray Charles*. Ray's care in creating a consistent mood pays off beautifully. The tempos are unrelentingly slow. The suite of ten songs, lasting a little less than forty minutes, has a strong sense of aesthetic integrity. It's all of a piece. The absence of brass and reeds, aside from a lilting oboe or lyrical flute, adds to the ambiance of heady romance. At age thirty-seven, Jimmy's voice remains pristine, vital, wonderfully responsive to the shading of the strings. At thirty-two, Ray's at the top of his game, a perceptive accompanist whose quiet funk brings out the bluest hues in each ballad. The lovely moments are many: the quiet resignation with which Jimmy interprets the haunting "Why Try to Change Me Now"; Ray's Erroll Garner–like tremolos echoing throughout "There Is No Greater Love"; Jimmy's plaintive reading of "Someone to Watch over Me," with Ray's sweet-and-salty support from below.

"When I was recording with Ray," says Jimmy, "I thought of Bird. Bird loved strings. Two of the songs I sang—'If I Should Lose You' and 'I Didn't Know What Time It Was'—were on *Bird with Strings*, the sessions he told me he valued above all others. I tried to do what Bird did—let the strings carry me to higher levels of expression. This was my way of remembering Bird.

"I'm critical of my own work. I'm not always happy with what I sing. And of course I've sung recording dates where the songs or the arrangements weren't right. But taking that long cross-country drive back home with little Tracy and Dad, I knew in my heart I had done my best work. I knew it had to succeed."

Jimmy took an upstairs flat for himself, Tracy, and his dad on Soika Avenue on the east side of Cleveland.

"Couple of weeks after I got home, I went to the local record shop to see if my album had arrived," he remembers. "It was there, and I was overjoyed. People were playing it. The dream was coming true."

"I got married in June of 1963," says producer Joel Dorn, then working as a deejay on WHAT-FM in Philadelphia, "and took off a week for my honeymoon. When I returned, a stack of new records were waiting for me, among them Jimmy's album on Tangerine. Without even reviewing it, I put it on the air, announcing, 'Ray Charles produced it, Jimmy Scott's singing it, and I know it has to be good.' It was better than good. In the seven years I was broadcasting, I never saw such a response. The phone lit up, requests came in like an avalanche. People called the station choked up with tears. Some people—maybe one out of three—wanted to know the name of the 'girl singer.' During my time on the air, I would only see a few jazz records cross over—Ramsey Lewis's 'The In Crowd,' Stan Getz's 'Girl from Ipanema'—but this looked like the biggest of them all. Then suddenly the station gets a call from ABC. The record has been withdrawn. Don't play it."

"My local store said they were told to ship all copies back," Jimmy explains. "I called out to California to see what was happening. Herman Lubinsky had produced some paper that said I was still under contract to him. If Ray didn't pull the album off the market, Lubinsky threatened to sue."

"When I signed Jimmy," Ray recalls, "he said he was contractually free. I had no reason to doubt him. But when Savoy came out of the woodwork, my lawyer said it could cost us a fortune. I withdrew. I wasn't interested in paying fancy legal fees to fight it."

Never one to waste money, Ray erased Jimmy's vocals and had organist Wild Bill Davis play over eight of the original tracks. The album—*Wonderful World of Love*—was released under Wild Bill's name on Tangerine. Listening to it is painful, especially when Jimmy's voice is still faintly audible on some songs.

"I understood why Ray pulled my record," Jimmy claims. "He had a new label and didn't want to start off tangled up in lawsuits. The cat I didn't understand was Herman. He might have advanced me a hundred bucks or so back in the late fifties and had me sign something, but after *The Fabulous Songs* flopped, he made it clear he wasn't interested in recording me again. Back in fifty-seven, when his friend Syd Nathan had me cut some sides for King, Herman didn't object. Why should he care now?"

"My father could be vindictive," says Herman, Jr. "He felt like he put good money into Jimmy with little results. When Jimmy suddenly turned up with an album distributed by ABC, Dad became incensed. If Jimmy had initially come to him and asked permission—made sure all legal constraints were lifted—I have a feeling my father would have agreed. In his long relationship with the Reverend James Cleveland, the great gospel singer who made a fortune at Savoy, Dad allowed James to cut records with other labels. But James knew how to handle Dad. He gave him respect. Dad felt Jimmy had gone behind his back. He was very hurt."

The Reverend Cleveland did, in fact, speak of Lubinsky with considerable gratitude. On the other hand, in Jimmy's case, Lubinsky clearly displayed an obstinacy bordering on the obsessive. He had it out for Jimmy. Yet for all Jimmy's bitter disappointment, he neither fought Lubinksy nor pushed Ray to do so.

"I didn't have a lawyer when I signed with Savoy," he says, "and didn't have one when I signed with Ray. Fact is, I still didn't know any entertainment lawyers. I'd spent the twenty-five-hundred-dollar advance from Ray and now had a little baby to support. Besides, fighting Lubinksy was like fighting City Hall. I knew I couldn't win. I had to let the thing go."

Falling in Love Is Wonderful, the greatest work of Jimmy Scott's career to date, quickly disappeared. There were no major reviews, no profiles of the singer, no media interest whatsoever. What should have been an artistic triumph became a personal disaster. In the same period of Andy Williams's "Days of Wine and Roses," Barbra Streisand's "Happy Days Are Here Again," Nat Cole's "That Sunday, That Summer," Tony Bennett's "I Left My Heart in San Francisco," Frank Sinatra's *All Alone* torch album, and Ella Fitzgerald's *Jerome Kern Song Book*, it's not inconceivable that Jimmy might have found success. It's doubly ironic that two singers deeply influenced by Jimmy had successful records with the same arrangers Ray used on *Falling in Love* just after the Tangerine album was recorded. In 1963, Gloria Lynne's "I Wish You Love" was such a hit off her album *Gloria, Marty and Strings* (Marty being Marty Paich) that she appeared on the *Ed Sullivan Show* along with Robert Goulet and Mae West. The album is superb, and at times her stylings sound more like Jimmy Scott than Jimmy Scott does. At Capitol, Nancy Wilson recorded *Yesterday's Love Songs . . . Today's Blues* with Gerald Wilson. Her exquisite interpretations, especially "Someone to Watch over Me," walk that thin line between imitation and emulation.

In the period between the assassination of John F. Kennedy and the arrival of the Beatles, big ballads and lush strings enjoyed a run of mainstream popularity that wouldn't last long. Soul and rock were on the verge of taking over. Jazz would soon experience a steep commercial decline, many of its young artists drawn to the avant-garde of Ornette Coleman and latter-day John Coltrane. Jazz singers would scramble for work. And in Cleveland, Jimmy Scott, among the most original of all jazz singers, would remain in obscurity for decades to come.

WHEN THE SUN COMES OUT

*J*immy and I are gorging ourselves on Judy Garland. He's at my house watching the new DVD collection of Judy's CBS TV shows from 1963. Some fans—Jimmy and I among them—consider this her finest moment. There are duets with Lena Horne, Diahann Carroll, Mel Torme, and Jack Jones. There's Vic Damone, Mickey Rooney, Tony Bennett, and Count Basie. Judy is reed thin, thoroughly charming, and neurotic at the same time. I think of Jimmy's devastating charm in selling a song and easily envision him on stage with Judy. I can't help believing she would have adored him. At the end of each show, she stands behind an open trunk, conjuring forth her roots in vaudeville. As she sings "When the Sun Comes Out," Jimmy hangs on her every note. Her vibrato has a strangely calming effect on him. Later that day Jimmy and I drive by Television Center, where the show was shot, and have lunch at Canter's Deli on Fairfax Avenue.

"Wintertime in Cleveland," says Jimmy, "was a good time to dream of California. I'd watch Judy's show every week and think about what I left in Los Angeles. It was difficult. Fish came back from her gig in Atlanta. She was as disappointed as me about *Falling in Love*'s falling through the cracks."

When the record was pulled, Jimmy had realized he couldn't afford to go back to California. Mary Ann had retrieved their belongings from California and joined Jimmy, his father, and Tracy in Cleveland six months after she had left for Atlanta. Nothing was the same as when she had left for Atlanta—not Jimmy's career and certainly not their relationship.

"I think we might have made it in L.A.," Mary Ann claims. "But Cleveland was impossible. Jimmy's family got all up in his business. They leaned on him so heavy. Jimmy's father was hell-bent on keeping us at odds. With his demanding attitude, he drove Jimmy crazy. Jimmy was just too sweet to back him down. Jimmy had many distractions, including drink. I'm not saying I was an angel, but I was clear-headed about my child. I'm not sure Jimmy was, because when I arrived in Cleveland, Tracy was dirty and needed new clothes."

"Fish was upset because she'd been gone for so long," says Jimmy. "Upset and a little guilty about going off and leaving the child. But Tracy was well cared for. I loved him."

"The love between me and Jimmy was in trouble," Mary Ann states. "Our relationship wasn't based on sex—the sex was never more than okay—it was about helping each other. He helped my confidence and I helped him find gigs and connect with Ray. But the gigs were drying up, the Ray record was dead, and living in Cleveland with him and his family wasn't anything I wanted. I decided I wanted to take Tracy and go home to Louisville."

"I couldn't argue with Fish," says Jimmy. "The mother–child bond is the strongest in life. Having had my mother taken from me, I could never do that to Tracy. Besides, aside from my sister Betsy, my own family really hadn't helped me care for the baby, and I felt he'd be better off with Mary Ann. It broke my heart to see them go. I'd been bathing Tracy, changing his diapers, and feeding him for a year. I felt like I'd been both his mom and dad. But I knew the little guy needed his mom, and she needed him. Sure enough, she turned out to be a beautiful mother and raised a beautiful son, all on her own."

Jimmy was back to where he started, playing Paddock's with Chickadee for $150 a week.

"My rent was eighty-five dollars, so I had enough to eat," he says. "I had to concentrate on whatever little gigs I could find around Cleveland because the out-of-town calls had dried up. Not long after I got home from California, Dinah Washington, who always gave me the gigs she couldn't make, died from an overdose of diet pills mixed with booze. She was thirty-nine. They called it an accident. I'd known Dinah since the forties, and I knew she got crazy when it came to weight. She'd weigh her background singers before each show, and if one of those girls was a pound over a hundred and ten, Dinah would fire her. Dinah fought herself when it came to her own body. She wanted to look a certain way and would do anything to achieve that look. She could be frantic. She could be cruel, especially to a young chick singer copying her. She took her role as Queen seriously. I've seen her bitch out a whole army of men, every one of them scared to say a word. She went through seven husbands. But I was her 'Fat Daddy,' and to me she was a pussycat. She heard what I was singing and understood my style when others scoffed. She was my sister.

"So was Big Maybelle, who also had the weight complex. Maybelle was going through changes with Lubinsky similar to my own. She was tired of his fifty-dollar advances, but when she changed labels—to Brunswick and Scepter—Herman came on with his cease-and-desist orders, arguing she was still signed to him. Whether he actually had legal papers on her or not, those labels would sooner drop her than fight. Like me, Maybelle wasn't a huge seller. Lubinksy's competitors weren't willing to pay lawyers to see whether Herman was bluffing. It was cheaper to drop us.

"Other friends, like Little Willie John, were also in trouble. King Records dropped him the same year *Falling in Love* fell apart. Then Willie fell apart. He got violent and was convicted for manslaughter. He died in prison a few years later. He was forty, and though he made some beautiful records, you had to hear him live to appreciate his greatness. Little Willie had musical genius in his soul—like Billie or Bird—but anger took him out. Like Dinah, he didn't like his looks. His size made him crazy.

"I had no interest in going crazy. I saw it was possible. It happened to Dinah and Willie and Maybelle. In a different way, it happened to Billie and Bird. It isn't easy being an outside artist. Being different can make you feel crazy. You want to get on the inside, but that's not always possible. Some were able to make it. Berry Gordy, for example, found a way. His Motown label finally took off. I knew Berry from the Detroit's Flame Showbar in the fifties, where his sisters had the photography concession and Berry was selling songs to Jackie Wilson. I knew his dad, Pops Gordy, when he had a print shop. We'd all hang out. Whenever I drifted over to Detroit for a gig, say, at some little club, the Gordys might drop in for old time's sake. I met all the kids—Marvin Gaye, Smokey Robinson, David Ruffin—and I loved their attitude. They showed me respect and still seemed interested in my style."

"In the early years of Motown," Marvin Gaye told me, "the only style that really interested me was a pure ballad approach. I didn't want to sing R&B. R&B meant getting out there and shaking my ass. To me, purity was everything. Jimmy Scott was the personification of ballad purity."

Marvin's failure to score as a balladeer underlined the marketing reality of the day: He became a hit maker only when he turned to rhythm and blues, singing songs like "Stubborn Kind of Fella" and "Can I Get a Witness."

"I knew there was nothing at Motown for me," says Jimmy. "But I still liked what they were doing. I could appreciate teenage music. Back in 1960, I'd even gone to Philly and appeared on Dick

Clark's *American Bandstand* singing 'The Masquerade Is Over.' Those teens, though, really didn't know what to make of me. That same weekend, I was more comfortable talking about jazz with drummer Max Roach and singer Abbey Lincoln on their radio interview show. Now Berry Gordy's productions were all over the radio. He called it 'The Sound of Young America,' and it was hardly a style I could adapt to. Other musicians could. Doc Pomus, for example, adapted beautifully. Doc was turning out rock and roll smashes—'Viva Las Vegas'—for Elvis. Doc and his friends in the Brill Building were writing hits for the Drifters and the Righteous Brothers. But I wasn't about to bother Berry in Detroit or lean on Doc in New York. Matter of fact, I'd rather withdraw than become a burden. I'd find other ways to survive."

"My father would tell me how Jimmy would disappear for years at a time," says Doc Pomus's daughter Sharyn Felder. "Dad would call Cleveland, but Jimmy either never answered or wasn't listed. 'He's a proud man,' Doc would say, 'and he isn't about to beg anyone for anything.'"

The question still remains: Because of his strong rapport with Ray, wouldn't Jimmy have called him to ask for help? If he couldn't have given Jimmy another record, perhaps Ray could have given him a slot in his show.

"I know Ray," Jimmy answers, "and I know he felt that he got burned. He put time, effort, and money into me, and when it turned bad I figured I'd used up my goodwill. Besides, I wasn't looking to be taken care of. My mother had taught me to care for myself. You see, her lessons never left me. During the gloomy years, I'd hear her say, 'The sun's going to come out. It always does. Might be covered by clouds, but those clouds are going to move on. The sun is God's creation. Light is God's creation. Light is hope. You keep that hope, you keep that faith, and nothing can bring you down.' At the same time, Mom was practical. 'God is a miracle worker,' she said, 'but he's not an employment agency. You go out and get your own job.' Mom never said that the job had to be music. She died way before I had any idea I could live on my singing. As the sixties went on and it looked like I couldn't live on my singing, I'd have to find other ways. Hard work is nothing to be ashamed of, Mom made clear. With that in mind, I went looking for work."

For another quarter-century, with few exceptions, Jimmy would be ignored by the jazz world. He'd work as a busboy, a cook, a nurse's aid, a hotel clerk; he'd experience another marriage of excruciating pain; he'd suffer a near-crippling accident. He'd withdraw into the isolated life of an isolated man, cutting himself off from the illustrious figures with whom he had worked. Lionel Hampton, Ray Charles, Quincy Jones, Stan Getz—no one heard a word from Jimmy. He never cried out for help. As far as the music business was concerned, he was dead.

In pressing questions about his reaction to this phenomenon, I look for signs of anger or bitterness. I find none.

"It goes back to this business of time," he says. "I saw it wasn't my time. Mom used to say that God might not be there when you want him, but He's always on time. I had one timetable that said my career would take off in the fifties. When that didn't happen, I had another timetable that said *Falling in Love* would kick-start my career in the sixties. When that didn't happen, I realized my timetable wasn't the one that mattered. What was God's timetable? I didn't know, but to find out required patience. I'm not exactly sure what wisdom is, but I know there's no wisdom without patience. Maybe wisdom *is* patience. Either way, the wise move was to find a job— any job—rather than go on welfare. That's how I became a busboy.

"I worked at Bob's Big Boy in Warrensville, Ohio, cleaning tables and washing dishes. Later I moved up to short-order cook. I didn't mind. I see singing as public service work—you're serving up entertainment—so serving food is related. I like to serve and greet the public. The pay was minimal, but the restaurant was busy and time passed quickly. With Fish back in Kentucky, I was still living with Kenny and Dad. Their work ethic was different than mine. Kenny had a gift for mechanics—he could fix anything—but couldn't concentrate on any career. He never made peace with the Deficiency, and for the rest of his life he'd go from doctor to doctor, looking for ways to get bigger. Kenny stayed unsettled. Dad wasn't interested in doing much work. After a lifetime of laying asphalt, he figured he was entitled to a break. That meant I was doing the heavy lifting. That also meant I needed more than one job.

"So I found extra work as a waiter at Elsner's Health Club, where members came to eat their thick steaks. If Bob's Big Boy was the low end of the food chain, this was the high end. Tips were better, and I usually could juggle my schedule and work both places, sometimes in the same day. I liked the variety of customers but didn't like the night shift. If I could find an occasional music gig, even at a neighborhood bar, I'd still rather sing than anything. So I kept looking for better-paying day jobs that freed up my evenings. The perfect one came—or so I thought—when I was hired as a nurse's assistant in a convalescent home.

"The home catered to the elderly. There were about sixty patients who lived there, mostly white, evenly divided between the men's and women's side. I liked the work for many reasons. Caring for people with serious conditions—people who lived in agonizing pain—put my own condition in perspective. If a man with liver cancer can tolerate his condition, who am I not to tolerate mine? I also found that my disposition was welcomed. A sick man who's down and depressed needs a smile and friendly hello more than anyone. My chores were basic— I helped the patients in and out of the shower; I changed those who soiled themselves; I aided those who couldn't feed themselves; I took the bus to various clinics with those who required special treatments; I helped with custodial duties. I did whatever I could to make their lives more pleasant and, as a result, gained satisfaction. I felt like I made a difference. One man donated a huge aquarium to the home out of appreciation for my attitude. The convalescent home gave my life steady purpose. Like everyone else, I need to feel useful.

"The home, where I worked for a couple of years, did something else to my life—it introduced me to a woman. Ruth Taylor worked as a nurse on the ladies' side. Turned out we knew each other as kids. I remembered her from the old neighborhood, down on Seventy-seventh and Central, when, after Mom died, we were living with Biddie Colone. Ruth was a snappy, independent woman with a nice appearance and well-spoken manner."

"I knew Ruth well," says Jimmy's sister Elsa. "She was an attractive, heavyset woman with dark brown skin. In that sense, she might have reminded Jimmy of our mom. She was very different from Channie. You could get close to Channie. Channie expressed her emotions. But Ruth was hard to read. She was a refined woman with good taste, but she kept you at a distance."

"When we met in 1965, she was recently divorced from a bass player," Jimmy recalls, "and her looks reminded me of pianist Mary Lou Williams, wide-faced and wide-bodied. Ruth had four children—two boys and two girls. The youngest girl was only six months old. Ruth and I started having lunch every day at the home. The conversations went easy. We came from the same place. We'd both been around. We understood how the world worked. I saw her as a reasonable and practical woman. She expressed an aggressiveness about what she wanted from life. I liked that aggressiveness. I saw how she was extremely devoted to the care of her family and unity of her children. I liked her children and didn't think being a stepfather would be a problem for them or me. Ruth and I both desired something stable. As our little lunches continued, it seemed clear that we were building a relationship. There was a physical attraction, but even stronger was a common hunger we both felt deep inside: the hunger for a home."

THINGS NOT SEEN

*I*t's Fashion Week in Milan, Italy, and Jimmy and I are walking through the Galleria on our way to the Duomo, the great cathedral that dominates the center of the city. Jimmy will be performing tonight, but now it's time for a little tourism. We enter the colossal edifice and slowly make our way around, stopping to study the magnificent stained-glass windows. Back outside, we sit at an outdoor café facing the forest of flying buttresses atop the church. Jimmy discusses religion.

"Maybe more than any time in my life, the sixties is when I sought religion. It's when I really needed it. I knew how to get myself together by finding regular work as a waiter or an orderly, but there was also spiritual work to do. After the excitement of being on the road and making records for a dozen years, the letdown was tremendous. The only way to avoid self-pity was to seek spiritual solutions. Mom used to say that God tests us. My test consisted of one question—could I deal with reality? My reality was clear: To get by, I needed faith. I found a nondenominational school that taught Christian theology out of Evanston, Illinois. I could take courses through the mail, meaning I could keep my jobs and study at night. For several years I concentrated on intense Bible study in pursuit of a ministerial license.

"Those years were not devoted exclusively to Christian thought. It wasn't that I felt that the New Testament was wanting. In fact, I loved reading the Gospels and found great comfort in the life of Jesus. The foundation constructed in my childhood by Prophet Hurley was still in place. He looked to Jesus as the antidote to ignorance. He presented the savior as an example of enlightened thought. My new studies confirmed all that—and more. Now I saw Jesus as a living example of someone carrying out the will of God. I saw Jesus as a symbol of abiding faith. I loved reading the poetic thoughts of Paul. When I found my faith faltering, I'd turn to 2 Corinthians 4:18, where Paul says, 'While we look not at the things which are seen, but at the things which are not seen; for the things which are seen are temporal; but the things which are not seen are eternal.'

"At the same time I was exploring the lessons of Jesus, I came upon a text from another culture. I was in a bookstore when these eyes, coming from a photograph adorning a paperback entitled *Autobiography of a Yogi*, seemed to penetrate my soul. The author was Paramahansa Yogananda. This was my first experience with Eastern thought. Though he died in 1952, Yogananda's message was carried on—and still is—by the Self-Realization Fellowship. I became absorbed with his message. The cosmic law of dharma pointed to the happiness of all living creatures. The teaching centered on inner peace, inner acceptance, and the quietude of meditative serenity. I saw no incompatibility between this guru from India and the carpenter from Galilee. In fact, I began to suspect, along with other Christians, that Jesus may have spent time in Eastern countries where he was exposed to the ancient be-here-now wisdom of spiritual teachers. Writing about Mahatma Gandhi, for example, Yogananda called him an 'apostle of Christian virtues.' In explaining the doctrine of nonviolence, Yogananda cited Jesus from Matthew 5:38–39: 'Ye have heard that it hath been said, an eye for an eye, and a tooth for a tooth: but I say unto you, that ye resist not evil with evil; but whosoever shall smite thee on thy right cheek, turn to him the other also.'

"In the light of these readings, I viewed the events of the times—and especially the life and radical, nonviolent work of Martin Luther King—with calm perspective. Gandhi and Jesus, Yogananda and King all seemed to be operating in cohesion. 'God is Love,' wrote the Yogi. 'His plan for creation can be rooted only in love. Does not that simple thought, rather than erudite reasonings, offer solace to the human heart? Every saint who has penetrated to the core of reality has testified that a divine universal plan exists and that it is beautiful and full of joy.'

"My spiritual journey comforted me in its unity. Two different cultures, one Western, one Eastern, were saying the same thing. God is within us, and peace is within God. As the sixties became less peaceful, I felt a greater need for spiritual study. I explored some churches and considered joining as a minister or maybe even starting a church of my own. But earthly politics always overwhelmed divine intent. Bickering and backbiting dominated. Those institutions seemed more driven by the ego of the elders than by the benevolence of God. I decided the only church I could count on was the church within my heart. My search for a spiritual connection stayed—as it remains today—a private concern.

"My main idea was to live a life based on love. The best sign of love is how we treat others. That's why I saw my work in the convalescent home as a blessing. That work let me offer loving assistance to those in need. It gave me a special kind of peace. Now I felt ready to enjoy the one thing I'd always missed—a peaceful family. Ruth was ready as well. In 1965 we decided to marry."

On another day in another season, Jimmy and I are standing in front of the house he bought with Ruth. It's a handsome, three-story structure at 1720 Lee Road in Cleveland Heights.

"We moved sometime in 1965," says Jimmy. "I remember that as a sad year for music. Tadd Dameron died that year, our hometown genius who had taken his place as one of the great architects of modern jazz. He was only forty-eight when he passed. Tadd was up there in the Bird category, the high-and-mighty category of cats who heard new harmonies and invented new sounds. Like Bird, Tadd had his dope problems. Like Mozart, he did it all when he was a young man. I believe he did enough to be remembered forever. Anyway, the Cleveland jazz scene had been quiet for a long, long time. With the news of Tadd's death, the quiet turned to grief for those of us who were touched by his advanced musical gifts.

"That was a period when I turned from music and concentrated on a home life. I dug this house on Lee Road. The neighborhood was a mix of Jewish and Italian with a sprinkling of other ethnic groups. It was—and still is—a desirable section of the city. I paid $17,500 for the house and, with Ruth's help, furnished and decorated it nicely. With my extra jobs, I'd been able to save money. The gig at the convalescent home turned bad, however, when I saw the owner churning the system. He secretly began instructing the nurses to angle certain patients in certain positions, which would expedite their demise. If doctor's orders said to keep the patient supine, the nurse might keep the patient sitting up. Or vice versa. The owner's plan was to free up beds for patients from wealthier families willing to pay bigger fees. I was horrified and refused to go along. It was a subtle system, though, and you could never prove the evil intent. Rather than participate—or even watch it happen—I quit. That was around 1967."

In 1967, the year of Aretha's "Respect" and the Beatles' *Sgt. Pepper's Lonely Hearts Club Band,* John Coltrane died of liver cancer at forty years old. The world of jazz was at loose ends. The avant-garde was in disarray; Miles was going electric while the mainstreamers and beboppers struggled to find work. The music world had completely forgotten Jimmy Scott, whose style remained an anomaly, now and for decades to come.

"I listened to Aretha and rejoiced at her success," says Jimmy. "Her father, the Reverend C. L. Franklin, had brought her to Cleveland in the fifties for his gospel shows. They set up a tent and sang on the corner not far from my house. Made a mighty impression. I was glad the public was ready for a female version of Ray Charles's invention of putting gospel into pop. I heard good music everywhere. Wilson Pickett, Sam and Dave, Stevie Wonder, Lou Rawls. I listened to all the kids with pleasure. But I also looked at the music business through the eyes of experience. I saw—at least for now—there was no place for me. It's not that I had given up. I always felt my time would come. But now was the time for patience.

"It was also time to find another job. Ruth's aunt was an elevator operator at the Sheraton Hotel at Terminal Tower, the same train station complex where I'd worked washing dishes at Fred Harvey's. She said there might be an opening and, sure enough, she hooked me up. It was a first-class hotel where everyone wore uniforms. The pay was decent and the benefits excellent."

"I was performing in Cleveland and staying at the Sheraton," remembers jazz singer Nancy Wilson. "While my manager checked me in, I was waiting in the lobby when, only a few feet away, an elevator opened. I quickly glanced at the operator. *I know that man*, I said to myself. His uniform, two sizes too large, hung on his thin frame. His demeanor was especially friendly and sweet. Then I realized who it was—*Little Jimmy Scott!* I was about to say something, but just couldn't. I didn't want to embarrass him. I myself felt embarrassed. I felt heartbroken. My idol, the man who taught me the art of singing, the most brilliant singer I'd ever heard, was running an elevator. *What a sad moment*, I thought to myself, *what an unjust world*. Yet the image that stuck in my mind was the smile on Jimmy's face. He seemed far from disgusted with his fate. He actually seemed happy."

"A job is a job," says Jimmy. "And my job at the Sheraton got better when they made me a shipping clerk in the receiving department. More responsibility, bigger pay. When the trucks pulled into the dock with their supplies of towels or linens, I was there to note the delivery. I did it for four years. Those were the same years that my marriage, which started out so strong, began to change."

"I lived with Jimmy and Ruth for a whole year," says sister Elsa. "I appreciated how my big brother was willing to take me into his family. I stayed on the third floor and kept to myself, but couldn't help but see signs of strain between Jimmy and Ruth. Ruth loved nice things, a trait she inherited from her own mother. She was also used to living well. Jimmy liked that about her. After some of his other women, he was ready for a lady with middle-class aspirations. But it turned out that, in the area of money, Ruth was far more driven than my brother. Her focus was her kids. She lived for them. She stayed at the nursing home, working hard to give her children the best—the best schools, the best clothes. Those children loved their mother but resented their stepfather. They disrespected Jimmy. They didn't understand his talent. They saw him only as a source of money. They didn't like how, from time to time, he drew their mother's attention away from them. Given Ruth's obsession with her children, Jimmy didn't have a chance in the competition. The children won hands down."

"Money became the issue between me and Ruth," Jimmy recalls. "Money and the children. The children weren't being raised right, but there was nothing that I as an outsider could do about it. To Ruth, those kids could do no wrong. When one of the grown kids decided to have a party and wound up jumping on my grand piano and pissing all over it, I lost it. I went looking for a gun. Maybe I'd had a few drinks, but believe me, it wasn't the liquor that upset me. It was the destruction of my piano.

"Well, Ruth went crazy and called Nadine, screaming, 'Your brother's gonna kill my kid!' Nadine's husband came over and calmed me down. But, man, I was still fit to be tied."

For all his introspection and genuine search for a spiritual connection, Jimmy's troubled relationship to liquor was more than marginal. His binges, even in the middle of a period of seeming tranquillity, were recurring and unpredictable. The inconsistency between his apparent inner calmness and outer chaos remained—and still remain—unresolved.

"Jimmy was still drinking," says Elsa. "He could be cool for a while, but then he might go off on a binge and lose his good sense, just like that."

"The problem wasn't my drinking," claims Jimmy. "It was the way Ruth and her kids worked against me. After a while, I accepted the reality that I was being had. I don't say that lightly. I wish it weren't true. For a long time I refused to believe it was true. Ruth's kids resented me. And Ruth was out to get everything she could for them and herself. As time passed, it became clear that Ruth was manipulating the money. Funds from our joint account ended up in accounts she'd set up for her kids. My earnings weren't huge, but they were steady. Besides the hotel and part-time waiter work, I'd find the occasional singing gig. So I had some money."

With his marriage in shambles, his dream of a happy home life destroyed, Jimmy made a few tentative steps toward resurrecting his career.

"There was a little spot in Cleveland called Isabel's across from Case Western Reserve University," he says. "Pay was next to nothing, but sometimes an old jazz fan would wander in and, out of nostalgia, give up a decent tip. Duke Wade, a friend from the Ray Charles days, would occasionally book me out of town. Duke had been a valet/manager for both Ruth Brown and Ray and knew his way around."

"When I learned that Jimmy was working as a hotel clerk in Cleveland," says Duke Wade, "I couldn't believe it. I called him—this was the late sixties—and said, 'You need to sing. You need to get your ass out of that Sheraton and start doing your thing again. I'll get you out of Cleveland if I have to drag you.'"

"Duke's a faithful friend," Jimmy testifies. "I told him that I'd be delighted to take whatever gigs he could find. But I wasn't about to leave the security of my Sheraton gig. There might be some demand for me in show business, but I was realistic enough to realize that the demand was very small."

"I could always book Jimmy at Lauretta's in Lawnside, New Jersey, just outside Camden," says Wade. "Lauretta was the woman who helped Kenny Gamble of Gamble/Huff, the famous Philly record producers, get started. Matter of fact, Kenny called her Mama. Well, Lauretta loved her some Little Jimmy Scott. She had a bar and barbecue place that brought in the best live music. I booked that room for years and, even during his down-and-out days, Lauretta hired Jimmy."

"Duke and Lauretta always believed in me," Jimmy recalls. "Lauretta would put me and Percy Mayfield on the same bill. The public had long lost interest in either of us, but Lauretta didn't care. Sometimes fans would come out, and sometimes Lauretta would be the only one cheering us on. Either way, Lauretta wouldn't give up. It was through Duke and Lauretta that, late in the sixties, I saw a thin ray of light break through the clouds. Remember, I hadn't cut a record since sixty-two. No record company in the country was interested—at least none I knew of. Turned out that Duke Wade knew differently. Duke Wade, you see, knew Joel Dorn."

THE SOURCE

"*I* went to work for Atlantic Records in 1967," says Joel Dorn, "after bothering one of the owners, Nesuhi Ertegun, for so long he had to give me a job. Through Nesuhi I met Doc Pomus, who became my closest friend. Doc and I had many musical passions in common, but none greater than Jimmy Scott. Doc had the highest regard for Jimmy, but he also used to talk about his streak of self-destructiveness. 'Fate hasn't been kind to Jimmy,' said Doc. 'But Jimmy isn't always kind to Jimmy. Just when things are going smoothly, he'll come out of a trick bag—hook up with the wrong woman, get drunk, disappear—and wind up shooting himself in the foot. When you hear him sing, though, you forget all that and just fall in love with that voice.' Well, I'd been in love with Jimmy's voice ever since I saw him at the Apollo and heard the Tangerine record with Ray. I'd been fanatical about his singing. From time to time, I'd ask Duke Wade about Jimmy's whereabouts. Duke was usually vague, but sometime in 1968, he said something about Jimmy appearing at Lauretta's in Lawnside.

"Next thing I knew, I was walking through the lobby at our offices on Eleven West Sixtieth Street, when who should be sitting on the couch but Lauretta herself with Kenny Gamble and Jimmy

Scott. They looked like they were waiting to see the dentist. I
scooped them up and brought them into my office. Duke wanted
Jerry Wexler, one of the Atlantic owners, to sign Jimmy, with
Kenny producing.

"I never knew why Duke sent them to see Wexler and not me,
but it didn't matter because Wexler wasn't interested. I was. I was
so excited about the idea of producing Jimmy Scott I drove my
bosses crazy. Whatever I lacked in talent I made up for in tenacity.
I had some success in producing Rashaan Roland Kirk, Les
McCann, and Yusef Lateef, so the powers-that-be weren't entirely
deaf to my ideas. 'Look,' I told Nesuhi, 'if it hadn't been pulled,
Falling in Love Is Wonderful would have gone through the roof. I
know Jimmy Scott can sell records.'"

"Duke Wade cut the deal with Dorn," Jimmy recalls. "I got
seven hundred fifty dollars up front, and another seven fifty when
the album was complete. I was so pleased about being back in the
studio, I would have taken less."

"I set up the sessions for three days in early March of 1969,"
says Dorn. "I wanted to keep the vibe of the Tangerine date—
strings, ballads, pure Jimmy Scott. I put together the best rhythm
section in the city—Junior Mance on piano, Eric Gale and Billy
Butler on guitars, Ron Carter on bass, and Bruno Carr, who'd play
with Ray, on drums. I also made sure Ray's man, Fathead Newman,
took the sax solos. I had two brilliant arrangers—Arif Mardin and
Bill Fischer—write the charts. In those days I was feeling my oats
and was certain I knew what songs Jimmy could sing. I selected all
eight of them. Because Jimmy is a gentleman, he went along with
the whole program. Because he hadn't recorded in years, he was
also especially anxious to please. And was especially pleased to be
on the label that was pumping out hits by everyone from Aretha
Franklin to Led Zeppelin. I couldn't wait to get started.

"First day of the first session, Jimmy turns up on time, only
with a serious problem. He didn't have any teeth. He'd ordered
new dentures but didn't have enough money to pay for them. I

scrambled around, found the bread, and by early evening Jimmy had his teeth. If you listen to those songs very carefully, you can hear a small whistle. Those are Jimmy's brand-new dentures. Didn't matter, though. All that mattered was that Jimmy still had his fastball. He *smoked*. After the first chorus of the first song, I just settled back and took it all in. Here was the most original ballad singer of the twentieth century back where he belonged—in a musical climate that brought out all the warmth and wonders of his invention."

"All the cats were wondering about Jimmy," says David Fathead Newman, "'cause it had been a while since we'd heard anything about him. Singers can get rusty. But Jimmy sounded like he'd been singing every night for the past ten years. He had that soft assurance that put us in the right space. He's the one singer who seems to create space, or expand space. By being so kicked back, he pushes the time limits and lets you linger in a way that new ideas have time to develop. As a musician, he allows for miracles."

The record contains at least one miracle—Jimmy's rendering of the Alex Stordahl/Sammy Cahn/Paul Weston song "Day by Day." It's fascinating to listen to Frank Sinatra's version, produced by Stordahl in 1945, next to Jimmy's. When Sinatra sang it—at age thirty—the United States was caught up in wartime romantic longing. Jimmy sang it in 1969, when he was forty-four and the nation was anguished by assassinations and conflict. Sinatra's version is exquisite, a straight and utterly sweet rendering of the story of a man in love. Jimmy's version is frightening, an elegy that goes deep into the mystery of desire. Frank floats on a cloud. With Newman's sweet promptings, Jimmy probes all heaven and earth. Jimmy takes it a tempo at least half the pace of Sinatra, elongating notes and rewriting melodies in a manner that seems to defy musical reason. The porous arrangement allows him to explore the text slowly, word by word, turning what was once light and lovely into an artifact of bold reinvention. Other ballad performances have reached this level of inspiration—Johnny Hodges's "Passion

Flower," Bird's "Just Friends," Gene Ammons's "A House Is Not a Home," Hank Crawford's "Angel Eyes," Billie's "I'm a Fool to Want You," Ray's "Don't Let the Sun Catch You Crying"—but only a very few. With "Day by Day," Jimmy enters the highest reaches of creativity. On *Falling in Love Is Wonderful,* he sang within the constraints of the Stordahl-like string charts of Gerald Wilson and Marty Paich. On "Day by Day," Bill Fischer's arrangement frees Jimmy's imagination. His vocals are stretched out, and like an impressionist, his pictures move from the representational to the subjective, even the experimental. His pictures are awash in new hues—faded pinks, soft ambers, glowing oranges, hazy blues.

Meanings abound. Day by day, for seven long years, Jimmy had been waiting to record. Day by day he had renewed his relationship with God. Day by day he had tried—and failed again—to sustain romance. Day by day he had considered the irony of being at the top of his vocal form and, at the same time, at the bottom of his career. Day by day he had brooded, prayed, waited. A lifetime of pent-up emotions is spent in that one song. "Day by Day" exists, for many, as Jimmy's greatest single creation.

"When we got through recording 'Day by Day,'" Dorn remembers, "the cats came in from the studio to hear the playback. Junior Mance kept shaking his head, 'I can't believe it, I can't believe I'm hearing what I'm hearing.'"

The rest of the album follows suit, proving that, if anything, Jimmy's long hiatus served to fire his audacity. The interpretations are all as free as "Day by Day," and the song selection, especially the inclusion of "Exodus" and "Unchained Melody," adds to the strangeness of the mood. Dorn doesn't like "On Broadway" or "Our Day Will Come," but the way Jimmy floats over a languorous rhythm section is unusually compelling. He takes whatever liberties suit his fancy.

"That kind of singing wasn't possible," Jimmy says, "when I recorded with Ray. It wasn't that Ray's supervision was strict, but those string arrangements restricted any extreme vocal movements.

Going to a record session is like going to a dance. You dance with the girl you brought. You sing with the charts you're given. Dorn had the cats write charts that let me wander. I liked that and tried to make the most of the wide-open mood."

There are echoes from Jimmy's past: another and even more introspective version of "Sometimes I Feel Like a Motherless Child," which he sang on Savoy in 1960, and the inclusion of Cissy Houston's vocal flourishes on "On Broadway," the same Cissy who sang on his original reading of "Someone to Watch over Me" in 1955. Then a gospel singer for Savoy, Cissy had since become part of the Sweet Inspirations, a soul group on Atlantic.

"I named it *The Source*," says Dorn, "because for modern jazz singing—especially modern *female* jazz singers—Jimmy really is the indisputable source. He seemed pleased with the title, and I was certain the album would reestablish him as a major voice in American music. Not only was his voice stronger than ever, his conception was broader and braver. Nancy Wilson agreed to write the liner notes, where she testified, 'The connotation "a singer's singer" has been applied to several artists. However, none deserves the title more than Jimmy Scott.' None of this impressed my superiors, however. They kept my title but some genius in the marketing department insisted that, instead of showing Jimmy on the cover, he should be replaced by a model. They compounded their stupidity by making the model a gorgeous young black woman with a huge Afro, all the rage back then. I hit the ceiling. It was an insult to Jimmy. Who cared that he didn't look like Harry Belafonte? He looked just fine—and besides, it was *his* goddamn record. For all my ranting, though, I just didn't have the juice to prevail. Their decision to go with the model made me feel very small. I was ashamed."

"I understood what they wanted," remembers Jimmy. "Naturally I would have preferred to see myself somewhere on the cover, but if they thought that would help sell the thing, I could only hope they were right."

"They were wrong," argues Dorn. "The model only added mind-bending confusion to the mix. Because Jimmy still wasn't well known, new listeners wondered whether the model was indeed 'Jimmy Scott,' a woman with a man's name. Add to that the fact that Jimmy's voice is often confused for a woman's anyway, and you have some idea of the mess we made. But even the packaging mess didn't compare to the legal mess that followed. Legal messes kept fucking with Jimmy's career."

"It was Herman Lubinksy again," says Jimmy. "Nine years after I made my last record for him, he was still claiming rights. The man was mad. He believed he owned me forever. He might have produced some old document that said, for a two-hundred-dollar advance, I was signed to him for life. Anyway, he came on with another cease-and-desist order. I was sure he was bluffing, but he managed to achieve his goal. He scared off Atlantic. That wasn't hard, because they apparently didn't really care about the record in the first place. The idea of a legal expense—even a small one to call Lubinsky's bluff—was all they needed to back out. At this point, it was clearly personal vindictiveness on Herman's part, but I still didn't have the means to hire an attorney to prove my case. I never even bothered to call Herman to plead my case, because I knew it'd make no difference."

"Like *Falling in Love*," says Dorn, "*The Source* died a painful death. I lacked the power to turn around our legal department. They weren't willing to fight for Jimmy. Meanwhile, the media didn't help. There were no big reviews. No articles on Jimmy in *Down Beat* or the *New York Times*. No nothing. Another Jimmy Scott masterpiece bit the dust. And just like that, Jimmy was back in Cleveland."

"I was back where I started," Jimmy concedes. "I had to assess the situation. For all my efforts—and the efforts of good people like Ray Charles and Joel Dorn—my singing career was still stuck in the mud. I had to look at that clearly. I also had to understand that my soul and my career were not the same. If God gave me the gift of singing, that gift remained. That gift didn't depend on the whims of moguls or the uncertainty of the marketplace. I could still express genuine gratitude for that gift. At the same time, Herman Lubinksy was real as rain. The man was intent on blocking me wherever I went. He had power. I had none. Rather than aggravate myself with ulcers, the cool move was to put the music game on hold. Concentrate on keeping body and soul whole."

After the three or four days it took to record *The Source*, Jimmy was back at the Sheraton.

"The people at the hotel knew about my singing," he says, "and let me arrange my schedule whenever I needed a little time off. I was a good shipping clerk, and they weren't about to let me go. I needed the job and worked it hard. I liked being busy. I liked when the days passed quickly. Here comes a truck with a load of laundry. Here comes the new chandelier for the lobby. Here are the kitchen supplies, and here's Max, the man who delivers shampoos and soaps. I liked all these people. Liked seeing them, liked helping them, liked how they gave my life a reason and rhyme. I could go on working at the Sheraton—and thought I would—until fate stepped in and knocked me on my ass. Literally."

THE HARDER THEY FALL

Cleveland winters are harsh and dreary. The gray-slate sky stays low, the lake freezes, time stands still. Hours can move as slowly as days, days as slowly as years.

"The seventies were the long years," says Jimmy.

His jazz life had turned to a family life, and the family wasn't working. More than ever, he and Ruth were fighting over money, and her children were fighting with him. Financial security became—and still is—an obsession for Jimmy. His trust of Ruth had crumbled, and yet he remained in the marriage.

"I decided to hang on as best I could," he says, "because I hated to see another family of mine fall apart, even if her kids were dead set against me. Our house was comfortable, and I wanted to find a way we all could live there in harmony. I wanted stability, but not at the price of constant bickering. Ruth was overreaching. She overreached for herself and her children. She reached in my pockets until my pockets were empty. Rather than dwell on her discontent—that I wasn't making more and giving her more—I turned my interests to politics. The city had been changing. In 1967 there was hope when we elected Carl Stokes, our first black mayor and brother of my Central High classmate Louis. Stokes served for two terms, but in 1971, when he decided not to run, hope turned to despair. I'd gotten a little involved in the Democratic leadership through my good friend Fanny Lewis, a councilwoman. I went to rallies and campaigned for certain candidates. I kept up on issues. The problem was bickering between the black caucus that had left the party and other black leaders who remained loyal Democrats. There was no unity."

"The decade of the 1970s witnessed a sharp transformation in the character and structure of black politics in Cleveland," writes William E. Nelson, Jr., professor of black studies at Ohio State University, in *Cleveland: A Metropolitan Reader*. "Black political leaders ceased to champion programs of social reform and community redevelopment, instead embracing more pragmatic programs that would enhance their access to high levels of material benefits."

"We went back to where we were when I was a kid," says Jimmy. "Neglecting the neighborhoods. Putting personal profits before helping the poor. It was hard not to be discouraged. I did my best, though, to simply do my job at the hotel. But that job ended with a crash in 1971. A co-worker in the laundry room asked me to bring him some soap. Someone had left open the door that housed the washing machines and dryers, which were going full blast. Moisture got all over the floor. I didn't realize that and took a bad tumble. My feet went out from under me, splaying in opposite directions. The major muscles in my pelvis ripped. The muscles were so severely dislodged I couldn't move. The pain was excruciating. They carried me out on a stretcher. After days in the hospital, the doctor recommended an operation, but with a stern warning: 'I can't guarantee you'll walk again.' I got up from the bed and saw that I could walk on my own. My walk had something of a limp—a limp I carry to this day—but whatever pain I felt was better than being confined to a wheelchair. I refused the operation. I've been walking ever since, although, as the years have passed, there's considerable discomfort along my legs and in my back. Old age has contributed to that pain, but I'm not complaining. I'm grateful to walk.

"I got a lawyer who wasn't too effective. Rather than a lump-sum settlement, he got me disability—three hundred dollars a month—and medical care for the rest of my life. Ruth's kids who were still in school got part of that disability. If I had any hope that the accident would bring me and my wife closer together, those hopes were dashed when Ruth wouldn't stop berating me for not getting more money out of the hotel. I spent more and more time outside the house, away from Ruth and the children, who were glad to see me gone. My only consolation was finding another woman in another city who was sweet enough to ease my emotional pain."

Without work, Jimmy was adrift in the early seventies, living off his small injury settlement and spending more time away from the home on Lee Road. There were no singing gigs. The only faint interest in Jimmy Scott came from, of all places, the Motown studios where Michael Jackson was recording his second solo record. The Jackson Five had scored a blaze of number-one hits since their debut in 1969. The group had been discovered and brought to Berry Gordy by Bobby Taylor, whose group, the Vancouvers, was signed to the label. A superb singer himself, Taylor was rooted in black music and saw Michael as the heir to Jackie Wilson and James Brown. As Michael's first producer, he didn't have any smashes—"I Want You Back," "ABC," and "The Love You Save" were later created by a group of writers called The Corporation—but Taylor kept feeding the young singer strong material from the past, including "Everybody's Somebody's Fool," Jimmy's hit from 1950.

"I thought of Jimmy Scott," says Taylor, "because Scott is the founding father of the school of high tenors. He's the standard by which others, including Frankie Lymon and Smokey Robinson, must be measured. Everyone with half an education in the history of our music knows 'Everybody's Somebody's Fool.' It was time to educate young Michael. He loved the song and the original phrasing. And he sang the shit out of it. It came out in 1972 on the album called *Ben*, after the silly movie song about the mouse. 'Ben' might have been the smash, but Michael's version of 'Fool' remains the classic off that album." (The song is included in Michael Jackson's *Love Songs*, released by Universal in 2002.)

The only other professional interest in Jimmy came in the form of a repeat performance by Joel Dorn, whose devotion, despite all obstacles, hadn't waned.

"Even though *The Source* had been blocked," says Dorn, "I couldn't stand the idea that Jimmy Scott, at his absolute prime, was still not being documented. In the meantime, I'd been lucky enough to have produced some hits for Bette Midler and Roberta Flack. Flack's 'First Time Ever I Saw Your Face' went to number one, and my bosses were finally cutting me some slack. Besides, our original promise to Jimmy was for two albums. Nesuhi Ertegun, with his old-school integrity, told me to go ahead with the second. I figured these new tracks wouldn't be issued—he still had the Lubinksy problem—but at least I could get them in the can and leave the rest to future fate. I knew Lubinsky wasn't going to live forever. In those days you could still cut ten tunes in three days for fourteen thousand dollars—arrangements, strings, rhythm section, the works. Jimmy got a couple of thousand, and we were off to the races."

"The second Atlantic sessions came at a good time for me," remembers Jimmy. "I needed to get out of Cleveland, and I needed the money. I had no illusions about a breakthrough album that would ignite my career. It was enough to know that Joel was getting together the best musicians with classy charts and beautiful songs."

In mid-October 1972, Jimmy returned to the Atlantic studios. With music arranged and conducted by Brazilian maestro Eumir Deodato, he continued in the inspired spirit of *The Source*. He recorded ten numbers; five were eventually released twenty-one years later on a CD called *Lost and Found*. According to Dorn, the other five were not worth releasing. But the five released are stunning.

"This was the freest that Jimmy ever sang," says Dorn, "and probably the best. We threw out all commercial considerations. No one mentioned the word 'airplay.' Jimmy was in his ultimate comfort zone. He approved and loved every song. He sang the verses when he wanted to sing the verses, and he picked the tempos—the world's *slowest* tempos—to suit his mood. We didn't worry about length. We didn't worry about anything. This was art for art's sake. I finally saw that the way to produce Jimmy Scott was to allow for his artistry. Don't push any songs on him. Give him all the time and space in the world, and he'll create a new world for you. When I heard him elongate those notes on 'I Have Dreamed,' for instance, all I could think was, *My man can pull some taffy.*"

Dorn put together another fine rhythm section, this one led by pianist Ray Bryant and including guitarist David Spinozza, bassist Richard Davis, and drummer Billy Cobham. Aretha Franklin, who recorded with Bryant in the early sixties, called the pianist "a model of sensitivity and skill." Jimmy responded to his accompaniment and the selection of songs with joyous appreciation.

"I took all these songs personally. They seemed to be telling the story of my life at that moment. 'For Once in My Life' is about the dream of righteous romance. I couldn't give up that dream—not then, not ever. I had first heard Stevie Wonder's version back in the sixties. That's when I met him in Detroit with the other Motown kids. He was still *Little* Stevie and told me that he had been listening to me. 'Well, I'm listening to *you*,' I let him know, 'and loving what I hear.'

"'I Have Dreamed' expresses my wish for a marriage that might have been. The same is true for 'The Folks Who Live on the Hill.' I remember Peggy Lee singing the song about how a couple lives happily ever after. They grow old, have kids, retire in perfect harmony. Peggy sings, 'When the kids grow up and leave us, we'll sit and look at that same old view, just we two, baby and Joe who used to be Jack and Jill.' I sang it as, 'Ruthie and Jim who used to be Jack and Jill.' I was still dreaming of making my marriage work.

I related to the song and its hopeful sentiment. 'Dedicated to You' had that same feeling—if only there were someone constant enough in my life to whom I could dedicate a book. I still believed in dedication. And the song 'Stay with Me' let me sing about the dedication that meant the most—spiritual dedication. 'Stay with Me' has jazz chords and jazz attitudes, but the story is about seeking God. 'Should my heart not be humble, should my eyes fail to see, should my feet sometimes stumble . . . stay with me.'"

The mixture of earthly and heavenly longing is what gives Jimmy his edge. To infuse sacred devotion into secular love songs is to raise the stakes from music to metaphysics. Jimmy's voice pierces and pleads with utter conviction. He is at the height of his powers, disarmingly personal, disarmingly confessional. All raw nerve ends are exposed. Dorn's brilliant productions and Deodato's exquisitely subtle voicings for horns and strings have a looseness that allows Jimmy, meditative by nature, to meditate in depth.

"I couldn't help but be encouraged by the second album I made with Joel," says Jimmy. "The music was where I wanted it. But I knew it wasn't going anywhere. Atlantic didn't even try to put it out. Back in Cleveland, it was clear that 'Ruthie and Jim' weren't going to be the folks who live on the hill. The end was coming. Ruth made the first move, hiring herself some slick lawyers and, after lots of fancy maneuvering, finding a way to get that big, beautiful house we had bought together. She also found a way to saddle me with debts that she had assumed. My lawyer was a pussycat; hers was a rottweiler. So you can imagine who won. She got it all and even managed to destroy my good credit in the process. Took years to straighten out the financial mess."

On another trip to Cleveland, this one during late summer under a warm sky, Jimmy and I again drive by the Lee Road house awarded to Ruth after long legal procedures. When I press Jimmy about his reluctance—both in personal and professional matters—to hire lawyers tough enough to protect his interests, he explains:

"I don't walk into conflicts. I walk away from them. I'm not one of these guys who can press a point by arguing. I can't remember winning an argument. But then again, I can't remember entering into an argument. So I guess I gravitated towards lawyers who weren't too aggressive, the way I'm not aggressive. I'm not saying that was smart. It was simply me. If I hire a guy to represent me, I have to feel comfortable with his behavior. In the world of courtrooms and conflicts, nice guys finish last. It takes a Lubinksy to fight a Lubinsky. Problem is, I'm not a fighter.

"I went on with my life, got a little apartment, lived on my disability. If I felt like singing, I'd go out to the old-age homes to sing for free. That's where you're really appreciated. If I needed extra money, I'd find work as a waiter. I'd hang out with the old musicians and, once in a while, even find a paying gig in some small club. I'd think about dear friends like Big Maybelle and the trouble they'd seen. Put my problems in perspective.

"Maybelle never recovered from her addiction. She never recovered from being mishandled by Lubinksy and mismanaged by Jimmy Evans. She got deeper into dope and, as if that wasn't bad enough, deeper into her obsession over eating. She had come to Cleveland in the late sixties to live out her last years, but, close as we'd been, she didn't want anyone to see her. She was ashamed. She moved into the upper quarters of her mother's two-family house on 132nd Street. Once she walked up those stairs, she never came down. She ate herself to death. That and dope and diabetes killed her. When they came to take her to the hospital, she had grown so enormous they had to cut off the door frames to carry her out. When Maybelle died in 1972, she was only forty-two.

"Underneath the complexes was nothing but a beautiful heart. A beautiful soul. Listen to her sing 'Say It Isn't So' or 'So Long.' Or when December comes and the family draws near, listen to her sing 'Silent Night' or 'White Christmas.' With all due respect, you can forget Bing Crosby. Maybelle had the voice of the century. Maybelle was Mahalia, Bessie Smith, and Dinah all wrapped up in one. The business did her in. Life did her in. She did herself in. But she gave her gift as well and as long as she could. I think back to the hundred one-nighters Maybelle and I played up and down the road, the laughs we shared, the respect we had for each other, the times she praised me and I praised her while others chose to scorn. I now praise her and the holy spirit that came through her voice. I praise her majesty as an artist. May lovers of music of the true soul never forget her."

"CAN'T WE BEGIN AGAIN?"

*L*ike the lives of most of us, the life of Jimmy Scott is riddled with ironies. Circumstances conspire to dash our dreams or exceed our expectations. What looks good turns bad; what's dark becomes light. Fate turns on a dime; fortune winks, then fades, then returns in a disguise we neither recognize nor trust. Never one to push, Jimmy played a waiting game when it came to fate. The great gap between 1973 and 1984 was, to use Thelonius Monk's phrase, the "un" years for Jimmy. Nothing happened. No comeback, no deals, few performances. He stayed in Cleveland, where he lived on the margins of middle-class life in utter obscurity.

"Somehow the years slipped away," Jimmy says. "Strange to think about it, but that was the period, as far as pure singing goes, when I was probably in peak form. Yet, with only one exception, I never made another record till 1990."

The exceptional irony came in May 1975, when Jimmy, about to turn fifty, went to Chicago to cut an album for Savoy Records, the same firm that had been blocking him for the past decade.

"It was Freddy Mendelsohn," says Jimmy. "I told you how Freddy was loyal. Well, he never gave up on me and felt terrible about how Lubinsky had treated me. Freddy still felt I could have hits. He still believed. When he first called me in 1974, Herman was dying of cancer. From all reports, cancer gave him a helluva licking on his way out. I was sorry to hear it. For all his craziness, I held no animosity towards Herman. I don't like hearing anyone has to suffer. 'It's the end of an era,' said Freddy, 'but it's an opportunity for me to make up a little of the wrong he did you. I have more control now and I can advance you fifteen hundred dollars for an album of new material. I've talked to your old friend Ace Carter, and he's ready to hire an orchestra and write charts. He wants to talk to you about tunes.'

"I was a little taken back by the good news/bad news. The bad news was that Herman was on his last legs. The good news was that Freddy wanted to front me an advance much bigger than Herman ever paid. There wasn't much to think about, because I had nothing else going on. Fifteen hundred bucks was fifteen hundred bucks. A record was a record, even if it came out on the label that had opposed me. I agreed.

"I'd known Ace Carter from when I was a kid in Youngstown. He once had a crush on my sister Nadine. Ace could play piano— for a while he replaced Basie in the Basie band after Count died—and he could write. Ace was a good choice. But when I showed up in Chicago at the studio, Ace was drunk. He'd convinced Freddy to buy him a bottle of Scotch and was practically falling off the piano bench. The sessions were chaotic. Despite the chaos, though, I had in mind an original song. I wanted to start off on an optimistic note, I wanted to let bygones be bygones, so I composed a set of lyrics based on the title 'Can't We Begin Again.' I was thinking of not only me and Freddy and me and Savoy, but all the people who have fallen out with loved ones. 'Can't We Begin Again' said it all for me. New start, new dedication, new reason for healing and hope."

The answer to the question posed by the album's title—*Can't We Begin Again*—is both yes and no. There are wonderful moments. Jimmy's title song makes me wonder why he didn't write more. He bends the word *begin* until you're certain it will break. But all that breaks is your heart. The song has the power and sustenance of a standard.

"I've written my share of songs," says Jimmy, "but only when the occasion arose. I think of myself more as an interpreter than a composer. But I considered this occasion auspicious, and I wanted to mark it with a personal statement."

Typical of Jimmy, that statement is filled with hope. He makes you believe that he *will* begin again. The other gem is "Close Your Eyes," taken at a tempo so slow that Quincy Jones has said, "you can shave between the beats." Producer Michael Cuscuna, who wrote the liner notes, calls it "an instant Scott classic." For the most part, though, the album is unfocused and unsatisfying.

"It was a mess," Jimmy remembers. "Ace was a good cat, but these sessions scared him and, for whatever reasons, triggered all his insecurities about arranging. He was too juiced to write. The charts were only half-finished, and the cats were making up parts as we went along. Alex Hamilton, a talented arranger who'd been working with James Cleveland on gospel records, added the strings afterwards. The record doesn't really gel. The tunes are fine—I sang 'I'll Be Around' and 'You've Changed' from Billie's *Lady in Satin*, an album I'd never forget—but we struggled with tempos and voicings."

There's a spirited reading of "The More I See You" and a plaintive "When I Fall in Love," but by the time Jimmy arrives at "What Are You Doing the Rest of Your Life" and "The Way We Were," he strains and struggles against the muddy orchestrations. Compared to the Dorn sessions from 1969 and 1972, Jimmy's last Savoy date is a sad affair. Ironically, unlike the Tangerine and Atlantic dates, indisputable masterpieces, this session had no problems being released.

"Savoy didn't put a penny into promotion," says Jimmy. "I don't even think they sent copies to deejays. It was simply a way for Freddy to get me money. I was grateful. I didn't expect much and didn't really suffer disappointment. The payday was enough."

Can't We Begin Again came and went without notice. Herman Lubinsky died in March 1974.

The seventies dragged on. The Vietnam War was over, Nixon in exile, Ford in the White House, *Jaws* in the movie houses. Soul music was rejuvenated by Earth, Wind and Fire. *Saturday Night Fever* and disco ran rampant. In 1975, Nancy Wilson covered Marvin Gaye's sexy "Come Get to This." Ray Charles recorded a double album of songs from *Porgy and Bess* with English singer Cleo Laine. Miles retreated—he didn't touch his horn from 1975 to early 1980—and in 1978, Quincy Jones supervised the score for *The Wiz* and began working with Michael Jackson. Jimmy Scott stayed in Cleveland.

"My disability checks, small as they were, anchored me," he says. "I found odd jobs and kept myself together. In 1979, Dad had a stroke and was put into a nursing home. Nadine was a nurse and made sure he had proper care. Betsy brought him meals. Kenny took him fishing. I'd come by every morning and have breakfast with him. We tried to keep him active. If he stayed in his house, he'd wind up sobbing. It was tough seeing Dad, always so proud, even cocky, reduced to the emotions of a young boy. We were caring for the father who could never take care of us. In doing so, we were honoring his wife, our mother, and her instructions about parental respect. I can't say I was emotionally close to my father, even in his last years, even being with him day after day. I can say, though, that in being a good son I felt close to my mother. I felt her by my side as I sat in his room. I felt her presence, comforting me as I tried to comfort him. That was all the comfort I needed.

"As long as my father was in this condition, I couldn't consider leaving Cleveland. But the truth is that I had no reason to leave. Even my most devoted friends in the music business, whether Freddy Mendelsohn or Joel Dorn, had done all they could. In

1980, I moved into University Tower, a high-rise at East Boulevard
and 105th Street. I was only fifty-five, but I was able to get senior
citizen status through my friend, councilwoman Fanny Lewis. I became active in the building as president of the tenants' association
and head of the grievance committee. I would report our various
complaints, whether plumbing or sanitation, to City Hall and,
through Fanny, was able to get some satisfaction.

"Meanwhile, I found no satisfaction on the local music scene.
Cleveland had gone go-go. The old jazz clubs were now nudie
bars. Great jazz and blues artists were replaced by topless dancers.
Most nights, I stayed home, read, watched TV, listened to old
records. Once in a while I'd hear from old friends."

"I started writing Jimmy in the late seventies," says Earlene,
his Newark girlfriend from the early fifties. "I wanted to know
how he was doing and whether he was singing. He wrote back and
said he'd been studying religion for years and was even licensed to
preach. I couldn't imagine Jimmy as a minister. I was sad he wasn't
performing and wrote him back saying that, no matter how styles
might change, his style would always be beautiful. I never stopped
loving him and never stopped encouraging him. Sometimes I'd
pick up the phone and call. If Jimmy was sober, we'd have a lovely
conversation. If Jimmy was drunk, I'd hang up in a hurry. Seems
like half the time he was drunk."

"People have a strange notion about my drinking," Jimmy contends. "When I'm not working I like to relax with a little drink and
a little smoke, but it never gets crazy."

Others disagree. "The only time Jimmy really gets crazy," says
sister Elsa, "is when he's drinking. Over the years, those times have
been plentiful. I think it's hurt him."

"It hurt me," claims Jimmy, "that I was consistently judged by
my family when, in fact, they didn't have firsthand knowledge of my
daily life. That life was well ordered and calm. I'd read my books,
take my walks, watch a little TV, maybe get a phone call from a
friend. One friend who never stopped calling was Doc Pomus. He

was like Earlene—always wanting to know why I wasn't singing. Doc also never stopped worrying the record companies to let me record. Doc was respected as a songwriter and music man, but the cats who ran the companies were cold-blooded. They weren't about to give a deal for old time's sake. In the seventies and eighties, the music business got more corporate and bottom-line. Sentiment was out."

"I got a little sentimental for Jimmy," says second wife Channie, "when my daughter died. When I went back to Cleveland for the funeral, I looked him up. Jimmy didn't know her well, but I knew he'd be feeling for me. He was living in the University Tower in a little one-bedroom apartment. Hadn't sung for years and didn't look like he ever would again. But he was just as sweet as ever. Hadn't changed. Didn't hold a grudge against me. He invited me up to his place like I was still the love of his life."

"I was glad to see Channie and heartbroken over her daughter," Jimmy recalls. "A blizzard hit the night she came over. We sat around, had a few drinks, and remembered those early days before things got twisted out of shape. As the storm got worse, I invited her to spend the night. She was reluctant, but I feared for her safety. I said I'd go stay with my brother Kenny, who lived nearby. 'No,' she said, 'tonight was nice. I want to keep it that way.' Then she went to her mother's. Her mother, by the way, called me sometime later, when Channie's brother died, to sing at the funeral. They wanted to pay me, but I wouldn't accept the money.

"There wasn't much drama during those long years in Cleveland. The seasons came and went. Someone might ask me to sing at a wedding, or a country club reception, or a neighborhood bar. They say go with the flow, even if the flow is slow. I wasn't disturbed by the slowness of life, but certain dreams did disturb me. In one, I saw my father in a wheelchair when the earth opened up and suddenly swallowed him whole. I woke up in a sweat. I called the home to see whether he was all right. That's when I learned he had died during the night.

"When I lost my mother, I had no time to absorb the feelings. We were pushed into orphanages, and that was that. The grief stuck. The grief stayed. The grief made me who I am today. But Dad's death was different. When he died in 1982, he was eighty-seven. He lived a long life and gave me all the time in the world to adjust to who he was—and wasn't. He wasn't an easy man. He had his ways, like we all have our ways. If he never found a way to keep his kids together under one roof, he never excluded us from his life. He knew where we were, and in his own good time, he came to see us. He had the good fortune of marrying our beloved Justine, who, sometime after his death, was declared a saint by the same church—the Hagar Universal Spiritual Church—he introduced her to during the Depression. Mom loved him. And so did we. To accept him, faults and all, was the lesson of a lifetime. I'm grateful for having learned that lesson. Once he was gone, I knew my life would shift. Death is a relief and a release. Energy shifts. Slowly, very slowly, I felt something shifting for me."

"I'M AFRAID
JIMMY SCOTT IS DEAD"

The signs that jazz might be shifting were subtle. In the late seventies, Scott Hamilton, a young tenor player, hit the New York scene with a style that emulated the masters of old, Coleman Hawkins and Lester Young. In the early eighties, trumpeter Wynton Marsalis joined Art Blakey's Messengers and would soon lead a quiet counterrevolution in which mainstream jazz—a refined, medium-cool bebop that mostly ignored the avant-garde—would take hold. The institutionalization of jazz instruction in high schools and especially colleges had spread across the United States, emphasizing the music's rich heritage. And Jimmy's contemporaries, jazz singers like Betty Carter and Carmen McRae, were enjoying newfound acceptance, playing university concerts as well as clubs. In short, the young were beginning to value the old.

Jimmy would eventually be embraced by the young. The young would rejuvenate his career and place him in a position he'd never before known—as an icon of style and an avatar of an earlier age. But like everything else in his life, the process would be excruciatingly long and fraught with obstacles. Jimmy's hard-fought reentry, like his music, was realized in a rhythm that fell far behind the beat of the average comeback. It began modestly with a phone call from Earlene Rodgers to a Newark jazz station in early 1984.

"I'd been working as a nurse for thirty years," says Earlene. "I stayed out at the House of Miriam, where I cared for the mother of New Jersey United States Senator Frank Lautenberg. The Senator and I were both contributors to WBGO, the Newark jazz station. I listened to it all the time and, as a member, wanted to hear more Jimmy Scott played on the air. One of their disc jockeys, Bob Porter, would interview musicians. I thought it would be great to interview Jimmy. I felt like I was representing all the Jimmy Scott fans, and I felt like we had waited long enough for Jimmy to get his due. I hoped this would convince Jimmy to come out of exile and start singing again. So I called over to the station and politely made my request."

Dorthaan Kirk, widow of Rashaan Roland Kirk and director of Special Events/Community Relations for the station, answered the phone. "I'd been living in Newark for ten years," says Dorthaan, "where Jimmy Scott is a legend. His legendary years, though, were back in the fifties. I knew that his fans held him in high esteem, but they were the same fans who told me he was deceased. So when this woman phoned to say she'd like to have him interviewed, I said, 'I'm afraid Jimmy Scott is dead.'"

"No, he's not dead," Earlene told Dorthaan. "I talked to him yesterday. He's alive and well and living in Cleveland. If Bob Porter will interview him, I believe I can convince him to come to Newark."

"I'd lost track of Jimmy Scott," says Porter, a successful jazz producer and Savoy Records scholar. "He'd disappeared long ago, and even his old friends didn't know whether he was alive or dead. When Dorthaan mentioned talking to a woman who'd just talked to Jimmy, I was delighted. I immediately invited him on the show."

"I wanted so badly to have Jimmy come to Newark that I bought him a plane ticket," says Earlene. "It was worth it, just to see him back in the limelight. He came and stayed with me and my mother. And sure enough, Bob Porter put him on the air."

"The interview went from noon to one," remembers Porter, "but that was just the beginning. The phones started ringing and wouldn't stop. Turned out that Jimmy was in our studio till midnight. Of course Jimmy is an enormously gracious and charming man. But it was more than charm that attracted the callers. His legacy was intact. Newark had not forgotten him. The goodwill he had created those years when he lived here, the musical thrills he had provided the jazz-loving community—the memories came roaring in from everyone and everywhere."

"I call it my glory day," says Jimmy. "I was overwhelmed. I had limited expectations. I thought it'd be nice to see Earlene, do a little interview, and go back home. Instead, the floodgates opened. One after another, fans started calling in. And stars as well—Al Hibbler, Quincy Jones, even Lionel Hampton. They all called with good wishes and loving support. After twelve hours of nonstop excitement, I was drained. And extremely grateful. I'd been living so quietly and so alone in Cleveland for so long, I presumed my name no longer meant a thing. It was wonderful to learn I was wrong. If Newark had embraced me in the fifties, the embrace was even warmer in the eighties. That night I was so excited I couldn't sleep."

"I wasn't surprised," says Earlene, "because once you hear Jimmy sing—no matter how many years may have passed—you never forget him. To have him back in Newark was a blessing for everyone. He flew home the next day, but he knew his life would never be the same. People wanted to hear him sing—and of course *he* wanted to sing. All those years in Cleveland didn't change that. A few weeks later, I made a trip to Cleveland to talk to him about his career. I stayed two weeks; I saw his sisters and his brother Kenny and felt part of the family. 'Jimmy,' I told him, 'if you promise to stop drinking, I'll help you. You can come live with me in Newark. Newark is where your career first got started, and Newark is where you'll get started again.' He looked at me and said he'd do all he could to make me proud. That was enough. The idea of having him in Newark, making a living as a singer and doing what God intended him to do, was a dream come true."

"Newark seemed the right move for many reasons," Jimmy reflects. "Newark was always a beat back from New York, which meant Newark suited my style. Newark was also the only city that had called me back. I felt moved to respond to that call. What's more, Earlene was making it easy by offering her home and her love. I saw her as someone to trust."

The old issue of trust would become critical to Jimmy's comeback. His history, where his trust was so often misplaced, left him unsure—and understandably suspicious—of people and their motives.

"I knew Jimmy felt like he'd been taken for a ride by his former wives," says Earlene. "He had bought two houses—one for Channie and another for Ruth—and lost them both. He was taken advantage of. I understood why, especially after Ruth, he kept his distance from women. I think Jimmy was always looking for someone like his mother. And maybe I reminded him of her. She was short like me, and Jimmy said she loved eating nuts just like I do. Unlike a lot of entertainers, Jimmy wasn't wild when it came to women. He was a one-woman man. He didn't want to play around. All he really wanted was a home. Every since he lost his mama, he'd been looking for a stable home."

"Earlene was offering me something I'd been seeking so long," says Jimmy. "Earlene was looking out for me. She cared more about my career than her own. Channie and Ruth never cared like that. They never offered the support a singer needs, especially a singer who can't be sure of his next gig. That made me grateful for Earlene. Besides, I'd been knowing Earlene since we were both practically children. I knew she was good through and through. Ruth had been a nurse, but not a loving nurse like Earlene. Earlene was sincere in everything she did. I saw her as a way to elevate my life—my home life *and* my work life. I probably should have stayed with her back in the early fifties, when we first met. Now fate was giving me a second chance. It felt right to marry Earlene."

"I have loved—and will love—only one man in my life," Earlene declares, "and his name is Jimmy Scott. When we got married in Newark on Valentine's Day 1985, it was all I ever wished for."

Jimmy was just short of sixty, Earlene fifty-seven.

"Twenty-two years had passed since I moved from Los Angeles to Cleveland," Jimmy recalls. "Twenty-two years is a long time. But Dad had died, and there was nothing holding me back. The signs looked good. If I wanted a career—and, to be honest, I never stopped wanting one—it was now or never. I knew it wouldn't be overnight, because overnight has been never my method. It was time to start putting myself out there again. Newark would be home base. Earlene and I lived in her home with her mother in the West Ward on Grove Street. From the start, though, I worried that Earlene was too close to her mom. Felt like her mom was in the middle of our relationship. I hoped that, with time, that would change. Meanwhile, their house was rat-infested. I could hear the rats scratching through the walls. The cats would kill them and pile them by the backdoor. I took my savings and got us a reasonably priced place in Georgia King Village: nice, clean, and rat-free. Then it was time to go to work."

"Jimmy needed help getting work," says Dorthaan Kirk, "and asked me if I'd assist. I said yes. After the interview with Bob Porter, I started taking him around town, introducing him to club owners, but despite his popularity, not everyone was willing to take a chance. So I decided to do it myself. I put up the money to rent the Mirage, an after-work bar on Broad Street in downtown Newark. They normally didn't have music, but were willing to make an exception. We put together a trio for Jimmy and spread the word: *Friday and Saturday only, Little Jimmy Scott returns to Newark.* This was March of 1985, just a month after he married Earlene. We charged ten dollars at the door and hoped for the best. Well, the straight of it is that Jimmy turned it out. We jammed over two hundred people in that club, both nights, and had to call an off-duty cop for crowd control. The cop had to literally lock the door. Seemed like the whole city wanted to get in to see and touch the great Little Jimmy Scott. The old-timers were there—Tiny Prince and his crowd—along with loads of young people who'd heard about Jimmy from their folks. Jimmy was sensational. That famous style had only gotten more individualized. He was fascinating to watch."

From those who were there—Dorthaan, Earlene, Bob Porter—it's clear that Jimmy had changed his physical presentation. In former times, he merely stood in front of the microphone and sang. But emerging from exile, embracing a new generation of jazz fans, he was more demonstrative. Like the latter-day Judy Garland, he was not in the least self-conscious about his unorthodox gestures. He sculpted the air with his hands. He waved his arms. He painted the picture, not simply with his voice, but with his fingers. Vocally, he was also freer.

"Like all great veteran jazz singers," says Bob Porter, "Jimmy's sense of improvisation had widened. He took more chances with melody and phrasing. If he was idiosyncratic before, his uniqueness had now reached another level."

"I had nothing to lose during that weekend at the Mirage," Jimmy reflects, "and everything to gain. When an artist takes the attitude that there's no downside, it's all up. I was thrilled that the club wasn't empty, and I simply said so with my singing. I sang the old songs—'Talk of the Town,' 'The Masquerade Is Over,' 'When Did You Leave Heaven,' and, naturally, 'Everybody's Somebody's Fool.' But when I sang them, they didn't feel old. And neither did I."

"The Mirage was a solid success," says Dorthaan. "People were grabbing at Jimmy like he was a hot star. After I paid the musicians and equipment and rental fee for the club, Jimmy got a nice sum. But he wasn't happy. I don't think he realized the extent of my expenses. He was looking for more. I saw that he had trust issues, and I understood why. He had wanted me to find him more work, but I decided not to. I saw that anyone who booked or managed Jimmy was going to have his or her hands full. He seemed to love everyone, but I saw that he also viewed everyone with a degree of suspicion."

Mistrust and suspicion, faith and optimism, caution and tenacity—these are the traits Jimmy displayed as he initiated his improbable and somewhat tortuous comeback. Misfortune still lay ahead; he would face several wrong turns and roadblocks. Jimmy would go through a half-dozen managers until he found the right one. Record companies were reluctant to sign him, club owners reluctant to book him. In the mideighties, though he found himself back in the music business, his struggles had just begun.

"I'VE SHED ENOUGH TEARS"

*I*n May 1985, two months after his comeback turn at the Mirage, Jimmy was booked into the Blue Note, a prestigious Greenwich Village jazz club, along with organist Charles Earland, under the banner "Uptown Comes Downtown." It was well over a decade since Jimmy had performed in Manhattan. *New York Times* critic Jon Pareles was enthusiastic: "Like a great Chinese calligrapher, Mr. Scott renders a song in spontaneous, impassioned, irrevocable strokes. He all but vaporizes the original melody to get straight to the heart of the lyrics, usually standards. . . . Even at the glacial tempos Mr. Scott prefers, he fills his songs with nearly unbearable tension." Three days later the *Times* ran a feature, its first ever on the singer, still referring to the sixty-year-old as "*Little* Jimmy Scott."

The publicity had no immediate impact. Jimmy found only scattered work in small clubs in Harlem followed by a concert in Louisville, Kentucky, arranged by his former girlfriend, Mary Ann Fisher, whom he hadn't spoken to in years.

"We might have been out of touch," says Mary Ann, "but I never lost my regard for him and his singing. Then this gig came up at the Kentucky Center for the Arts. It was perfect for Jimmy.

We called it the Midnight Ramble Stage Show, and it featured Jimmy, myself, a comic who imitated Moms Mabley, and an exotic dancer."

"It was like being back with Caldonia," remembers Jimmy. "But I didn't mind. I figured if I was coming back, I might as well go all the way back to the beginning."

"I loved seeing him," Mary Ann reports. "The fact is, when I heard Jimmy was singing again, I jumped at the chance to have him visit me and my son Tracy. There were no hard feelings. Only the devil could stay mad at Jimmy Scott, and even the devil would finally melt. Especially when Jimmy starts to sing. His voice was even more beautiful, and his presentation was more dramatic. He was throwing his arms around in all different directions. It was exciting to watch him."

Back in New York, he played the West End Café across from Columbia University, where Pareles gave him another plug in the *Times*: "Diminutive and bespectacled, Mr. Scott is a bold singer indeed. Singing in a voice so high it might almost be considered a soprano—a voice that sounds slightly more frayed, and less ethereal, than it did on his 1950's albums—Mr. Scott specializes in ballads of desperate love, capturing melancholy feelings by completely reshaping his songs."

"The songs I was singing," says Jimmy, "were the ones I've always sung—and always will sing. 'There, I've Said It Again,' 'This Love of Mine,' 'Moonglow.' The tried-and-true songs. The stories of my life. I thought that, with all the good publicity, I was off and running. But it was more like crawling. Still not many gigs. A nice one happened in D.C. at the Capital City Jazz Festival, where I got to play with my friend from the bebop days at Minton's, Milt Jackson. My buddy from Hamp's band, Betty Carter, was on the same bill, and it was good to hear her sounding better than ever. Emotionally, these reunions were beautiful. Financially, they were modest. Once in a while, I'd see a sign of hope. Bill Cosby featured 'An Evening in Paradise,' one of my old Savoy records, on his TV sitcom in 1986. It was flattering, but it didn't bring work. I didn't despair, though, because too many friends were rallying around me. I remember going to one of Doc Pomus's big birthday parties. We were born only a month apart and loved to celebrate together. 'Goddamnit, Jimmy,' he said, 'this time you're not getting away from us. This time it's going to happen if I have to take a gun to their heads.'"

In the September 21, 1987, issue of *Billboard* magazine, Doc Pomus wrote this letter to the editor under the headline "Before It's Too Late":

I've been singer Jimmy Scott's fan and friend for almost 40 years. When I first met him he was coming off R&B tunes like "Dearest Darling," "My Mother's Eyes" and "Hands Across the Table." At that time, black records were called "race records" and seldom crossed over to the white charts. His career then was at a semi-standstill and he was already starting to fall through the cracks. Then he disappeared and for the next twenty years I heard very little about him. Later I heard that Jimmy was working in the shipping department of a Cleveland hotel and singing at senior citizen homes and at hospitals. These gigs went on until the mideighties. Then two years ago he suddenly turned up in Newark, New Jersey. I heard him sing and he was great as ever. He looks healthy and acts fairly wise, but wealthy—forget about it. He's just barely hanging in. If you want to know more about his singing ask Quincy Jones or Stevie Wonder or Frankie Valli or Nancy Wilson—they idolize him. When we talk about Jimmy Scott we're talking about somebody who might be the best singer of contemporary or vintage ballads around. There must be some space somewhere for him. What's everyone waiting for? He's sixty-two years old, he'll die and there'll be a hot funeral. Everybody will show up in hip mourning clothes and talk about how great he was. Let's do something now. I've shed enough tears for enormously talented friends who died penniless in relative obscurity. I'm getting good and pissed at the affluent members of the music community who sit around and pontificate and let such tragedies happen again and again.

"My father went on a campaign," says Doc's daughter Sharyn Felder. "He was so happy to see Jimmy back in action and, at the same time, so angry no one was recording him, that he was dead-set on doing something about it. He didn't want to see history repeat itself."

"For twenty years, Doc and I spoke on the phone fourteen times a day," Joel Dorn recalls. "At least three of those daily conversations concerned Jimmy Scott. He was obsessed with seeing Jimmy make it."

For all Doc's determination, Jimmy's career languished. Not a single "affluent member of the music community" heeded Doc's call. Not a single record deal. In 1987, Gary Jardim produced *The Ballad of Jimmy Scott*, a low-budget documentary video on Jimmy, featuring author Nathan Heard, who knew Jimmy from the old days in Newark. The documentary showed the singer looking forlorn while performing before a handful of people. The film never found distribution.

That same year, Joe Fields of Muse Records, a respected jazz label, turned him down cold. "He let me know in no uncertain terms," says Jimmy, "that no one had any interest in recording an old man."

In many ways, Jimmy's new life in Newark resembled his old life in Cleveland. Things were low-key. He and Earlene moved into the Stephen Crane projects on Sixth Street in north Newark.

"It was a simple high-rise apartment," remembers Earlene, "but big enough for the two of us. Jimmy wouldn't let me bring my mother. I've always taken care of her, so it was an adjustment for me."

"I thought a marriage should be between two people," says Jimmy, "not three. Earlene was so tied to her mother that I felt left out."

"Somehow I managed," continues Earlene, "running back and forth, caring for both Mom and Jimmy. Jimmy's spirits were good. When we had sex, it was satisfying. I still believe I felt closer to him than he felt to me, but we were together and that's all that mattered. Jimmy was still drinking and smoking weed every day, yet I couldn't complain. He seemed controlled and concentrated on finding work. There was some action after that big weekend at the Mirage, but then the phone stopped ringing."

"I knew the process would be long," Jimmy asserts, "so I can't say I was worried. You can live quietly and cheaply in Newark— and that's what I was doing. I went to a senior citizen's center where they gave free courses on the use of computers. I studied those courses, figuring I might as well make good use of my time. My friend Tiny Prince, the promoter from the fifties, was still around. He still might point me to a little gig now and then. Even better, though, Tiny was working for the Housing Authority. That's how Earlene and I managed to move out of the Stephen Crane projects and get an apartment in the Arlington House, which was for low-income or no-income senior citizens. Given the slow movement of my career, I qualified. That's another way Newark kept me going. If I wasn't getting gigs, at least I was getting inexpensive housing."

Jimmy's frugality has always been part of his strategy for survival. It worked in the fifties and, to a large degree, was working again in the eighties. But thirty years had brought major changes to the city that sat on the Passaic River eight miles west of Manhattan. In the fifties, Newark was a vital center of black music. The effects of the riots in the summer of 1967, though, were catastrophic and long-lasting. Residents fled to the suburbs, leaving central Newark in ruins. Poverty, unemployment, and crime had ravaged the cityscape.

"When I returned to Newark," says Jimmy, "I could see hardship everywhere. Urban renewal had turned into urban removal. It was flat-out urban destruction. The city looked like one big ghetto. I wasn't shocked, though, because the same thing had happened to

Cleveland. White flight and inner-city decay went hand in hand. It was sad, but it also meant you could live cheaply. In spite of the bleakness, I was still cool. I always found the people and places I needed to find. Newarkers protected me. Even when I couldn't buy a gig, Earlene would take me out to the House of Miriam, where she was nursing. I'd help out with chores or maybe sing a few songs for the old folks. No matter how raggedy the city had gotten, Newark had a large core of good folks. Newark had soul. Over the next ten years or so, the city sustained me."

Meanwhile, a striking trend was developing in black music: a return to the reign of high male voices. Michael Jackson and Prince dominated the charts in the eighties with styles marked by sexual ambiguity. Whether consciously or not, they both bore the influence of Jimmy Scott, who, decades earlier, had captivated audiences with a sound—and a look—blurring traditional distinctions between female and male. In the field of pop, Linda Ronstadt's three albums with Nelson Riddle devoted to pre-rock standards were enormously successful. The mood of the music and the style of the packaging were drenched in nostalgia for the forties and fifties. The eagerness of young trendsetters to sing standards— everyone from Carly Simon to Joni Mitchell to George Michael to Harry Connick, Jr.—continues to this day and undoubtedly predisposed the youth market to veteran vocalists. Straight-ahead jazz singing was also enjoying a renaissance. "The best of the new generation," according to jazz historian Ted Gioa, "Bobby McFerrin, Dianne Schuur, Ian Shaw, Cassandra Wilson—found ways of revitalizing the tradition."

Yet, for all the retro shifts in taste and movement in the music markets, Jimmy remained unemployed. His first big break didn't come until the winter of 1988, with the publication of Jimmy McDonough's impassioned "All the Way with Jimmy Scott: For Whatever the Reason," a full-blown profile that appeared in New York's *Village Voice*. With deep sympathy and great affection, McDonough told the tale. For the first time in print, Jimmy discussed the Deficiency. McDonough talked to a number of the major characters, including Channie, and didn't shy away from the horror stories. He spent extended time with Jimmy and Earlene, reporting how at one nightclub the audience consisted of three members—McDonough, Earlene, and Earlene's mom. He characterized Jimmy with the admiration nearly all Scott profilers bring to the task. The Jimmy Scott described by McDonough was clearly down and out and, by the end of the profile, appeared helpless. McDonough was so moved by Jimmy's dilemma that he put his fee for the article into producing a demo he hoped would get the singer a deal. Quincy Jones had told McDonough that, if the demo was good, he'd help. But it would be another three long years before a deal was realized. When it did happen, Quincy was not the catalyst.

But McDonough's article made a difference. The *Voice*'s hip demographics reached Jimmy's potential audience. And even more significantly, a few record executives took note. Bill Bentley was working as a publicist at Warner Records in Los Angeles when he read McDonough's article. "My next trip to New York," says Bentley, "I saw an item that Jimmy was appearing at the Ballroom and made a point to see him."

"The Ballroom is where I opened for Johnnie Ray," Jimmy recalls. "This was the same Johnnie Ray who, early in the fifties, came out with those huge hits like 'Cry' that people said were imitating me. I never held a grudge and saw Johnny as a nice cat. We had wound up in the same boat. Like me, he was looking for a comeback. But the public had forgotten him, and the Ballroom was practically empty. Johnnie's life hadn't been easy. I felt for him. His band didn't show, and also like me, he had to use pickup musicians who didn't know his material. It was sad to see him at loose ends. He wasn't well. A couple of months later he died, and I couldn't help but think—there but for the grace of God . . . "

"Seeing Jimmy at the Ballroom," says Bentley, "was an epiphany, an experience of spiritual and emotional dimension I didn't know music could provide. I couldn't believe this guy didn't have a deal. I wasn't a big shot at Warner, but at least I could send memos to the big shots. I reasoned that if anyone would go for Jimmy it would be Seymour Stein, head of Sire Records, an independent label within the Warner Group. Seymour had made his fortune in new wave/punk. He'd signed Talking Heads and the Ramones. He'd also signed Madonna. More significantly, Stein has an encyclopedic knowledge of early R&B. He loves the old stuff. Because he's an eccentric executive, I thought he'd appreciate an eccentric talent like Jimmy Scott. If only Seymour would go see Jimmy—that would do the trick. No one can see Jimmy and resist conversion. But in spite of the endless memos I sent, I couldn't get him to any of Jimmy's shows. I enlisted the help of Joe McEwen, an A&R guy at Sire, who felt as strongly about Jimmy as I did. Joe is another man with great taste and expertise about black music. But not even Joe could get Seymour to see Jimmy."

While Bentley and McEwen were campaigning for Jimmy at Warner Records, an unrelated development aided the cause: the comeback of another singer who had also paid deep dues—Ruth Brown.

"During what I call my wilderness years," says Ruth, "I'd gone through the same changes as Jimmy. I'd worked as a domestic, I'd mopped floors, I'd bathed the sick and elderly. I made do. In the mideighties, though, things started turning around. John Waters cast me in his hit movie *Hairspray* as Motormouth Maybelle. I also starred in *Black and Blue* on Broadway, where I won a Tony. At the same time, I met a lawyer named Howell Begle, who listened to my story about being cheated by record companies over the years. I wasn't just speaking for myself, but for hundreds of artists, Jimmy included. Howell took on the cause. He became our legal knight in shining armor. Through his killer persistence and use of public relations and public pressure, he turned the thing around. In 1988, Atlantic Records said it would recalculate royalties back to 1970. I got my first royalty check in more than twenty-five years. Even better, when we started up the Rhythm and Blues Foundation—in part to recognize and help artists fallen on hard times—Atlantic gave the first major corporate grant, nearly two million dollars."

"Eventually some of my royalties were also refigured," says Jimmy. "I never got huge checks, but I did receive some modest income as a result of the foundation's work."

The foundation would play a large role in Jimmy's future—as would Ruth's presence in New York.

"When *Black and Blue* was dark on Monday nights," says Jimmy, "Ruth played the Lone Star Roadhouse. It got so popular that the joint was called 'Ruth's House' on Mondays. Many a time she asked me to open for her. Everyone started coming 'round, and when Ruth couldn't make it, she loaned me her band and let me headline. The Lone Star was a good lift for me."

An even bigger lift was the Blue Note's Eighth Anniversary Celebration in November 1989, honoring Cab Calloway. Jimmy attended as a fan, but was called to the bandstand by Illinois Jacquet, who led a big band as the former Hampton vocalist sang "I Cried for You" and "All of Me." According to *Down Beat*, "the star-studded event brought together Tony Bennett, who sang 'Don't Get Around Much Anymore,' Jon Faddis with a rap in honor of emcee Illinois Jacquet, Milt Jackson, and Gerry Mulligan. But for pure emotion, the night belonged to singer Jimmy Scott, whose vocal styling bridged the changes of jazz into R&B and rock & roll; his falsetto a model for Frankie Lymon, Michael Jackson and even Diana Ross."

That Jimmy has never sung in falsetto—his high voice remains in his natural range—hardly matters. He was garnering good press. Gradually word was being spread. The forces of benevolence were gaining strength. When white blues singer Bonnie Raitt swept the 1989 Grammy awards, forging a remarkable comeback of her own, she used her new prestige to aid older black artists. Raitt became a power behind the Rhythm and Blues Foundation,

whose initial Pioneer Award winners, each of whom received
$15,000, included Jimmy, Ruth Brown, Charles Brown, the
Clovers, Etta James, LaVern Baker, Mary Wells, and Percy Sledge.

"I had never won an award in my life," he says, "and much less
one for cash. Soon as I won and said thank you to my peers, I knew
what to do with the money. I paid off my debts and then went out
and did what I'd been longing to do for years—I made a record."

At the end of the eighties, approaching sixty-five, Jimmy had
reason to hope. But hope had always been part of his emotional ar-
senal, whether reasonable or not.

J'S WAY

*J*immy and I are in Manhattan in late summer. The surround-
ings are serene. We sit on a bench in Gramercy Park and watch
little children scurry after pigeons. Jimmy sips hot tea, chain-
smokes, fidgets, and smiles adoringly at the kids, who approach
him without hesitation. They're drawn to his gentleness. In a couple of hours, we'll go to a studio in SoHo, where he'll begin a new
record. For now, though, his memories have rewound back to the
start of the nineties, when this intimidating city, for the first time
since the fifties, began opening its heart to Jimmy's sound.

"I found a few warm spots," he says. "The Lone Star was defi-
nitely one. Doc Pomus's apartment on Seventy-second and Broadway was another. Doc would have me over and invite every record
exec he knew, with the hope of getting me signed. It didn't work,
but I didn't lose any sleep. I could see things gradually opening up.
New York was more hospitable, but still beyond my means. For all
my little successes, I wasn't ready to move to the city. I started J's
Way Records in Jersey because studio time was cheaper over there.
Since I had some income, Earlene and I had to move out of the no-
income Arlington House. We found an apartment on South Munn
Avenue in East Orange, just outside Newark. That's where I put

together my first group—ever—the Jazz Expressions. For years I'd been bothered by rhythm sections who didn't understand my rhythms. I'd been disappointed that many of the young cats hadn't learned the lessons of the masters. But the Jazz Expressions rekindled my faith. I'd heard them around town and knew they'd fit with my style. Hilliard Greene, a brilliant bassist, eventually became my musical director and still anchors me to this day. Kenichi Shimazu, a wonderful pianist from Japan, had the right touch and those heavenly harmonies. With Brian Kirk on drums and Alvin Flythe on sax, I was set to record. It had been fifteen years since I'd cut *Can't We Begin Again* for Savoy. I called the new one *Doesn't Love Mean More.*"

Another unanswerable question, *Doesn't Love Mean More*, released in 1990, went nowhere. Jimmy's efforts as an entrepreneur were naive, patently unsuccessful, and, at the same time, endearingly genuine. J's Way was a record company in name only. There were no employees, no marketing, no distribution. Jimmy used his $15,000 Pioneer Award money to make not only *Doesn't Love Mean More*, but a dozen other no-budget CDs, using local Jersey studios that charged below-bargain rates.

"He was eager to help anybody who wanted to record," says Earlene. "If you had a hard-luck story, Jimmy would fall for it. He related to artists who were dying to record. He was an easy touch."

"I didn't do it to make money," Jimmy claims, "but to help others get recognition."

He chose little-known artists he had met over the years—singers Arthur Leeks, Connie Speed, Lander Coleman—aging veterans who, in Jimmy's estimation, needed a break. There were also J's Way CDs by tenor saxophonist Harold Ousley, pianist Kenichi Shimazu, the vocal–piano duo of Janet Tenjaz and Sven Anderson, and singer Larry Browne.

"Seems like Jimmy was recording everyone," recalls Earlene. "He had a deal with the studios where it hardly cost anything to make the albums. But without a real company behind them, they went nowhere. At the same time, there were lots of hangers-on around Jimmy. Jimmy had a hard time figuring out who was worthy and who wasn't. You see, the Pioneer Award got him all excited. His newfound fame got him overstimulated. Got him to thinking that he could do more business than he was capable of doing. It woke up all his hustling energy. Jimmy's strange about money. At times he doesn't seem to care. At times he can be a spendthrift. He can be generous. Then there are times when all he wants to do is save. He can also start making big plans to make big money. Those plans usually flop. One of those plans was the concert he produced in the early nineties."

Jimmy's prime effort in the promotional arena was something he called "The Infancy of Jazz: The Hottest Musical Revue to Hit Newark," featuring his J's Way artists at Newark Symphony Hall. The concert, like the CDs, was sparsely attended and lost money.

"Jimmy would call me and Doc," remembers Joel Dorn, "and talk about some fruit farmer he had just signed from Outer Slovenia who played great alto. As a producer, he didn't know what he was doing. He had a kind heart, he couldn't refuse anyone anything, but his instincts for production were nonexistent. His business instincts were even worse. He'd meet a bartender, and the next thing you know, the bartender would be booking his gigs. He changed managers and booking agents more frequently than he changed clothes. Underneath it all was that strange paradox that Doc had recognized years before—for all Jimmy's quiet tenacity, he had a powerful tendency to do himself in."

The most important J's Way product—*Doesn't Love Mean More*—is significant, not for the lackluster production or mediocre songs (all of which are originals by Jimmy, Leeks, or Shimazu), but because it announces Jimmy's return. His voice has changed, sometimes shockingly so. His pitch is no longer absolutely reliable, his vibrato no longer steady. He wavers; at times he falters. For those of us raised on the piercing purity of his voice and its soaring power, this new voice requires adjustment. At sixty-five, he is a different singer.

"I was a different man," he says. "I was an old man. Just as I didn't walk the same as I once did, I couldn't sing the same. But that was no reason not to perform. Senior artists have every right to express themselves. The world of music shouldn't be restricted to the young."

What remained, of course—what always remains—is the phrasing. Jimmy's genius resides in the high art of storytelling. Young or old, his voice is so wedded to his sincerity, so sweetly sad and poignantly introspective that technical deterioration—as in the case of the latter-day Billie Holiday—is hardly the point.

In spite of the disaster of J's Way, Jimmy scraped by. John Goddard, a record store owner and devotee of jazz and blues, booked him into clubs in northern California, opening a new market to the singer. In southern California, Ruth Brown arranged a gig for Jimmy in November 1991 at the prestigious Cinegrill in the Hollywood Roosevelt Hotel, where she had performed to standing-room-only crowds. She and Nancy Wilson threw a champagne party at the club to celebrate the opening-night performance of, as the invitation read, "their friend and inspiration—Little Jimmy Scott."

Writer Bill Reed was there:

"It was an auspicious moment, a glamorous affair. I had discovered Jimmy through *The Source* a few years earlier. I remember asking Gerald Wilson, one of the arrangers of Jimmy's Tangerine album, whatever happened to Jimmy. 'He's dead,' Wilson said. So when I learned he was alive and well, I was thrilled. We became fast friends. I'd never met an artist so friendly and open. On opening night, all the stars came out. Bonnie Raitt was there, and so was Paul Gayten, Jimmy's musical partner from the early fifties. There was widespread media coverage, big crowds and enthusiastic response. Jimmy looked resplendent in his tux. It was a happy occasion but also sad. For all the hoopla, Jimmy was so broke he didn't have enough money for food. I had to give him and Earlene fifty bucks to buy dinner. I also helped him set up a stand in the hotel lobby to sell his CDs and tapes."

In addition to *Love Doesn't Mean More*, Jimmy sold tapes on the J's Way label. *The Songs I Sing* and *Listen to Jimmy Scott Sing* were compilations of his Tangerine and Savoy material he duped off the original LPs. This was the low level of Jimmy's business affairs. On a far higher level, through Ruth Brown, he had forged an association with Howell Begle, the powerful Washington, D.C., attorney and major R&B fan. Begle was working miracles in reclaiming royalties for Ruth and other artists from the forties and fifties.

"I helped Ruth put her career back together in the early eighties," says Begle. "That's how I entered the universe of Doc Pomus and Jimmy Scott. I was motivated to make a difference, so, in addition to my work as unpaid director of the Rhythm and Blues Foundation, I did what I could to help individual artists. Many, like Jimmy and Charles Brown, were in desperate need of strong legal representation. I also tried to help in extra-legal ways. In 1989, I arranged for Jimmy and Charles to perform at Columbia University. And in the winter of 1990, Jimmy appeared with Ruth at the Kennedy Center for the Performing Arts in Washington. Before the concert, there was a reception with the Black Caucus, where Jimmy spoke with Congressman Louis Stokes, his classmate from Central High. Jimmy shined at these events. He was gracious and charming. After decades of playing dives, he was grateful for the high-prestige venues and handled himself with dignity. His friends and supporters remained baffled why in the world he couldn't get a record contract."

Although a few writers were slowly warming up to Jimmy, major critics continued to give him short shrift. In Will Friedwald's ambitious *Jazz Singing: America's Great Voices from Bessie Smith to Bebop and Beyond,* Jimmy is mentioned only in a passing foot-note, whereas Betty Carter, his cohort from Hamp's band, domi-nates an entire chapter. And in Gary Giddins's mammoth *Visions of Jazz: The First Century,* Jimmy's name never appears.

Even an appearance on the final episode of David Lynch's widely watched television series *Twin Peaks* in 1991 wasn't enough to convince music executives of his commercial viability. That appearance, however, marked Jimmy's entrance into the field of edgy art. In the coming decade, young hipsters—singers, actors, directors, and artists—would form an unofficial but wildly enthu-siastic Jimmy Scott fan club. They saw him as the ultimate outsider with an artistic sensibility defying middle-class conformity. His strange appearance, his pedigree credentials as an original bal-ladeer and bebopper, even the intriguing imperfections of his aging voice, resonated with a slew of influential rockers—Michael Stipe, Elvis Costello, Flea, Nick Cave, David Byrne, Bruce Springsteen, and especially Lou Reed—for whom intriguing imperfection is a hallmark of merit.

"David Lynch had come to the Cinegrill to see me perform," says Jimmy. "He told me afterwards that he liked my aura and had to have me in his show. Naturally I agreed. I wasn't too famil-iar with the program, but someone said that millions of young people watched it, so I was grateful for the shot. I didn't quite un-derstand the story line. David had me wearing a bow tie and singing to a dwarf."

In the twenty-ninth episode of *Twin Peaks*—"Beyond Life and Death"—Jimmy appears as a ghost in the Black Lodge, the most mysterious setting of this most mysterious series. Singing "Syca-more Trees," a song by Lynch, he looks ethereal.

As an avatar of post-noir cinematic narrative, Lynch under-stood something about Jimmy that struck a chord with other artists working on the fringes of conventional storytelling: Jimmy's sense of alienation, of lost love and romantic angst, was captivating. Those who rejected standard heroes accepted Jimmy as unequivocally heroic. Yet it wasn't a postmodern *artiste* or underground superstar who was responsible for Jimmy's breakthrough. Young hipsters remained a powerful part of his comeback, but they couldn't get him the one thing he'd been seeking since Atlantic dropped him eighteen years earlier—a major record deal. That job was left to an old hipster who, ironically enough, could only open the door by virtue of his own demise.

HAND FROM THE GRAVE

The breakthrough came on Sunday, March 17, 1991, in the Riverside Funeral Home on Amsterdam Avenue in New York City. It happened during the funeral service for Doc Pomus, the same Doc Pomus who had prophesied three and one-half years earlier in his letter to *Billboard* that Jimmy Scott would be mourned and re-membered only after death. Now it was Doc's death that set the scene for the emotional and financial transaction that Jimmy had sought so long.

"It was as though Doc could do in death what he couldn't do in life," says producer Joel Dorn. "The karmic implications were astounding. The funeral was the most amazing any of us had ever seen."

"In making arrangements for the service, I wanted to honor my father and the music he loved most," says Sharyn Felder. "The first person who came to mind was, of course, Jimmy Scott. Then I called two of Dad's closest collaborators—Doctor John, aka Mac Rebennack, and David Fathead Newman. It was important that the live music at the funeral be the music my father considered the most spiritual. Jimmy, Mac, and Fathead were the first three people I asked to perform. I remember Jimmy and his wife, Earlene, arriving before anyone else. They were at least ninety minutes early. Jimmy came and offered me a condolence hug. Then he and Earlene found a place in the back and sat quietly, their hands folded in their laps."

By the time the service began, hundreds of mourners had crowded into the sanctuary. Hundreds more were forced to stand outside and listen over loudspeakers. Doc Pomus was widely revered by the industry as a man of wisdom and integrity. He had attained the status of a music-business guru. "If the music business had a heart," said Jerry Wexler, "it would be Doc Pomus."

"Bookies, Broadway stars, moguls, elevator operators, rock icons—everyone was there," says Dorn. "Everyone loved Doc. We all took turns speaking. The high-toned eulogists, like Ahmet Ertegun, were overshadowed by the street people. A black bartender from Brooklyn broke it up when he said, 'In a box of cheap cigars, Doc Pomus was a five-dollar Corona.'"

"We were all deeply moved," remembers Seymour Stein, the head of Sire Records and the man whom Bill Bentley and Joe McEwen had been lobbying for years to sign Jimmy. "Doc was more than a gifted songwriter or close friend. He was a spirit, the true spirit of rhythm and blues. As I was sitting there and remembering what a life force this man had been, I began hearing someone singing 'Someone to Watch over Me.' I couldn't quite place it. The voice was very high, very haunting. I stretched to look, but the singer was too short to be seen. Mac was playing organ, and Fathead was playing tenor, but who was singing? It had more emotion and sweetness than I had ever heard. It was absolutely angelic. The voice was singing, 'I hope that she . . . turns out to be . . . someone to watch over me. . . . ' The old standard was being turned into a hymn. Other people were wondering about the singer as well. Soon whispers went from row to row—'Who is it?' 'Who's singing?'—when suddenly I realized it could only be Little Jimmy Scott. *My God*, I thought to myself, *no one in the world can sing this soulfully. I've got to sign him.*"

Stein doesn't recall the urgings from Bentley or McEwen. "If Joe wanted to sign him," says Stein, "Joe had the power to do so. To tell you the truth, until I went to Doc's funeral, I didn't think Jimmy Scott was even alive. It's not my practice to do business at funeral services, but as soon as this one was over, I made some quick inquiries and decided to offer the man a deal. It was criminal that someone singing so beautifully didn't have a major label behind him. I told my staff, 'We're not only signing him, but we're making a major commitment to Jimmy Scott.'"

"Quite literally," adds Bentley, "Doc Pomus did what none of us could do—force Seymour to hear Jimmy live. I'd always contended that this would do the trick. Well, it did. It didn't matter to me and Joe whether Seymour remembered how we bugged him. He signed Jimmy and put good money behind him."

"The day after the funeral, Seymour called me," says Jimmy. "I had him talking to my lawyer, Howell Begle. I saw the deal as Doc's last act on my behalf. His hand came out of the grave and tapped Seymour on the shoulder, saying, 'Give my pal a break.' At the same time, I couldn't get all giddy over the deal. Mourning requires time and patience, and I wanted to give Doc the respectful mourning he deserved."

"Jimmy and Earlene came to Dad's apartment on Broadway and Seventy-second Street every single night to sit shivah," says Sharyn Felder, describing the week-long period of formal mourning observed by Jews after the funeral of a close relative. "They arrived just as they'd arrived at the service—hours before anyone else, always formally dressed, extremely quiet and extremely polite. They'd sit in the corner, their hands folded. Jimmy would say how much he respected my father. Out of respect, I'd play all the Jimmy Scott records my father owned. As they played, Earlene would close her eyes, her head slowly turning to the rhythm of the songs, her lips mouthing the lyrics. She had every song memorized. There were tears in her eyes. I felt those tears had to do with her love of Jimmy. I've never seen anyone so deeply into a singer as

Earlene was into Jimmy. Now I know that during this period, Jimmy had learned that Sire wanted to sign him. Another artist might have boasted or bragged about the good news. But, in sitting shivah with us, night after night, Jimmy never mentioned himself, only the love he felt for my father."

"Warner Records treated Jimmy like a star," says Howell Begle, who cut the deal. "He was signed to their Sire label for one album with an option for four more. The initial advance was fifteen thousand dollars for the first album, twenty thousand for the second, twenty-five thousand for the third, thirty-five for the fourth, and forty-five for the fifth."

"It was far more money than I'd ever gotten for recording," Jimmy states unequivocally. "I was finally in the five-figure range. More important than the bread, though, was the idea that these people really understood me. They understood the musical mood I needed to do what I do best."

"In considering how to record Jimmy," says Stein, "I turned to Tommy LiPuma. He had the expertise and taste required."

LiPuma was the perfect choice, the one producer who would understand, and enlarge, the legacy of Jimmy's great Tangerine and Atlantic ballad sessions. Essentially a jazz producer, LiPuma had a particular knack for overlaying lush pop ingredients onto a jazz palette. Moreover, his productions—whether George Benson's *Breezin'*, Dr. John's *City Lights,* or João Gilberto's *Amoroso*—were unabashedly romantic, awash in extravagant strings, relaxed meters, and reflective moods. His best-selling productions for Diana Krall—*When I Look in Your Eyes* and *The Look of Love*—capture the same feeling of sensuous understatement.

"Jimmy is a genius," LiPuma is quick to say, "and I jumped at the chance to get him in the studio. The first job was to get the best rhythm section. I chose Kenny Barron, Stan Getz's favorite pianist and a model of sensitivity. With Ron Carter on bass, Grady Tate on drums, and John Pisano on guitar, the foundation was laid. I wanted Fathead Newman, who had known and played with Jimmy longer than anyone, to take the sax solos. And I wanted Johnny Mandel, Dale Oehler, and John Clayton to write the charts, knowing they had an especially fine feel for strings. As far as tunes, I had Jimmy sing over forty songs as piano/vocal demos. From those forty, we chose nine. If a tune wasn't right, he'd say, 'Man, I just can't get a relationship with that song.' So we dropped it. I wanted little variation in tempo because, in essence, we were sustaining a single frame of mind—that unique Jimmy Scott frame of mind."

"It was a pleasure from start to finish," says Jimmy. "Grady Tate got a little bit of an attitude, slightly reminding me of what I'd gone through with Charlie Mingus in the fifties. Grady was convinced he had the line on a rhythm I was missing, but Tommy cooled him out. Tommy made it clear the cats had to follow me."

"To be honest," admits LiPuma, "Jimmy had pitch problems that we had to straighten out afterwards electronically. Those were strictly technical matters, though. For feeling and phrasing, Jimmy's vocals were incomparable."

LiPuma's impeccable taste and generous sense of open space gave Jimmy the freedom he required. Though some fans were bothered by his unsteady vibrato, the album, called *All the Way*, was an unqualified triumph, representing the critical and commercial zenith of his career. Jimmy went for straight-ahead standards—"All the Way," "Angel Eyes," "Embraceable You" (the same song he cut live with Bird in 1950), "At Last," and, as a nod to Doc Pomus, "Someone to Watch over Me." Jimmy had recorded both "Someone to Watch over Me" and "I'm Getting Sentimental over You" on the Ray Charles–produced Tangerine album. And "Every Time We Say Goodbye" is his favorite track from the Ray Charles/Betty Carter album, also from the early sixties, creating a continuity that's especially satisfying.

"Many elements of my life came together in this record," he says. "It was the one time I had the right producer, the right songs, and the right company behind me."

At age sixty-eight, Jimmy had his first real success—at least by jazz standards—since he'd recorded "Everybody's Somebody's Fool" when he was twenty-five. *All the Way* would appear on the *Billboard* top-ten chart for jazz albums and go on to sell nearly forty-four thousand copies, a feat he'd never come close to duplicating. Warner publicists and distributors worked overtime to make certain the album was noticed. The credits listed McEwen, Bentley, and Stein as coexecutive producers.

"I consider those guys saints," says Howell Begle. "They spent some $190,000 on producing the record. They did it knowing that they'd never recoup. Money wasn't the point. Art was."

"We had a sense of history with *All the Way*," explains McEwen. "We had a tremendous sense of achievement when it was complete."

In October 1992, the album was launched with a party at the Bottom Line in New York City, where Jimmy performed. *Down Beat* gave *All the Way* five stars, its highest rating, calling Scott "one of the great jazz singers, fully worthy of comparison with Dinah Washington or Betty Carter." Phyl Garland, in *Stereo Review*, wrote, "While no recording could capture the full effect of Jimmy Scott live, this one comes close enough. Though some of the control has been eroded by age, his voice still retains its plangent quality, and the heart is still there, the soul, the artistry. That should be enough for anyone." Bob Blumenthal of the *Boston Globe* cited the album as "an instance of a legend meeting high expectations." In an overview of all Jimmy's recordings, *Stereophile* called *All the Way* "the defining record of his career."

His career had finally caught fire. Liz Smith devoted an entire column to Jimmy, hailing his comeback and calling his voice "one of the great mesmerizing instruments in contemporary music." She also mentioned "Street of Dreams," the song Jimmy recorded in 1992, with Fathead's fine accompaniment, for the LiPuma-produced soundtrack of the motion picture *Glengarry Glen Ross*. In the same period, Jimmy also performed on the soundtrack for the film *Rage in Harlem*. Celebrities asked to be photographed with him. Madonna saw him at New York's Tavern on the Green, where she claimed he was the only singer who could make her cry. Liza Minnelli said all other singers should kiss his feet. Jimmy's old friend Joe Pesci brought in Robert DeNiro, Christopher Walken, and Mikhail Barishnikov to hear him sing.

The stars came around to relish Jimmy's extraordinary theatricality. But one star did more than simply appreciate Jimmy's artistry; he made an enormous difference in Jimmy's career. For years Lou Reed had been hearing about Jimmy through Doc Pomus. Deeply moved by Jimmy's performance at Doc's funeral, Lou called him soon afterward, looking to collaborate.

"I didn't know too much about Lou," says Jimmy, "except that Doc had been his confidante. Doc would give him advice and try to keep him sane. Doc had told me that Lou had been in the Velvet Underground, he was a singer and a writer and a major cat in the world of arty rock and roll. Then I met Lou for the first time the day we buried Doc and later learned he was a serious poet."

"To hear Doc speak of Jimmy was one thing," says Reed. "But to hear Jimmy himself was quite another. I saw him as Hamlet and Lear rolled up in one. I was honored when he agreed to record with me and sing with me on a short tour of Europe to promote *Magic and Loss*, my album that came out in 1992."

"Lou dedicated *Magic and Loss* to Doc," explains Jimmy. "I sang some background parts on the record and did the same on the tour."

"There was some racist bullshit from the press on that tour," says Reed. "A writer in London said Jimmy looked like a bellboy on stage. But Jimmy was too dignified to be concerned with putdowns. He was above all that. During those European dates, he changed my life as a singer. Without offering formal lessons, he was tutoring me in the art. I learned more about vocalizing during that tour than any time before or since. I call Jimmy the Generous King because he bequeathed his approval of me. I consider my songs outsider stuff, and though he sings in a different genre, Jimmy is a complete outsider himself. On that level we connected. The crowd connected as well. Many hadn't heard of Jimmy, but when he came out, the sun came out."

"Anyone Lou introduced would have gotten a big audience reaction," claims Jimmy. "It was a helluva introduction to Europe—not through jazz but this far-out rock-and-roll poetry. That's the only way I could have developed a young audience—through Lou. The kids got to know me, and little by little, Europe started opening up to my music."

Jimmy's role in *Magic and Loss* is extremely limited. He repeats the enigmatic line "I want all of it—not some of it" in the song "Power and Glory." On the live show, Jimmy's participation was also restricted to a few numbers. "I felt as though the roles should have been reversed," says Reed. "Jimmy should have been the predominant voice, with me in the background."

"I was cool singing background," Jimmy contends. "Anything to get me over to Europe. Anything to keep the career rolling. Besides, Doc liked Lou. Doc calmed him down. I felt like Doc expected me to do the same."

"I saw there were times when Jimmy was calm and times when he wasn't," says Reed. "He's really two guys. The first is almost beatific. When he drinks, though, he becomes that other guy. A few times I saw that other guy in Europe. It didn't impact his performances, but it did make me appreciate his complexity."

A video clip of Jimmy performing with Reed leaves a strange impression. Dressed casually, Jimmy looks and sounds out of place next to the underground rocker. He doesn't get the quirky syncopations or the enigmatic lyrics. Nonetheless he gives it his all—Jimmy always gives it his all—but the two make an especially odd couple. One wonders what Jimmy, accustomed to the straight-ahead sincerity of the standards he'd been singing for fifty years, makes of Reed's ironic sensibility.

"There's a part of Lou that's a little twisted," says Jimmy, "and a part that's very sweet. Even when I didn't understand his lyrics, though, I understood his genuine feeling for me. And I'll always be grateful that he introduced me to Europe."

In the early nineties, in addition to Europe, Jimmy toured Japan. The gigs were arranged by jazz producer Todd Barkan, a longtime Jimmy Scott admirer.

"Jimmy took me along," remembers Earlene. "It was a good trip because the Japanese fell in love with him. Some Americans see Jimmy as strange, but not the Japanese. They saw his beauty. I was happy for his success even though I felt him moving away from me. Our marriage had become strained. So much was happening so quickly that Jimmy was getting more high-strung, more nervous. When he was on the road he was okay. But when he came home and said he had to relax, that meant liquor and pot. That stuff didn't relax him. In my opinion, that stuff only agitated him.

"When my uncle died, Jimmy really got worked up because he knew an inheritance was involved. Through relatives, I learned that my uncle was my father, a fact my mother had been denying all my life—and still does. Well, as my husband, Jimmy figured he was entitled to the inheritance. He went over to my uncle's place and took whatever he wanted. He hauled off the furniture and took the mirrors off the wall. He moved the stuff to an apartment he had rented on Mount Prospect Street. He moved in alone, without me. He said he needed time to think things over. He wanted his space and his own privacy. I've always been willing to give Jimmy whatever he wants, so I didn't argue. But I couldn't deny what was happening. I saw the move as proof of something I'd long believed. Jimmy has never loved me, not like I love him. That makes me sad, but it doesn't make me love him any less."

"For all the good things Earlene did for me," says Jimmy, "I left her because I felt she was too tied to her mother. I saw that going into the marriage but was hoping it would change. It never did. Fact is, it got worse. Earlene's mother was always in the middle of our relationship. Earlene could never leave that woman. She still can't. I felt like I was the man in the marriage and deserved my wife's full attention. But it was her mother calling the shots."

"I think Earlene's mother reminded Jimmy of our grand-mother, the one who rejected our mom and tried to run our mom's life," speculates Jimmy's sister Adoree. "It's easy to set Jimmy off, especially when it comes to family issues. And Earlene's mom sure did set him off."

The mystery of Jimmy's marriages—and of all his romantic liaisons—remains a mystery. He undoubtedly saw many of these relationships in a practical light: Channie would become a barber and help his financial position; as a nurse, Ruthie would bring in considerable income; and as an untiring booster of his career, Earlene would give him the support he had lacked. At the same time, he yearned for domestic tranquillity. He wanted to trust these women to bring him happiness. That trust, though, proved elusive.

Things were moving quickly. It had been seven years since Earlene called WBGO, the Newark jazz station, and declared that Jimmy Scott was not dead. That single call set off a series of events that gradually led to a comeback of considerable magnitude. Jimmy's ambition had been reawakened. His art was being valued across generational lines. The media, once indifferent, had embraced his story. He went from living on social security to earning fifty to sixty thousand dollars a year. How did he handle it? He was certainly grateful. Gratitude is as much a part of Jimmy's makeup as his penchant to languish behind the beat. But he was also anxious because the tempo was picking up at a rate that left him uncomfortable.

"After all that waiting," he says, "things started popping quicker than I had expected. I had to make my adjustments and hurry along. Here's Europe, here's Japan, here's a record deal, here's a movie soundtrack. After so many years in isolation, being in demand was strange. My policy, though, was clear—I took what was offered and charged ahead."

A fundamental change in rhythm, especially for a sixty-eight-year-old man, can be disconcerting. Jimmy adjusted to the change as well as he could. But the result was a profound confusion. Who to trust professionally? Who to trust personally? He needed fresh energy to put together a career at an age when most men are deep into retirement. Miraculously, he found that energy. But with it came a slew of new problems.

SOUND OF PAIN

Separated from Earlene, living alone in Newark, periodically switching agents and managers, Jimmy struggled to sustain his comeback and secure his finances. Not since the fifties had he worked so consistently. The buzz about his return to the business was still strong.

In January 1993, his celebrity was bolstered by an invitation, arranged through the good offices of Howell Begle, by newly elected President Bill Clinton to perform at his first inaugural ball at Washington D.C.'s Union Station. Jimmy appeared on stage with Manhattan Transfer and sang "Someone to Watch over Me." That same year, Jimmy entertained at the Alec Baldwin/Kim Basinger wedding in East Hampton. And Bruce Springsteen featured him on the soundtrack of the hit movie *Philadelphia*.

"When Tom Hanks asks Denzel Washington to take his case and Denzel turns him down," says Jimmy, "you can see by the look on Tom's face he's about to burst—that's when I start singing. I was the sound of his spirit crying. Bruce brought me in as the sound of pain."

Madonna was also moved by Jimmy's plaintive style. She visited him during one of his New York engagements and used him in her video *Secret*.

"It was shot at the Lenox Lounge, where I was sitting with two chicks in this thirties décor," Jimmy explains. "I didn't sing or speak, but God bless Madonna for putting me on MTV."

When Tony Bennett did the *MTV Unplugged* show in the mid-nineties, it sent Bennett's career skyrocketing. The MTV audience embraced Bennett with unrestrained enthusiasm. In a far more modest way, Jimmy benefited from the same trend. The nineties were shaping up as a decade steeped in retro. The lounge lizard and the saloon singer—Sinatra's favorite self-characterization—were being celebrated as never before. Movies like *Swingers* bathed in the nostalgia of an earlier era when the Rat Pack defined cool and balladeers wore their hearts on their sleeves. The fad produced its fair share of frauds, but among the genuine articles, Jimmy Scott, along with Shirley Horn, held high honors.

Horn's comeback paralleled Jimmy's. Having made a brief stir in the early sixties, she disappeared from national view, only to reemerge in the mideighties, when a series of fine albums on Verve revived her career and gave her a new audience. She performed on the same *Glengarry Glen Ross* soundtrack that Jimmy did. And in 1992, her masterpiece, *Here's to Life,* was arranged by Johnny Mandel, who also arranged several songs on Jimmy's *All the Way,* released the same year. The albums are close in quality and sensibility. Jimmy and Shirley sang on the same nightclub circuit and in many of the same festivals. And perhaps more than any other female jazz singer, Horn shared Jimmy's penchant for slower-than-slow tempos and delayed back-phrasing. Both singers also bring to mind the latter-day Lady Day, the Billie Holiday of the poignant *Lady in Satin* period. Scott and Horn mirror one another with intriguing distortion: Jimmy's high, male voice often sounding female; Shirley's low, female voice sometimes sounding male; Jimmy's extroverted emotionality; Shirley's salty shyness; two singers whose uncanny ability to invent melodies and rearrange rhythms is the product of long lives spent in isolated reflection.

For all the similarities, the sales of the two albums differed sharply: *Here's to Life* sold 135,500 copies, whereas *All the Way* sold a little more than one-third that number. But *All the Way* garnered Jimmy his first-ever Grammy nomination. He attended the ceremonies in February 1993 in Los Angeles, where Bobby McFerrin won the award for best jazz vocalist. By then Jimmy's comeback seemed to have peaked. Jazz critic Gene Santoro attended Jimmy's performance at Tavern on the Green in Manhattan ("Scott wrung every number dry of nuance"), and noted that the club was half-empty. Matthew Buzzell, a gifted filmmaker who would begin directing *If You Only Knew*, an insightful documentary on Jimmy in 1999, attended some of those same dates.

"I was in awe of his persona," says Buzzell. "I'd never met anyone like him. No self-consciousness, no hubris. His talent seemed matched by his humility. He didn't know me from Adam, I was just another twenty-something fan, but he treated me like a long-lost friend. I was also stunned to see that Arthur Leeks, a singer Jimmy had signed to his own label, had set up a table at the club, where he was selling J's Way CDs and tapes."

In spite of his major-league deal, Jimmy continued to operate in minor-league ways, peddling his own J's Way recordings. He continued producing J's Way records by Harold Ousley and Connie Speed, in addition to holding homegrown concerts in Newark featuring his J's Way roster. All of this cost him money.

"In my own little way," he says, "I was still trying to build up my own little company."

That little company would soon fold. Not ready to abandon all his entrepreneurial ambitions, though, Jimmy bought a used limousine with the idea of starting a side business.

"It was a big 1985 Lincoln," Jimmy relates. "The idea was to turn the business over to my brother Kenny. I partnered up with a friend who put up half the money."

"I remember Jimmy coming by and picking us up in this funky limo," says Sharyn Felder. "The driver was so small I was afraid he couldn't see over the steering wheel. Jimmy was so sweet, though. He wanted to take us around town in style."

"I had hopes for a good supplementary income," Jimmy contends. "But before we really got started, my partner smashed up the limo. There went the business. . . . "

"Seemed like everyone had a scheme for Jimmy to sponsor," says brother Kenny. "Everyone had a scheme for him to get rich."

Many of his friends agreed and worried about his being exploited.

"Some slick dude talked him into buying a house in Vegas," says Lou Reed. "He got Jimmy to put down twenty-five thousand, convincing him that this was the purchase price when it was really just the down payment."

"I know the difference between a down payment and a purchase price," Jimmy insists. "It angers me when people presume I've been taken. I decided not to move to Vegas, not because I was hoodwinked, but because spending two hundred and fifty thousand on a house was just out of my range. For a while I thought getting off the East Coast and living in the desert might be relaxing. The warm weather might do me good. But the deal never went through, and I only lost a few bucks."

Meanwhile, his management relationships remained volatile. After working with Harriet Sternberg, he switched to Lupe DeLeon, who managed, among others, Etta James and Charles Brown.

"Jimmy liked to work," says DeLeon, "and we did the best we could. We booked him into prestige venues, like the Venetian Room at the Fairmont Hotel in San Francisco. Everyone in our office loved him and worked hard to find him gigs, but in spite of his big media comeback, club owners were still reluctant. He was still an oddity and, outside of New York and L.A., not a proven draw. Booking Jimmy was a struggle."

"Jimmy was a delight," exclaims Ross Locke, who worked out of DeLeon's office as the singer's tour manager. "He's a wonderful human being, and we were dedicated to his career. Jimmy just doesn't become another artist to manage; he becomes a cause. He never missed a performance, never failed to deliver, but when he was off the road and we needed to talk business, we knew to call him before noon. After that, he was usually too wasted to be coherent."

Despite everything—the busted limo, the aborted move to Vegas, the failure of J's Way, the drinking—Jimmy's art never faltered. His second Warner album, *Dream*, a far more modest affair than *All the Way*, was recorded in New York City during a blizzard in the winter of 1993. It's an exquisitely languorous colloquy between Jimmy and a select group of jazz veterans, including Junior Mance, Ron Carter, Red Holloway, and Milt Jackson.

"We were all huddled up in the studio," says Jimmy, "where making music was our way of beating back the freezing world outside. Maybe that's why the music sounds so warm. You can also feel the warm friendship I had with my friend Milt Jackson, who I knew from the forties. I love hearing vibes behind me, that sound that Hamp first started, and Milt is up there with the greats. The company proposed that the sessions be low-budget and simple, and I went along with the program."

The least demanding of artists, Jimmy usually goes along with the program. This program involved drastically cutting production overhead.

"Despite the reviews and the Grammy nomination, Warner couldn't recoup the cost of *All the Way*," says Howell Begle. "So we understood when the second album involved only a rhythm section and a couple of horns."

Devoted friend and supporter Jimmy McDonough served as executive producer, and Mitchell Froom was called to produce. Froom was an eccentric choice. Known for his work with decidedly nonjazz artists like Los Lobos, Crowded House, Sheryl Crow, and Elvis Costello, Froom proved a good choice. He had the right feel. He created a winter solstice of sorrow, a snowfall of solemn ballads, sparsely charted or not charted at all, and allowed Jimmy to select songs from his deepest past—"Talk of the Town," "Laughing on the Outside," "I'm Through with Love," "You'll Never Miss the Water" (with Froom himself playing a most mournful organ)—all numbers that Jimmy had recorded in the fifties. Froom created an ambiance that allowed the singer to do what he does best: suspend time, liberate himself from the tension of time, treating it not as a restriction but as a license to wander at will.

"There was little editing," says Froom. "Jimmy did the songs in one or two takes. With a singer like Jimmy, you don't punch in one or two notes. As a storyteller, Jimmy has a continuum, a style of musical narration that is tied together like a tapestry. If you pull out one element and try to alter it, the tapestry unravels. There are times when he sings slightly off tune, but I didn't object. Being strictly in tune can be overvalued. Many of the jazz greats are a little sharp or flat. That, too, is a unique part of the power and poignancy of jazz storytelling. The entire album is, after all, Jimmy's sense of what it means to dream."

Dream is an apt title. The dreamy packaging is the finest of any Scott album, an atmospheric photo essay of a snowbound city at night, Jimmy walking through the lonely landscape, a pilgrim in search of the same bliss he had sought throughout life: domestic peace.

"I didn't have peace with Earlene," he confesses. "And I can't say it was her fault. Because she's a caretaker and a nurse, she just had to nurse her mom to the point where I didn't feel like I had a wife."

Although he separated from Earlene in 1993, he didn't file for divorce until 2001.

"After he left me, he started calling and saying he wanted me back," says Earlene. "But by then it was too late. I'd gone back to be with my mother, who really did depend on me more than ever. I regretted what happened. I see Jimmy as a good man, a gentle man. Oh, there were a few times when he got wild and once even violent. When I asked him not to step on a new bedspread, he grew defiant and hauled off and smacked me, though it really didn't hurt. What hurt was his mistrust. He didn't trust that I loved him as much as I loved my mother. And he didn't always trust me with money. Maybe because of his other women—like Channie and Ruth—he just couldn't trust any woman. I don't know. All I know is that he's a complicated guy who's not easy to live with. To writers and fans, he's a doll. But to the ladies who love him, the ones who live with him, he's a piece of work."

THE JAZZ LIFE REDUX

*B*y the midnineties, Jimmy's comeback story had been told and retold in any number of Sunday supplements. He sang on the Charlie Rose television show. His old recordings were being reissued in new packaging. *The Source* sessions were re-released twice—first with bonus tracks on *Jimmy Scott: Lost and Found*, by Rhino in 1993, and in 2001 in original form with its original title on Joel Dorn's Label M. In 1999, Billy Vera's comprehensive *Little Jimmy Scott: The Savoy Years and More* (Atlantic) was issued, as well as *Everybody's Somebody's Fool* (Universal), a retrospective of Jimmy's first recordings on Decca and Coral.

Meanwhile, his new recordings hit a sales snag. *Dream* sold only half as well as *All the Way*. The Warner promotional machine had worked on *All the Way* with full force. But by the time *Dream* came out, the buzz had died down and Jimmy had returned to the role he played so long at Savoy—a singer garnering great professional respect but making little commercial impact. Finally, in assessing Jimmy's modest sales, one is forced to conclude that the fault lies neither with the production nor the promotion. For all his wonders as a transcendent artist, Jimmy simply has limited appeal. "Not everybody gets him," says Joel Dorn. "Not everyone wants to deal with the pain and angst he brings to a song. Listeners like it easy. Well, there's nothing easy about Jimmy Scott."

His third Warner release, *Heaven*, a somewhat lugubrious collection of spiritually minded songs released in 1996, dropped even more precipitously to sales of a little more than six thousand. In spite of its lukewarm reception, Jimmy was especially enthusiastic about the album.

"I love *Heaven* because my producer, Craig Street, teamed me with pianist Jackie Terrasson," says Jimmy. "Jackie had been with Betty Carter. Betty ran the best training camp for jazz musicians since Art Blakey. Through Betty, Jackie learned everything there is to know about accompanying singers. The man gave me his heart. Most of the record is just him and me, with minimal or no rhythm. The only problem was my cold. I'd just played Tavern on the Green the week before. I thought I needed a rest between the gig and the sessions, but Warner had it scheduled and said changing would cost too much. I didn't argue."

In spite of Terrasson's inventive play and the strong support of Hilliard Greene, musical director of Jimmy's touring combo, the Jazz Expressionists, *Heaven* suffers from a string of amorphous songs ill suited to Jimmy's style. Jimmy requires standards, motifs that resonate with emotional history. He also requires rhythmic syncopation as a counterpoint to his rhythmic idiosyncrasies. On *Heaven*, he sounds lost.

"At that point we were lost for ideas," says Joe McEwen, then Warner's A&R man. "After *Heaven*, we didn't really have anywhere else to go with Jimmy. Our enduring accomplishment was *All the Way*. But to duplicate that record was impossible."

After three albums, Warner dropped Jimmy in 1997, declining its final two options. Given the downward slide of sales, the move hardly came as a shock.

"I was disappointed but I understood," Jimmy says with typical equanimity. "A new regime of executives had taken over, who didn't have the same feeling for me or for jazz. By then, Seymour Stein had lost interest. Actually I didn't see that much of Seymour after he signed me at Doc's funeral. There was only that one warm meeting. Years passed before I heard from him again. I remember singing somewhere in Paris, when I looked up and saw Seymour's smiling face. He said wonderful things about me and then disappeared into the crowd."

The young hipsters helped keep him visible. Flea, the spirited bassist of the Red Hot Chili Peppers, accompanied Jimmy on an improbable version of Captain and Tennille's "Love Will Keep Us Together." Jimmy and Michael Stipe of R.E.M. sang "Ill Wind" as a duet on the soundtrack of the film *Albino Alligator*. Actor Ethan Hawke gave him a small part in *Chelsea Walls*, a low-budget movie he was directing. And saxophonist David Sanborn had him sing a heart-stopping version of "For All We Know" on *Pearls*, an album produced by Tommy LiPuma and Johnny Mandel.

"The Warner rejection wasn't the end of the world," Jimmy reflects. "I had faced a lot worse in my career. Besides, I could still make a decent five-figure income. By then I was a semiregular on the jazz club circuit. I had no reason to complain. Especially when I was offered a deal by a small label, Artists Only Records. They wanted me to cut rock songs—no jazz tunes, no standards. They thought it would appeal to a younger crowd. And I thought, *Why not?* The advance was decent—ten thousand dollars—and the record, which had me singing with a string quartet, was interesting."

The album, released in 1998, was called *Holding Back the Years*, after the Simply Red song by Mick Hucknall. In addition to the title tune, Jimmy sang compositions by John Lennon ("Jealous Guy"), Elvis Costello ("Almost Blue"), Prince ("Nothing Compares 2U"), Elton John ("Sorry Seems to Be the Hardest Word"), and Bryan Ferry ("Slave to Love"). Stalwart Scott supporters of the old school didn't like the record. Billy Vera, busy compiling a superb three-CD box of Jimmy's work on Savoy, found it "unlistenable."

Joel Dorn, busy preparing a reissue of *The Source*, called it "the wrong songs for the wrong singer—Jimmy trying to be something he just ain't." Jimmy's sensibility seems to clash with that of the songwriters. And the lack of rhythmic structure, reminiscent of *Heaven*, leaves him at loose ends. The record *is* rough going. If anything, one would guess the album would have damaged his career.

That guess would have been wrong. In spite of a smaller distribution network, *Holding Back the Years* outsold *Heaven* two to one. What's more, it not only pleased a young rock market, but enjoyed considerable popularity in Europe. When I accompanied Jimmy to Italy in 2000, his promoter, Isio Saba, set me straight: "If it weren't for *Holding Back the Years*, Jimmy wouldn't have the European audience he enjoys today. Singing that material brought out a dimension in him, a flair for drama, that reminded us of Charles Aznavour and Edith Piaf. We saw Jimmy Scott as a great tragedian. You call them cabaret singers; we call them actors, actors with the gift of song."

By the end of the decade, Europe became a steady source of work for Jimmy. He was invited to festivals through the Continent, made a splash at Montreux, and was especially popular in Italy.

In 2001, Saverio Palatella, an Italian designer of elegant, high-fashion women's clothes, invited Jimmy to sing at the heavily publicized presentation of his fall line in Milan. "When I heard him sing 'The Crying Game' from *Holding Back the Years,* I was transfixed," says Palatella. "I'd never heard a voice like that. I had to learn about him. I was dying to meet him. He gave me a feeling no other musical artist had ever given. He inspired my designs and soon had me designing clothes just for him."

"I was facing the ocean at an outdoor festival, singing in southern Spain," Jimmy remembers, "watching the moon race across the sky. It was a beautiful moment. The audience knew me, not from the old stuff, but from the songs by Prince and Bryan Ferry. It was then that I realized I made the right decision to take that deal on Artists Only."

But the simple truth is that Jimmy—leading the jazz life, making it up as he goes along—takes virtually any deal. He took the Artists Only deal, not just because he needed the money, but because no one else was offering. He sang the songs suggested by *Holding Back the Years* producers Gerry McCarthy and Dale Ashley for the same reason that he sang "Everybody's Somebody's Fool" forty-seven years earlier: It was a chance to record, a way to survive. Not one to overscrutinize material, Jimmy's easygoing way in the studio may have misguided him when, during his Savoy days, he agreed to interpret material beneath him. But that same attitude of adaptability resulted in expanding his appeal overseas. It wasn't a conscious decision but more the work of a man who simply loves to work.

The freewheeling jazz life also led to another surprise—Jimmy's move from Newark back to Cleveland in 1997. It had been more than a decade since he'd lived in the city of his birth.

"Newark was always good to me," Jimmy is quick to say, "but it didn't hold the appeal it once had. My thing with Earlene was over. I was living in an apartment but longed for a house. Once I got over the crazy idea of living in Las Vegas, I started to reason things out: For seventy or eighty thousand dollars, where could you still buy a nice house in a good neighborhood with two or three bedrooms and a little lawn out front and in back? I thought of Cleveland. I thought of my brothers and my sisters. I thought of going home and being close to family. The winters were still cold and the city still wasn't rolling out the red carpet for me. But the airport was big enough for me to go wherever I needed. And there were a few signs that I was still welcome."

The first was a cover story, "The Comeback Kid," in the Sunday magazine of the *Cleveland Plain Dealer*. Later, another cover story, Carlo Wolff's "Little Big Man," appeared in *Cleveland Scene*.

"As far as I was concerned," says Jimmy, "they were both a day late and a dollar short. I always appreciate the publicity—I'd be a fool not to—but it took the city an awfully long time to give me any recognition. I remember being invited to a Grateful Dead concert in Cleveland where Bob Weir invited me up to sing with the band. The next day a local paper described me as an unknown female vocalist. I thought of that song by Percy Mayfield, 'Stranger in My Own Home Town.'"

Jimmy and I are standing in front of the attractive house he purchased in 1997 in Euclid, a quiet community alongside Lake Erie just east of Cleveland. It's a solidly middle-class home on a solidly middle-class street, a well-maintained brick structure, two stories plus finished basement, finished attic, glassed-in porch, and white picket fence. The neighborhood is predominantly white—Jimmy reports that prejudiced neighbors shot BBs through his windows when he first arrived—with a smattering of black and Latino families. The place is big enough for a large family. It's an unlikely domicile for a single man. But if that man is Jimmy Scott, and if the place reminds him, as he is quick to say, of the house he and his family had to abandon when his mother died in 1938, it all makes sense.

"I'm working hard to pay off the house," says Jimmy, "so they can never take it away from me. I'm trying to do something my father could never do—own something of substance. I've lost houses to women before, but this is a house I intend to keep. This is what I've been working for."

In retrospect, the move back to Cleveland seemed to coincide with Jimmy's move toward a more stable life. In his seventies, his search for a simple, happy home took on new importance. In 1999, through writer Richard Skelly, he finally found a manager whom he trusts completely. He calls Maxine Harvard "the only real guide I've ever had in my career, and certainly the most honest."

"I worked in New Jersey a large part of my life," says Maxine. "And I was there at the Mirage in Newark when Jimmy first reappeared on the scene in 1985. I adore him personally and artistically. But when he asked me to manage him, I did so on the condition that his drinking not interfere with his performances or our business. He said it wouldn't, and for the most part it hasn't."

Maxine brought him to Todd Barkan, a producer with a clear vision for recording Jimmy. His interest was in preserving the essence of Jimmy as a pure jazz singer. In a trilogy of meticulously crafted records made for Fantasy—*Moon Indigo, Over the Rainbow,* and *But Beautiful*—Barkan surrounded Jimmy with the finest studio musicians, creating an ambiance of excellence and a repertoire taken from the Great American Songbook. Barkan's late-century productions were similar to Norman Granz's fabled mid-century productions of Billie Holiday—a singer given the space to breathe, a company of seasoned and sympathetic cohorts given room to stretch, and a slate of time-tested standards. Lovingly backed by Wynton Marsalis, Hank Crawford, Joe Beck, Eric Alexander, Lewis Nash, Cyrus Chestnut, George Mraz, David Fathead Newman, Bob Kindred, Lew Soloff, and Renee Rosnos, Jimmy's Fantasy albums acquired the status of classics.

The net sales of each of these releases have been modest, in the range of five thousand to ten thousand copies, but Fantasy, a major jazz label, promoted him like a star and the reviews were invariably superb. Jimmy's career attained a quiet steadiness he had never before enjoyed. For many years, he kept the same members of his fine backing band, the Jazz Expressionists—pianist Michael Kanan, bassist Hilliard Greene, drummer Dwayne Broadnax, saxophonist Justin Robinson. (Jon Regen replaced Kanan in 2002.) Jimmy and the group worked the United States, Japan, Europe, and Latin America with regularity. He was the subject of a major documentary *Why Was I Born?* directed by Melodie McDaniel and broadcast on Bravo cable television in 1998. Fifty-one years after the start of his career, *Down Beat* finally devoted a feature to him (though it was Diana Krall who graced the cover). He even won an award, his first ever: Best Male Jazz Vocalist, presented by the Jazz Journalists Association. He was not getting rich, still worked tirelessly to earn at most eighty thousand dollars a year, but had survived with a certain aplomb. And yet, during the most recent years that I interview him about his life and times . . .

He fidgets. He scratches his palms until they bleed. During long afternoons at home in Cleveland, he might start drinking and smoking and falling into semicoherent reveries about his former loves and future plans. Mostly, though, he is clearheaded. He sits calmly and listens to the ballads of Ben Webster and Dexter Gordon. He speaks of his great family trauma, the one from sixty years ago that destroyed sibling unity, as though it happened yesterday. His family remains the source of ongoing frustration, late-night soliloquies, and quiet ranting about what went wrong and what still goes wrong. His obsessions remain obsessions—mother Justine, father Arthur, his brothers and sisters. There is also the matter of romantic love. Late in the course of his life, he has entered a new and all-consuming relationship with a white woman in her fifties who once trained wolves. To see Jimmy through her eyes, to hear the story of their love affair, is to grapple with the question of whether or not this book will have a happy ending.

JEANIE

When Jeanie McCarthy speaks of the love nest, she is referring to the third story/attic that has been converted to a large, cozy bedroom she and Jimmy share in his Euclid home. The room is awash in purple and lavender, Jeanie's favorite colors. There are purple Tiffany lamps, purple picture frames holding images of Jimmy at every juncture of his career. The focal point is the queen-size bed covered with a lavender bed comforter and oversized matching pillow shams. The scent of lavender incense fills the air. The stereo continually plays CDs by Jimmy, Dinah, Billie, Big Maybelle, Walter Jackson, Marvin Gaye. Elaborate scrapbooks, put together by Jeanie, document Jimmy's career. One wall contains cases housing all of Jimmy's releases since the early fifties on 45s, LPs, cassettes, and CDs. Laminated Jimmy Scott album covers are strewn here and there. Purple candles glow. Jimmy and Jeanie are sitting on the bed, openly affectionate with one another, sometimes embarrassingly so.

"No woman," says Jimmy, "has ever taken the time to study my life like Jeanie. No woman has ever taken the time to set up my house like Jeanie has done. Her artistic touches are everywhere. Even with my wives, we never talked in depth, never had two- or three-hours discussions about my past or my relationship to God. Jeanie and I don't just listen to music together, we listen to an individual instrument on the track—the violin, the harp, the flute. Jeanie hears everything. She hears my heartbeat. She was the first woman in my life who wrote me letters of pleading love."

Jean McCarthy was born July 23, 1946, and was raised in small towns in northern New Jersey. She tells her story in the East Coast accent of a young girl. The sweetness of her personality mirrors the sweetness of Jimmy's. When she started dating Jimmy, a friend told her, "Now you'll be called Little Jeanie, just like he's Little Jimmy."

"Jimmy was always part of my consciousness," she says. "In the fifties, it was his voice singing 'Someone to Watch over Me.' In the sixties, it was 'The Masquerade Is Over.' Now he calls me his 'rock and roll baby,' but my thing was always rhythm and blues. He doesn't distinguish between the two. I do. I was an R&B fanatic. Through sheer persistence, I met James Brown as well as James's family. James became a close friend. I spent lots of time with him in his house on Linden Boulevard in St. Albans, Queens. I called him 'Skates' because of how he slid across stage as if on ice. Jackie Wilson was another friend. I frequently visited him when he came to the city and stayed at the Alvin Hotel. Jackie had a golden heart, and I loved him. I had a Wall Street office job by day but at night I lived the R&B life. I became the common-law wife of George 'Smitty' Smith of the great soul group the Manhattans. Smitty is now singing with the angels. He passed away from a brain hemorrhage on December 16, 1970. After his death, I continued living in his home with his mother, who remains extremely close to me today.

"I swore never again to get involved with the world of music and, instead, turned to animals, the other great passion of my life. I learned to train German shepherds and Alaskan malamutes. That led to an interest in wolf hybrids and pure wolves. I worked with renowned researchers in the field and went west, where I learned about wolf preservation and habitat. The best part was going to the Yukon, befriending a dog musher, driving a dogsled, and interacting with the wolves, even raising a pack of my own. I became a wolf behaviorist and felt a mysterious kinship with their strong and gentle souls. I learned that if you love and respect them for who they are and not try to change, humanize, or dominate them, they'll respect and love you as well.

"After Smitty, there were two other powerful, long-term relationships with men, but by the late eighties the second of those romances had run out of steam. I began seeing notices around the city for club appearances by Jimmy Scott. I found some of his early records. The sound of his young voice thrilled me. When I heard *All the Way*, the thrill was even greater. He'd aged with a maturity that melted my heart. Through Felix Hernandez, then the deejay of WBGO's *Rhythm Revue,* the best R&B show ever, I met Steve Nicholas, who managed an R&B oldies store in midtown called Downstairs Records. Steve was a friend of Jimmy and kept encouraging me to see him live. By then I was listening to Jimmy night and day. I saw him on PBS, singing 'Sorry Seems to Be the Hardest Word' from *Holding Back the Years,* on *Sessions at Fifty-fourth Street* when David Byrne was the host. I had heard everything he had recorded and read everything written about him. Watching him on TV, I remember thinking, *He looks so frail and weak; he's depressed; his emotional needs aren't being met; he looks lonely and in need of love. I'd better hurry and see him because he's not going to be around for long.*

"It wasn't until August 1999 when I actually went to hear him in person. I was living in Jersey City, where I was partners in an auto repair business. Turned out to be one of the most memorable nights of my life. There I was, standing outside Birdland, waiting for Steve and his girlfriend, Mary, when here comes this cat diddy-boppin' down the street. He looked straight out of the fifties, a shiny satin blue do-rag tied around his head. I couldn't take my eyes off Jimmy Scott. My impression from TV was all wrong.

Jimmy was energized like a teenager, happy and friendly and frisky as a kitten. He gave me the smile of life and, after the show, when Steve introduced us, he gave me a warm hug. Our cheeks pressed together like magnets. Electricity shot through my body. My heart was racing, my knees were weak. I was a goner. I couldn't help myself; I turned to kiss his cheek, and as I did, he turned towards me. Unexpectedly our lips touched. Inside my head he was singing the song 'My Foolish Heart . . . beware my foolish heart.'

"I couldn't sleep that night. For the weeks that followed, I did nothing but think about Jimmy. I bought a purple notebook, where I started jotting down ways to help his career. I started making my Jimmy Scott scrapbooks. After six weeks, I couldn't take it anymore and asked Steve for Jimmy's address in Cleveland. I wrote him a long letter, pouring my heart out, explaining that because we're both Cancers, our signs are in close alliance. We both require loads of love."

"Those are the letters," Jimmy explains, "that touched me to my core."

"During his next trip to New York," Jeanie continues, "he called me in Jersey City and invited me to his hotel. I spent an entire day with him, both of us seated in his bed, just talking. Talking about anything and everything. I'd never met anyone so open, so willing to discuss his deepest hurts and desires. We were attracted to each other physically, but the spiritual bond was even deeper. I gave him a silver anchor on a long chain—silver is the metal of our astrological sign—and placed it around his neck. He asked me whether I knew his song 'Anchored by My Side.' 'I know it and I love it,' I answered. 'It's from *Can't We Begin Again*, your last album on Savoy.' He was amazed I knew so much about his career. We embraced, we held each other for hours, but never made love. There was no hurry.

"Jimmy went off to Europe, then Japan. Months passed before he returned to New York. He played a reunion concert with his old boss Lionel Hampton and invited me along, introducing me as his lady. I was in heaven. That night, back in his hotel, the spiritual turned physical. Before we undressed, before we consummated our love, he turned to me and said, 'I hope I don't offend you.' 'Why would you even say something like that?' I asked. 'I have a short joint,' he said. 'I know about Kallmann's Syndrome,' I told him. 'Size doesn't matter to me. Desire does. And I desire you.' Jimmy was a wonderful lover with a masterful use of his manhood. He was tender and considerate, sensitive and strong. It was better than I could have dreamed of. When it was time for him to leave for Cleveland, he wanted me to go with him—right then and there. It was impossible, but Jimmy can be persuasive.

"A few weeks later I made up mind. I gave up my interest in the auto repair business, packed up my things, rented a truck, and, nine hours later, arrived at his house in Euclid at three thirty in the morning. For the first three weeks that we were together, Jimmy made love to me every night, sometimes twice or three times a day. It was a perpetual honeymoon. We bathed each other, combed each other's hair, gave each other massages. He even told me he had a cemetery plot for me right next to his so I'll never have to be apart from him. I said we only need one, so we could be in each other's arms forever, the way we sleep together every night. I began calling him by his middle name, Victor, because I wanted to relate to James Scott the man, not Jimmy the entertainer. He introduced me to his family, who for the most part treated me like a sister."

Before long, though, tension developed between Jeanie and Kenny, Jimmy's younger brother. Kenny had been helping Jimmy put together the new house. After giving up driving, Jimmy had also bought Kenny a car. Kenny had become Jimmy's driver and, on one level, his chief confidante. Now Jeanie was replacing him. When Jimmy and I were in Europe during 2001, leaving Jeanie behind in Cleveland, Kenny planted seeds of doubt in Jimmy's mind about Jeanie's motives. I saw Jimmy grow paranoid, exhibiting the same extreme suspicion he had expressed to me about his former wives. He wondered whether Jeanie was exploiting him in nefarious ways.

For a time, he was convinced she had to leave. But when he returned to Cleveland, he saw that he had been overly concerned. The love-birds were back in their nest.

During the many times I was in Cleveland and Jimmy was in Los Angeles, he went off on verbal binges about his family. The un-willingness of his older siblings, Arthur and Shirley, to keep the kids together became a subject upon which he'd ruminate for hours. On one hand, he was generous with his siblings to a fault, lavishing them with gifts. At the same time, he complained about their disinterest and disapproval of him. For over a year, Jimmy was reluctant to have me meet his siblings. When I finally inter-viewed them, I found them, like Jimmy, highly intelligent. They were proud of their brother, but, once we moved beyond a superfi-cial discussion to the real issues, they spoke about the problem that was never quite vanquished—his drinking. Throughout their lives, his drunken harangues, though intermittent, never stopped.

Jeanie had her own problems with Jimmy's drinking. Once in New York, he jumped out of a cab as it sped through Columbus Circle. "It was a miracle that he wasn't killed," says Jeanie. Later that night, even drunker, he began choking her, screaming, "You hurt Justine! You hurt Justine!" The reference, of course, was to his mother. "When he woke up the next morning," says Jeanie, "he was sweet as pie and didn't remember a thing." That was only one of several incidents.

In entertaining questions about booze and pot, Jimmy is al-ways patient, never dismissive. He calls it a weakness, but in the end argues, "You've been with me for years now. Have you ever seen me mess up a show? Have you ever seen me late for a gig?"

The answer is no. When traveling with Jimmy, I always found him downstairs in the lobby, his suitcase neatly packed, a half-hour before anyone else. His work ethic never lags. Though he is in his late seventies, his energy remains dynamic. His good nature and docile disposition endear him to everyone who crosses his path. His complexities are hidden by layers of genuine goodwill.

Jeanie is increasingly challenged by his inscrutable ways. In addition to being his lover, she is clearly his caretaker. Days go by when he'll eat little more than a few potatoes and a handful of candy. From the road, he calls her every night with sweet words of love. Back home for an extended stay, his mood can turn sour. He grows restless, returning to the theme of his fractured family, going off on endless tirades. He coughs continually. His health seems precarious. He fears doctors and needles and hasn't had a checkup in years.

Tragedy struck in the winter of 2001, when Kenny, who was estranged from Jimmy during his final months, died of kidney failure. "I'm glad I talked Jimmy into seeing Kenny in the hospital," says Jeanie. "I'd been visiting Kenny there and knew how he longed for a reconciliation with his big brother."

Jeanie has deepened her relationship, not only with Jimmy, but with his sisters, with whom she grows increasingly close. Surprisingly, although Jimmy left Earlene in the early nineties, they still hadn't divorced by 2000. Now he feels the need. The process takes a year. There are delicate negotiations over money, but both parties compromise and at the end of 2001, a divorce is decreed. With a fourth marriage behind him, Jimmy considers a fifth. His relationship with Jeanie fluctuates wildly—on Monday it's all sweetness and light; on Tuesday he talks of sending her back to Jersey. Jeanie considers the challenge of living with a man whose loving charm is matched only by his irascibility. "As long as I get more of the good Jimmy than the bad," she says, "I'm here to stay."

I consider the question of his lifelong search for domestic happiness. When Jeanie first came on the scene, I was convinced that such happiness was at hand and that Jimmy's story would conclude blissfully. Of course I wanted to believe this, because, like anyone who has been with Jimmy for any length of time, I had learned to love him. Not only did Jeanie know and value Jimmy's art, she seemed to assuage his anxiety about the Deficiency. As the three of us ate pizza in Greenwich Village or dined at fish joints in

Cleveland's Flats, I saw them as a couple comforting each other with outlandish affection. My hope was that after a lifetime of sour romantic relationships, Jimmy would be able to keep this one sweet.

But sweetness is not an easy condition to sustain. And I wonder whether the condition expressed by the most powerful part of Jimmy's being—his art—is the condition that most accurately reflects his soul. That condition intimates sadness. His songs are pleadings and prayers, studies in pain. The generous medium of jazz allows him—even insists upon—the spontaneity of his moods. But as I examine those moods, beginning with his songs from the forties all the way up to today, I see a consistency. Like Billie and Bird, the consistency lies in the cry. His style is about heartache. The metaphysics of the blues—in slow-moving ballad form—frames the mystery of his songs.

I admire Jimmy's ability to cope. He copes with physical conditions that would have driven a lesser man to madness. He copes with ongoing humiliation. At a convenience store, the cashier hands him a pack of cigarettes and change, saying, "Thank you, Miss." Under his skullcap, Jimmy's visage can project the profile of an old woman. He doesn't correct the clerk and later reports that he has silently absorbed such blows practically every day of his life. Similarly, he has coped with professional circumstances with an almost serene acceptance. I marvel at the tenacity with which he pursued—and still pursues—the cold-blooded world of show business. I marvel at the wisdom of his relaxed approach to time. I treasure the hundreds of hours spent listening to his conversation and music. Like Wordsworth's "Composed upon Westminster Bridge," Keats's "This Living Hand," and Yeats's "Among School Children," Jimmy's "Why Try to Change Me Now," "Day by Day," and "The Folks Who Live on the Hill" are sacred texts of my spiritual life. The plain facts of his story as a jazz survivor over the course of a half-dozen different epochs is enough to inspire the most cynical observer of U.S. commerce. To emerge free of bitterness is testimony to the God he calls Jesus.

Yet I'm left with the same nagging questions I asked myself after working with other troubled geniuses. How do we understand the tear in Jimmy's voice? Marvin Gaye had it. So does Ray Charles and, for that matter, Aretha Franklin. That tear is not technical. It is no mere gimmick or fluke of nature. Does the tear symbolize a fate that excludes normal contentment? Is the tear the price paid to achieve immortality in the land of jazz? I don't know the answer. But I do know that when it comes to living the jazz life, Jimmy Scott has done so with rare integrity. You feel the integrity in his singing. You feel it in his style. His faith in his own style, virtually unchanged over a half-century, is tied to his faith in time. He can take his time, even control his time, by relinquishing control. He surrenders to the moment. Hearing him, we can do the same. His is an art based on the emotional truth that accompanies vulnerability. Such truth endures.

ACKNOWLEDGMENTS

Thanks to Jimmy Scott, who opened up his heart and trusted me with his life; Andrea Schulz, for lovingly shepherding the book from start to finish and contributing substantially to its final structure; Maxine Harvard, for asking me to write the book and holding my hand while I did; Jeanie McCarthy, whose archives and insights into Jimmy were invaluable; my wonderful wife, Roberta, and daughters, Alison and Jessica; my dad, who led me to the music; Scott scholars Billy Vera, Matthew Buzzell, Bob Porter, Bill Bentley, Richard Reicheg, and Todd Barkan, who generously shared their knowledge; Joel Dorn, whose enthusiasm and encouragement sustained me; the brilliant photographer Nicola Goode; Jane Snyder; Alex Smithline; Lisa Erbach Vance; Aaron Priest; Dan Strone; Terri Hinte; Chuck Stewart for the great photo; Leah Mirakhor for her invaluable research; Joel Dufour for his friendship and scholarly assistance; Mathieu Bitton for artistic input; and Jim Henke, Howard Kramer, Terry Stewart, Maryann Janosik, and Cleveland's own Ruth Brown for their support at the Rock and Roll Hall of Fame; counselor and beloved cousin Steve Ritz; my dear friends Alan Eisenstock, Leo Sacks, Harry Weinger, Richard

Cohen, Richard Freed, Philip Maxwell, Herb Boyd, Patrick Henderson, John Bryant, Glenn Kiser, Erina Siciliani, Massimo and Frieda Dalla Torre, and the Barbieris of Parma.

The following interviewees entertained my questions and generously granted me their time: Jimmy's brother Kenny, who died before he could see the major part he played in this book; Jimmy's sisters Elsa, Betsy, Nadine, and Adoree; Sharyn Felder, who opened up her home and her father's files; Zee Mannsur; Professor George H. Latimer-Knight; Celotes Clark; Lionel Hampton; Harold Arnold; Eli Adams; Ruth Brown; Illinois Jacquet; Howell Begle; Gil Bernal; Jimmy Cleveland; Quincy Jones; Jerry Wexler; Aretha Franklin; Etta James; Betty Carter; Dr. Billy Taylor; B. B. King; John Goddard; Rosemarie McCoy; Joe Pesci; Frankie Valli; Clifford Solomon; Lee Magid; Ozzie Cadena; Earlene Rodgers; Channie Blanchfield; Tiny Prince; Nancy Wilson; Lou Reed; Barbara Kukla; Lionel Hampton; Duke Wade; Dorthaan Kirk; Bobby Taylor; Hilliard Greene; Dwayne Broadnax; Michael Kanan; Mary Ann Fisher; Ray Charles; Gerald Wilson; Mitchell Froom; Tommy LiPuma; Herman Lubinsky, Jr.; Gil Askey; David Fathead Newman; Hank Crawford; Isio Saba; Saverio Palatella; Dan Marx; Bill Reed; Orrin Keepnews; Bob Porter; Bill Bentley; Bill Reed; Lupe DeLeon; and Ross Locke.

BIBLIOGRAPHY

BOOKS

Baraka, Amiri. *The Autobiography of LeRoi Jones*. New York: Freundlich Books, 1984.

Bennett, Tony, with Will Friedwald. *The Good Life*. New York: Pocket Books, 1998.

Brown, Ruth, with Andrew Yule. *Miss Rhythm*. New York: Da Capo, 1999.

Buchmann-Moller, Frank. *You Just Fight for Your Life: The Story of Lester Young*. New York: Praeger, 1990.

Catalano, Nick. *Clifford Brown*. New York: Oxford University Press, 2000.

Chilton, John. *Let the Good Times Roll: The Story of Louis Jordan and His Music*. Ann Arbor: University of Michigan Press, 1994.

Clarke, Gerald. *Get Happy: The Life of Judy Garland*. New York: Random House, 2000.

Cohodas, Nadine. *Spinning Blues into Gold*. New York: St. Martin's Press, 2000.

Coleman, Robin R. Means. *African American Viewers and the Black Situation Comedy*. New York: Garland, 2000.

Dance, Stanley. *The World of Count Basie*. New York: Da Capo, 2001.

_____. *The World of Swing*. New York: Da Capo, 2001.

Davis, Miles, with Quincy Troupe. *The Autobiography*. New York: Simon and Schuster, 1989.

Deffaa, Chip. *Blue Rhythms: Six Lives in Rhythm and Blues*. New York: Da Capo, 1996.

DeVeaux, Scott. *The Birth of Bebop*. Berkeley: University of California Press, 1997.

Duberman, Martin Bauml. *Paul Robeson*. New York: Alfred A. Knopf, 1988.

Edwards, Joe. *Top Tens and Trivia of Rock and Roll and Rhythm and Blues, 1950–1980*. St. Louis: Blueberry Hill Publishing, 1981.

Epstein, Daniel Mark. *Nat King Cole*. New York: Farrar, Straus Giroux, 1999.

Fox, Ted. *Showtime at the Apollo*. New York: Holt, Rinehart and Winston, 1983.

Friedwald, Will. *Jazz Singing: America's Great Voices from Bessie Smith to Bebop and Beyond*. New York: Da Capo, 1996.

_____. *Sinatra! The Song Is You*. New York: Da Capo, 1997.

_____. *I Paid My Dues*. New York: Lancer Books, 1967.

Giddins, Gary. *Visions of Jazz: The First Century*. New York: Oxford University Press, 1998.

Gioia, Ted. *The History of Jazz*. New York: Oxford University Press, 1997.

Gitler, Ira. *Swing to Bop*. New York: Da Capo, 1987.

Gonzales, Babs. *Bebop Dictionary and History of Its Famous Stars*. Newark, N.J.: Expudidence Publishing, 1967.

Gourse, Leslie. *Sassy: The Life of Sarah Vaughan*. New York: Da Capo, 1994.

Hampton, Lionel, with James Haskins. *Hamp*. New York: Warner Books, 1989.

Haskins, Jim. *Queen of the Blues: A Biography of Dinah Washington*. New York: William Morrow, 1987.

Heard, Nathan. *Howard Street*. Los Angeles: Amok, 1968.

Holiday, Billie, with William Dufty. *Lady Sings the Blues*. Garden City: Doubleday, 1956.

Jones, Quincy. *Q: The Autobiography*. New York: Doubleday, 2001.

Keating, W. Dennis, and Norman Krumholz and David C. Perry, eds. *Cleveland: A Metropolitan Reader*. Kent, Ohio: Kent State University Press, 1995.

Kennedy, Rick, and Randy McNutt. *Little Labels—Big Sound.* Bloomington: University of Indiana Press, 1999.

Kukla, Barbara J. *Swing City: Newark Nightlife, 1925–50.* Philadelphia: Temple University Press, 1991.

Lydon, Michael. *Ray Charles: Man and Music.* New York: Riverhead, 1998.

Lynne, Gloria, with Karen Chilton. *I Wish You Love.* New York: Forge, 2000.

Maggin, Donald I. *Stan Getz.* New York: Morrow, 1996.

Mosbrook, Joe. *Cleveland Jazz History.* Cleveland Heights, Ohio: Northeast Ohio Jazz Society, 1993.

O'Meally, Robert. *Lady Day.* New York: Da Capo, 2000.

Passman, Arnold. *The Deejays.* New York: Macmillan, 1971.

Petkov, Steven, and Leonard Mustazza, eds. *The Frank Sinatra Reader.* New York: Oxford University Press, 1995.

Porter, Lewis. *Lester Young.* Boston: Twayne, 1985.

Reig, Teddy, with Edward Berger. *Reminiscing in Tempo.* Metuchen, N.J.: Scarecrow Press and Institute of Jazz Studies, Rutgers University, 1990.

Rosenthal, David H. *Hard Bop.* New York: Oxford University Press, 1992.

Shaw, Arnold. *The Street That Never Slept.* New York: Coward, McCann and Geoghegan, 1971.

_____. *Honkers and Shouters.* New York: Collier, 1978.

Stearns, Marshall, and Jean Stearns. *Jazz Dance.* New York: Da Capo, 1994.

Vail, Ken. *Bird's Diary: The Life of Charlie Parker, 1945–1955.* Chessington, Surrey: Castle, 1996.

_____. *Lady Day's Diary: The Life of Billie Holiday, 1937–1959.* Chessington, Surrey: Castle, 1996.

Watkins, Mel. *On the Real Side.* New York: Simon and Schuster, 1994.

Whitburn, Joel. *Top R&B Singles, 1942–1988.* Menomonee Falls, Wisconsin: Record Research, 1988.

Whiteside, Jonny. *Cry: The Johnnie Ray Story.* New York: Barricade, 1994.

Yogananda, Paramahansa. *Autobiography of a Yogi.* Los Angeles: Self-Realization Fellowship, 1974.

ARTICLES

Aigest, Scott. "Backtalk." *Offbeat*, May 2001.

_____. "The Crying Game." *Down Beat*, September 2001.

Asnaghi, Laura. "Montenapo, La Boutique del 2001." *La Repubblica*, March 3, 2001.

Baird, Robert. "Jimmy Scott Reveals the Secrets of the Universe." *Pulse!* September 1994.

_____. "Jimmy Scott." *Stereophile*, September 2000.

_____. "The Source and Over the Rainbow." *Stereophile*, June 2001.

_____. "Back in Style." *Schwann Inside Jazz and Classical*, September 2002.

Barol, Bill. "One for the Soul Survivors." *Newsweek*, November 7, 1988.

Begle, Howell. "I Smell a Rat: Royalty Practices of Classic R&B Recording Companies." *Rhythm and Blues Foundation News* 4, October 1994.

Bindert, Dan. Interview with Jimmy Scott. *Cleveland Public Radio*, December 1999.

Birnbaum, Larry. "Little Jimmy Scott." *Down Beat*, August 1992.

Blumenthal, Bob. "Jimmy Scott: A Torch Singer Triumphs." *Boston Globe*, June 16, 1995.

Braun, Jennifer. "Musician Recalls Newark's Days as Jazz Mecca." *Star Ledger*, August 24, 1992.

Cahill, Greg. "Great Scott." *Northern California Bohemian*, April 12, 2001.

Cohen, Aaron. "Jimmy Scott." *Offbeat*, June 2001.

_____. "Over the Rainbow and the Source." *Down Beat*, August 2001.

Dorn, Joel. Liner notes for *Jimmy Scott: Lost and Found*. Rhino Records, 1993.

_____. Liner notes for *The Source*. Label M, 2000.

Escott, Colin. Liner notes for *Big Maybelle Candy!* Savoy/Atlantic Records, 2001.

Feather, Leonard. "Jimmy Scott Enthralls Before Packed House at Catalina." *Los Angeles Times*, November 19, 1992.

Garland, Phyl. "The Burning Ballads of Jimmy Scott." *Stereo Review*, January 1993.

Goodman, George. "Little Jimmy Scott Seeks to Evoke a Happier Past." *New York Times*, May 5, 1985.

Harrington, Bob. "Little Jimmy's Hypnotic Effect." *New York Post*, July 12, 1989.

Harrington, Richard. "Atlantic Expands Royalty Reform." *Washington Post*, March 5, 1997.

Heckman, Don. "Jimmy Scott Withstands Test of Time." *Los Angeles Times*, November 30, 1990.

_____. "Over the Rainbow." *Los Angeles Times*, May 27, 2001.

_____. "Jimmy Scott Delivers High Drama." *Los Angeles Times*, June 13, 2001.

Hernandez, Raoul. "Motherless Child." *Austin Chronicle*, July 6, 2001.

Hildebrand, Lee. "Jimmy Scott Is No Fool: He's Back Singing." *Tribune*, July 1990.

Hinckley, David. "Little Jimmy Offers Big Show at Tavern." *New York Daily News*, February 3, 1995.

Holland, Jan. "Jimmy Scott: Heaven or Hell Are Up to You." *Venice*, May 1997.

Hooper, Joe. "The Ballad of Little Jimmy Scott." *New York Times Magazine*, August 27, 2000.

Ingham, Chris. "It Takes Two, Baby." *Mojo*, August 1999.

Jardim, Gary. "Power of Love." *Village Voice*, March 1985.

Johnson, Phil. "It'll Make a Grown Man Cry." *Newspaper Publishing Independent*, May 25, 1999.

Kanzler, George, and Jay Lustig. "Symphony Hall Hosts Scott's 'Infancy of Jazz.'" *Star Ledger*, February 11, 1993.

Kochakian, Dan. "Great Scott—It's Jimmy." *Blues & Rhythm*, March 1999.

Kukla, Barbara. "Vocalist Jimmy Scott to Launch His 'Infancy of Jazz' Revue." *This Week*, February 8, 1993.

MacArthur, Paul J. "Little Jimmy Scott and the Roads Less Traveled." *Event*, January 6, 2000.

McDonough, Jimmy. "For Whatever the Reason: All the Way with Jimmy Scott." *Village Voice*, winter 1988.

_____. Liner notes for *All the Way*. Sire Records, 1992.

Morris, Chris. "Declarations of Independence." *Billboard*, March 11, 2000.

Niesel, Jeff. "Regional Beat." *Cleveland Scene*, March 15, 2001.

Pareles, Jon. "Pop: Little Jimmy Scott." *New York Times*, May 2, 1985.

_____. "Jazz." *New York Times*, November 24, 1985.

Pledger, Marcia. "The Comeback Kid." *Cleveland Plain Dealer Sunday Magazine*, December 14, 1997.

Pomus, Doc. Letter to the Editor. *Billboard*, September 21, 1987.

_____. "Remembrance of Cookie's Caravan and Jimmy Scott," Personal papers of Doc Pomus, Private Collection of Sharyn Felder, 1986.

Porter, Bob. "The Savoy Story." Liner notes for *The Savoy Story*. Atlantic Records, 1999.

Ramsey, David. "Singer Spurs Strong Reaction." *Syracuse Herald American*, August 14, 1994.

Resta, Francesco. "Little Scott." *Uomo*, April 2001.

Richardson, Derk. "Jimmy Scott Beats the Clock." *San Francisco Examiner Magazine*, October 1, 2000.

Rogers, Ray. "The Return of Jimmy's Jazz." *Out*, October 1994.

_____. "Great Scott, It's Jimmy." *New York Post*, August 17, 1996.

Romero, Michele. "Jimmy Scott: His Big Break Came at Sixty Five." *Entertainment Weekly*, June 24–July 1, 1994.

Santoro, Gene. "Little Jimmy Scott Goes for Baroque at the Tavern." *Now*, August 1993.

_____. "Two Fine Singers, One Terrific Voice." *New York Daily News*, April 19, 2001.

Schoemer, Karen. "A Singer Puts His Stamp on Well-Known Songs." *New York Times*, October 1, 1992.

_____. "A Voice Born of Emotion and Care." *New York Times*, December 11, 1992.

Silsbee, Kirk. "Little Jimmy Scott." *Los Angeles Reader*, November 23, 1990.

Skelly, Richard. "The King of Jazz Balladeers Is Back." *Goldmine*, November 4, 1992.

_____. "Jump into Jazz at Lincoln Center." *Asbury Park Press*, April 3, 2001.

Smith, Liz. "The Ploys of Summer." *New York Post*, October 2, 1992.

Snook, Debbi. "Prominent Cleveland Blacks Buried in Lake View Cemetery." *Cleveland Plain Dealer*, February 4, 2001.

Soeder, John. "The Jazz Singer." *Cleveland Plain Dealer*, July 8, 2000.

Townsend, Eunice, and Risasi Dais. "Newark Jazz Festival." *New York Amsterdam News*, December 3, 1994.

Troup, Stuart. "Little Jimmy Scott's Voice Still Wails." *Newsday*, May 3, 1985.

Vera, Billy. Liner notes for *Little Jimmy Scott with Paul Gayten Band*. Specialty Records, 1991.

_____. Liner notes for *Little Jimmy Scott: Everybody's Somebody's Fool*. Universal Music, 1999.

_____. Liner notes for *Little Jimmy Scott: The Savoy Years and More*. Savoy/Atlantic Records, 1999.

Verh, Duane. "The Source." *Cleveland Times*, July 11, 2001.

Williamson, Don. "The Source." *All About Jazz*, March 2001.

Wolff, Carlo. "Jimmy Scott: Over the Rainbow and the Source." *Metroland*, March 29, 2001.

_____. "Little Big Man." *Cleveland Scene*, July 6–12, 2000.

Zacharek, Stephanie. "All the Way Back." *Boston Phoenix*, August 7, 1992.

DISCOGRAPHY

The following discography lists the recordings available on CD.

DECCA AND CORAL

Jimmy Scott: Everybody's Somebody's Fool (Universal)
Original issue 1950–1952; reissue 1999. Invaluable. Jimmy's first hit, plus three other recordings with the Hampton big band. Dates with Billy Taylor, Stan Getz, and Lucky Thompson.

SWAN

New Bird
Original recording 1950; first reissue 1977 as *One Night at Birdland* (Columbia); second reissue 2000 as *New Bird* (Swan).
The out-of-print Columbia LP got the information wrong; the newer Swan CD has no information at all. But it's Jimmy, and it's Bird, and it's quite amazing.

SAVOY, REGAL, AND ROOST

Little Jimmy Scott: The Paul Gayten Band—Regal Records Live in New Orleans (Specialty)
Reissue 1991. Uneven. A rare example, though, of Jimmy live in the early fifties. He sings five songs, including "Fool."

Little Jimmy Scott: The Savoy Years and More (Savoy/Atlantic)
Original issue 1952–1975; reissue 1999. The three-CD box is the
most comprehensive overview of Jimmy's work on Roost and
Savoy. All the jewels are here, with the exception of "Can't We Begin Again," from his final Savoy session in 1975.

Very Truly Yours (Denon/Japan—Savoy)
Original issue 1955; first reissue 1984 as *Little Jimmy Scott* (Savoy,
United States); second reissue 1993 in Japan. The first Scott album
ever. Includes "Imagination," "When Did You Leave Heaven?" and
"Street of Dreams." Heartbreakingly beautiful.

If You Only Knew (Denon/Japan—Savoy/Atlantic)
Original issue 1956; first reissue 2000 in Japan; second reissue
2002 in United States. Some hits, some misses. A strong "I'm
Through with Love." In addition to the original songs, the U.S.
reissue includes three bonus tracks.

The Fabulous Songs of Jimmy Scott (Denon/Japan)
Original issue 1959; first reissue 1994 as *All Over Again* (Nip-
pon/Japan); second reissue 2000 as *The Fabulous Songs of Jimmy
Scott*. The earlier reissue includes the original album plus twelve
other Savoy sides. The second reissue is restricted to the original album only. Both include "Sometimes I Feel Like a Motherless
Child" and "The Masquerade Is Over."

Can't We Begin Again (Denon/Japan)
Original issue 1975; reissue 2000. A mess. Jimmy's final and saddest session for Savoy. But worth it for the title track.

TANGERINE

Falling in Love Is Wonderful
Original issue 1962; reissue scheduled for 2002 by Rhino. A price-
less gem.

ATLANTIC

The Source
Original issue 1969; first reissue 1993 as *Jimmy Scott: Lost and Found* (Rhino); second reissue 2000 as *The Source* (Label M). You need both reissues. The first doesn't include "This Love of Mine"; the second doesn't include "Dedicated to You." Both include the mind-altering "Day by Day," which is also available on *Head Jazz* (Label M, 2001), a miscellaneous collection.

J'S WAY

Jimmy Scott: Doesn't Love Mean More, 1990
Jimmy's own label and some of his own songs, with the Jazz Expressions, his own combo for the first time ever. Not his most satisfying effort.

Harold Ousley: That's When We Thought of Love, 1994
Recorded in 1986, this CD has Jimmy singing on three tracks. In spite of a lovely "Time after Time," the CD is only for the most diehard Jimmy fans.

SIRE

Lou Reed: Magic and Loss, 1992
Jimmy sings background on one song, "Power and Glory."

All the Way, 1992
The great comeback moment. Tommy LiPuma's triumph and Jimmy's biggest seller.

Dream, 1994
The dreamiest of Jimmy's work in the nineties. A noble and compelling follow-up to *All the Way*. Jimmy's reunion with Milt Jackson is a blessing.

Heaven, 1996
Ethereal abstractions on spiritual themes. Not my favorite.

FOR ARTISTS ONLY

Holding Back the Years, 1998
Jimmy sings Prince, John Lennon, Elvis Costello, Elton John. This is the CD that got him over in Europe. Young hipsters love it.

MISCELLANEOUS RECORDINGS IN THE NINETIES

Glengarry Glen Ross, soundtrack, Elektra, 1992
Jimmy's chilling version of the Tommy LiPuma–produced "Street of Dreams." David Fathead Newman solos from heaven.

Twin Peaks: Fire Walk with Me, Warner, 1992
Jimmy performs David Lynch's "Sycamore Trees."

Jazz Passengers: In Love, Windham Hill Records, 1994
Hal Willner and Hugo Dwyer produce Jimmy singing "Imitation of a Kiss."

David Sanborn: Pearls, Elektra, 1995
Magnificent version of "For All We Know." Production by Tommy LiPuma and Johnny Mandel.

Albino Alligator, soundtrack, Warner, 1997
Jimmy sings "Ill Wind" with Michael Stipe of R.E.M.

Lounge-a-Palooza, Hollywood Records, 1997
A collaboration with Flea of the Red Hot Chili Peppers on Captain and Tennille's "Love Will Keep Us Together."

Eastwood After Hours, Live at Carnegie Hall, Malpaso/Warner, 1997
Jimmy sings "The First Time Ever I Saw Your Face" in this tribute to the music from Clint Eastwood movies.

Bravo Profiles a Jazz Master: Little Jimmy Scott, Rhino, 1999
Compilation by Billy Vera centering on songs from *The Source*.

FANTASY

Moon Indigo, 2000
The first CD of Todd Barkan's superbly produced trilogy. Jimmy interprets the Great American Songbook with straight-ahead jazz backed by, among others, Hank Crawford and Cyrus Chestnut.

Over the Rainbow, 2001
With Joe Beck, Grady Tate, David Fathead Newman. Jimmy finally sings the Judy Garland song of his childhood as well as revisiting "When Did You Leave Heaven?"

But Beautiful, 2002
The most moving of the three Fantasy discs. Pianist Renee Rosnes is superb, along with George Mraz and Lewis Nash. Wynton Marsalis solos on "Darn That Dream." The highlight is Jimmy's duet with cohort Freddie Cole on "When You Wish Upon a Star."

VIDEOS

"The Ballad of Jimmy Scott," directed by Gary Jardim, 1987.
"Why Was I Born?" Directed by Melodie McDaniel, 1998.
"If You Only Knew," directed by Matthew Buzzell, 2002.

INDEX